Writing Women
since the Renaissance

Writing Women's History since the Renaissance

Mary Spongberg

© Mary Spongberg 2002

All rights reserved. No. reproduction, copy or transmission of this publication may be made without written permission.

No paragraph of this publication may be reproduced, copied or transmitted save with written permission or in accordance with the provisions of the Copyright, Designs and Patents Act 1988, or under the terms of any licence permitting limited copying issued by the Copyright Licensing Agency, 90 Tottenham Court Road, London W1T 4LP.

Any person who does any unauthorised act in relation to this publication may be liable to criminal prosecution and civil claims for damages.

The author has asserted her right to be identified as the author of this work in accordance with the Copyright, Designs and Patents Act 1988.

First published 2002 by
PALGRAVE MACMILLAN
Houndmills, Basingstoke, Hampshire RG21 6XS and
175 Fifth Avenue, New York, N.Y. 10010
Companies and representatives throughout the world

PALGRAVE MACMILLAN is the global academic imprint of the Palgrave Macmillan division of St. Martin's Press, LLC and of Palgrave Macmillan Ltd. Macmillan® is a registered trademark in the United States, United Kingdom and other countries. Palgrave is a registered trademark in the European Union and other countries.

ISBN 0-333-72667-7 hardcover
ISBN 0-333-72668-5 paperback

This book is printed on paper suitable for recycling and made from fully managed and sustained forest sources.

A catalogue record for this book is available from the British Library.

A catalogue record for this book is available from the Library of Congress.

10 9 8 7 6 5 4 3 2 1
11 10 09 08 07 06 05 04 03 02

Typeset by Aarontype Limited Easton, Bristol, England
Printed in China

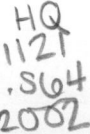

For Barbara and Judith

The one duty we owe to history is to rewrite it
Oscar Wilde

Contents

Acknowledgements   x

Introduction: 'Hardly Any Women At All?'? Women Writers and the Gender of History   1
    Gendering History   1
    Gender and Genre   5
    Women Writing History   8

Part I   Men's History

1 The Classical Inheritance   15
    The Classical Heritage   16
    Ancient Historians and the Gendering of History   20

2 'All Histories Are Against You': Women and the History Men   34
    Reforming History   35
    The Historical Defence of Women   38
    The Science of History   44
    Enlightened History?   46
    The Romantic Reaction   51
    The History Men   57

Part II   Women's History

3 'Above Their Sex'? Women's History 'before' Feminism   63
    History as Feminine Pedagogy   64
    Before Feminism   65
    Reforming Women   67
    Local Heroines   77
    The History Women   80

4 **History's Romantic Heroines: Women's History and Revolutionary Feminism** 86
   The Salon   87
   Revolutionary Feminism   89
   Foreign Correspondence   93
   Romantic Revolutionaries   101
   The Staëlian Legacy   105

5 **'Heroines of Domestic Life': Women's History and Female Biography** 109
   Domestic Woman   110
   Domestic Heroism   113
   Female Biography   115
   History as Domestic Science   118
   Feminising History   124

6 **Women's History and the 'Woman Question'** 130
   Women's History and Feminist Consciousness   131
   Before Suffrage   134
   First-wave Feminism   136
   First-wave Feminism and the Social Sciences   142
   The Social Sciences and Social History   145

7 **Amateurs or Professionals? Women's History in the Academy** 150
   Women and Higher Education   151
   The European Experience   155
   The Impact of War   160
   Women's History in the Academy   165
   History and the Feminine Mystique   167

8 **'Clio's Consciousness Raised'? Women's Liberation and Women's History** 172
   The Emergence of Women's Liberation   173
   Radical History?   176

Contents ix

    Women's Historians and Women's Liberation   179
    Clio's Consciousness Raised?   184

9 Liberating Women's History? Feminism and the Reconstruction of History   189
    Radical Feminism and the History of Women's Oppression   189
    Victim History?   192
    The Culture of True Womanhood   194
    The Class Challenge   199
    Women's Culture and Cultural Feminism   203

10 Surpassing the History of Men: Women's History and Lesbian History   209
    Sex Wars   209
    Women's History and the Lesbian Continuum   212
    The Elusive Qustion of Female Friendship   213
    Lesbian Sex and Sexology   217
    Sex Radical, Butch/Femme   221
    Doing 'It'?   225
    Making Things Perfectly Queer?   227

Conclusion: Dealing with Difference   229
    All the Women Were White?   231
    Dealing with Difference   236
    Poststructuralist Postscript   239

Notes   241
Index   293

Acknowledgements

> To be at so much trouble in filling great volumes, [with history] which, as I used to think, nobody would be willing ever to look into, to be labouring only for the torment of little boys and girls, always struck me as a hard fate; and though I know it is all very right and necessary, I have often wondered at the person's courage that could sit down on purpose to do it.
>
> Jane Austen, Northanger Abbey, 1818

When I first began this book I was blissfully ignorant of the enormity of the subject upon which I was about to enter. Although I was aware that some women had written history before the 1970s I thought that I could probably summarise these rare creatures in a chapter or two, before moving on to the 1970s when women's history really began. I thought I had a very clear picture in my head of what women's history was, why women needed to write history and how women had been excluded from historical discourse because the pre-eminent historical subject was man. In the course of writing this book many of my ideas about both women's history and women as historians have changed rather dramatically. While I still believe that man has been the pre-eminent historical subject, I am now also aware that not merely since the 1970s, or even since the end of the nineteenth century, but for almost as long as men have been writing history women have been creating alternate narratives, telling different stories, producing other facts. In fact since antiquity women have been writing women's history.

In the course of my re-education in this subject I have incurred considerable debts that now must be acknowledged. Firstly and most importantly I would like to thank Barbara Caine and Judith Keene, who first inspired my interest in women's history and who have endured lengthy discussions about this book since its inception. The University of Sydney was an excellent training ground for both women's history and feminist historiography and I need to thank Carole Adams, Heather Radi, Jan Kociumbus, Penny Russell and Stephen Garton for their support and encouragement over the years.

Colleagues at Macquarie have provided a cosy but also critical environment for this book's gestation and it has been enriched by seminar questions and corridor discussions with David Christian, Jill Roe, Marnie Hughes-Warrington, Chris Cunneen, Michael Roberts, Alison Holland, Hsu-Ming Teo, Michelle Arrow, Tom Hillard, Lea Benness, Alana Nobbs and Ian Plant. Colleagues beyond Macquarie must also be thanked and I am grateful to Michael Neve, Caroline Overy, Sally Alexander, Sophie Watson, Jerry Johnson and various others who have made my London trips less lonely.

Barbara Caine, Ann Curthoys, Marnie Hughes-Warrington, Joy Damousi, Lisa Featherstone, Michelle Lyons and Susan Magarey have all read various stages of the manuscript. Their comments have been invaluable. My research assistants Lisa Featherstone and Michelle Arrow have been critical to the completion of this project and have been excellent sources of feedback and good humour during this time.

Since much of this book makes use of materials that are rare it could not have been written without the support of the staff at the British Library, the Public Library of New York, the State Library of New South Wales, and the Fisher Library at the University of Sydney. The inter-library loans librarians at Macquarie have also been enormously helpful and I am most grateful for their efforts.

This book took much longer to complete than I originally anticipated so I need to thank my editor, Terka Acton, who has been infinitely patient and good-humoured in the face of my difficulties in completing it. I would also like to thank Amanda Capern whose generous comments greatly assisted the editing process.

I would like to thank my family Don and Cath Spongberg, Josie Spongberg, Patricia Drew, Michaela Buckland and Matthew Spongberg, all of whom have helped me in ways too numerous to mention. The staff at Toddler's Junction Connie Ters, Steve Cunico and Kylie Smith provided excellent care for my other production, Tallulah, while the manuscript was being completed. My husband Guy Fitzroy too has been incredibly supportive of my work. Finally, thanks to my daughter Tallulah, who has had to live with this book her whole life and whose existence has enriched both the book and my life beyond measure.

INTRODUCTION

'Hardly Any Women At All'? Women Writers and the Gender of History

> History, real solemn history, I cannot be interested in .... I read it a little as duty, but it tells me nothing that does not either vex or weary me. The quarrels of popes and kings, with wars or pestilences, in every page; the men all so good for nothing, and hardly any women at all.
> Jane Austen, *Northanger Abbey*, 1818

Gendering History?

The complaint of Catherine Morland in Jane Austen's *Northanger Abbey*, that history has 'hardly any women at all', is not an uncommon one and until fairly recently few historians would have disagreed. That is not to say that women were entirely absent from history or that historians of women did not exist before the 1970s. On the contrary, it is possible to document women in history from the time of Herodotus, and there is evidence to suggest that women have engaged in historical writing from the first century CE.[1] Since the 1960s historians of women have continually reclaimed the lives of individual women historians, 'recovered' women's historical writings from the past and established traditions of women's history dating back to ancient times. An overarching impression remains, however, that women are somehow situated outside 'history'.[2]

It is not the case that women have failed to engage with history, but that their historical endeavours have not been regarded as 'proper' history. Women who attempted to write history were rarely considered 'real' historians: rather they have been characterised as biographers, historical novelists, political satirists, genealogists, writers of travellers' tales, collectors of folklore and antiquarians. Occasionally a woman, such as Catherine Sawbridge Macaulay, would be allowed the title 'historian' because she engaged in the masculine activity of writing political history. Such rare figures were regarded as the exceptions that proved the rule. More often than not, women's writings about the past, regardless of their historicity, have not been treated seriously as history.

For the most part those interested in studying women's historical writing did little to dispute this idea in the wake of women's liberation. Framing their own discussions in pioneering tropes of discovery and exploration, women's historians in the 1970s were quick to distance the 'new' women's history from earlier feminine traditions.[3] Lumped together under the title 'the history of women worthies', these earlier works were rarely examined and readily dismissed.[4] This disavowal of earlier traditions of women's historical writing failed adequately to account for the ways in which gender has shaped history as a discipline. While contemporary feminist historians were quick to establish that women had been excluded from history, the idea that such exclusion was integral to the development of the discipline of history was not initially considered. Women's history written in the early 1970s was primarily concerned to correct the absence of women from history.[5] This was a radical endeavour in itself, as it recognised the need to claim a space for women's subjectivity within a masculinist discourse. The 'add women and stir approach' to women's history did, however, have its limitations, as it did not necessarily 'revise previous historiographies in feminist terms'.[6] Although this new women's history accumulated a wealth of detail about women's lives in the past, its impact on history more generally was limited.

With this recognition came the belief that it might not be possible to merely insert women into history without fundamentally changing the nature of the discipline. Women's history written at this time drew upon the methodologies of social history which were framed by Marxist paradigms such as oppression, consciousness and agency. While this drew much attention to certain aspects of women's historical experience, the dependence on an ostensibly masculinist theoretical framework limited the possibility of creating a truly woman-centred historical approach. As Joan Wallach Scott has observed, 'new facts might document the existence of women in the past, but they did not necessarily change the importance (or lack of it) attributed to women's activities'.[7]

Contemporary historians of women found themselves in a similar predicament to women historians in the past, as they saw women's history marginalised, treated as 'particular history', a specialist area of interest, but again placed outside 'history'.[8] In response, feminist theorists demonstrated how the absence of women from history had become integral to the very definition of history itself. Compelling critiques of the intrinsically masculinist nature of the discipline were made, as feminist historians argued that many aspects of historical practice were essentially 'phallocentric'.[9] Historical methodology, chronology, periodisation and the rhetorical practices of historians were all shown to favour masculinist interpretations of the past.[10] As Judith Allen argued, this commitment to a masculinist vision of the past was 'not a contingent or provisional feature of the discipline, amenable to simple reform of content or approach'.[11] For women to gain historical subjectivity, both as agents of history and as writers of history, feminist historians needed to create new ways of understanding the past and to embrace new methodologies and theoretical positions.

Joan Wallach Scott drew all these arguments together in her essay 'Gender: A Useful Category of Historical Analysis' delivered to the American Historical Association's conference in 1985. Borrowing from feminist theorists who argued that sexual identity was primarily a social and cultural construction, and feminist historians who insisted that relations between the sexes were contingent and changed over time, Scott reasserted the idea that gender must become a critical category of analysis within history. Defining gender as the 'social organisation of the sexes', Scott challenged feminist historians to investigate the multiple and contradictory meanings attributed to 'sexual difference' and to uncover how differences between the sexes came to be constituted by hierarchical social structures.[12] Scott argued that there could be no separate history of women. Instead she suggested a new history must evolve that focused primarily on the changing nature of relations between the sexes.

Following historians such as Natalie Zemon Davis, Joan Kelly-Gadol, Linda Gordon and Michelle Perrot, Scott considered history an intrinsically masculinist discipline and was critical of the gender-blindness of much historical writing. Drawing on the work of the French theorist of deconstruction Jacques Derrida, Scott argued that the language historians used had generated an idea of a universal subject, which was not universal, but rather white, male and middle-class. Deconstructionists maintain that such systems of thought are falsely constructed and they operate in an oppressive and excluding manner. By refusing to gender this subject male, historians had produced a system of meaning that not only necessarily excluded women, but naturalised women's subordination to men and normalised their historical marginalisation or invisibility. Such ideas allowed Scott to challenge the [male] historian's claim to 'objectivity' and 'universality' by gendering as male the 'single prototypical figure' that had previously 'represented the historical subject'.[13] Masculinist history, history that represented the views of the white, middle-class male, had become 'general' history, while history about women or other marginalised groups had become 'particular' history. By insisting upon the historical particularity and specificity of men, Scott threatened traditional historical paradigms and undercut the [male] 'historian's ability to claim neutral mastery or to present any particular story as if it were complete, universal and objectively determined'.[14]

Textuality or the study of the way arguments are structured became a critical tool in Scott's analysis of how gender functioned in historical writing. Drawing on Derrida, she argued that '[P]ositive definitions rest always on the negation or repression of something represented as antithetical to it.' In this context the positive definition of man was always dependent on a negative definition of woman. 'Such oppositions', Scott argued, 'both conceal the heterogeneity of either category', but also 'the extent to which the terms presented as oppositional are interdependent'.[15] The term 'man' derives meaning from some internally established contrast with the term 'woman': there is no real or inherent opposition between the two terms. More significantly, Scott showed how this interdependence was usually hierarchical, one term being dominant and visible, with the opposite term being subordinate, secondary and invisible, as in man/woman, public/private, state/family, production/re-production.

Drawing on the extensive feminist critiques of the ways in which such oppositions have shaped the conceptualisation of historical knowledge enabled Scott to argue that history too was a participant in 'the organisation of knowledge about sexual difference'.[16] Whereas the masculinist historical tradition has assumed that the category 'man' was inclusive, a 'generic, universal category typifying everything human', Scott's work suggested that this universal subject has been 'constituted through violently hierarchical differences'.[17] Moving beyond the criticisms previously offered by feminist historians, Scott contended that history should not be critiqued because it offered an incomplete record of the past, or a masculinist vision of the past, but because history and historians were responsible for the production of knowledge that legitimised the exclusion and subordination of women. Moreover, she demonstrated how these gendered oppositions and hierarchical differences consistently and necessarily placed women, both as historical subjects and as historians, outside history.

Gender and Genre

While feminist critiques of history allowed historians of women to recognise how gender shaped historical writing and methodology, gender as a category of analysis offered no unifying theoretical structure for women's history. Feminists deconstructed masculinist historical methodology, chronology and rhetoric, yet failed to generate androgynous historical practice. Their analysis was critically important, however, in that it allowed for re-evaluation of earlier traditions of women's historical writings. Insisting that gender has shaped historical practice allowed feminist historians to reassess the ways in which women had participated in the creation of history in the past. Feminist criticism of masculinist historiography suggested that what had constituted 'history' or 'historicity' was not necessarily 'objectivity' or 'empirical research' or any of the other criteria used to differentiate history from other genres, but rather the sex of the author.

This insight has meant that it was no longer possible to simply dismiss earlier historical writing as the 'history of women worthies' or pale imitations of 'manly' history. Gendering history made it possible to see women as innovative shapers of the medium, subtly manipulating the expectations of gender and genre to carve out their own particular history. This has resulted in the considerable expansion of our knowledge of the women who wrote history in the past and raised questions about what forms of women's writings constituted women's history in both the past and the present. With this profusion of information about women historians came an understanding that 'women's history' in the past took multiple forms, and evolved both in relation to and in reaction to masculinist conceptions of history and the prevailing prescriptions of gender.

In 1985 Bonnie G. Smith published in the *American Historical Review* the first major study of women as historical writers prior to the rise of second-wave feminism. Although several minor surveys had been produced before this, they were largely biographical and bibliographical studies, devoted to women who had succeeded in practising history 'as a masculine craft'.[18] Smith's work was new and important because she did not focus on historians such as Catherine Sawbridge Macaulay and Mercy Otis Warren, who produced political history, or Margaret Cavendish and Charlotte Arbaleste, who wrote the biography of male kin. Instead Smith looked to women historians who had contributed to the history of women. In so doing she argued for the first time that a separate feminine historical tradition existed, distinct from the historical practices of men. Natalie Zemon Davis had described a tradition of women's history existing since Plutarch that was composed of 'little biographies of great women'.[19] But this was a tradition dominated by male scholars, such as Boccaccio, Thomas Heywood and

George Ballard. Moreover, such biographical writing was dismissed by contemporary women's historians, who referred to it unkindly as the history of 'women worthies'.[20]

Instead of limiting women's historical practice to an archaic tradition of 'women worthies', Smith argued that the production of women's history by women in the past had 'relevance for contemporary research' into the history of women and its associated problems.[21] Unlike earlier historians who had sought to distance the 'new' women's history from the 'old', Smith saw the importance of establishing continuities with the past. Shifting focus away from biographical studies, she showed that women historians in the past had engaged in all forms of historical production, often developing innovative methodology or skilfully manipulating the genre to allow a woman-centred perspective.[22]

Smith's insights have allowed contemporary historians of women to reinterpret the legacy of women's history in the past. The work of women historians from earlier periods could no longer be dismissed as quaint and antiquarian, because it was different from that produced by male historians. Rather Smith's argument suggested that the work of women historians was necessarily different because it pushed against the masculinist boundaries that defined history in earlier periods. According to Smith, women's innovation in historical writing in the past made possible women's history in the present. In later works Smith rearticulated the idea that the production of history was 'gendered', demonstrating that a separate and long-established tradition of women's historiography has always existed. Moreover, she showed that the practices associated with the development of history as a modern professionalised discipline excluded women from history as both subjects and practitioners.[23]

While Smith opened the field, it has been left for other historians to draw out greater discussion about women historians in the past and their relationship to women's history in the present. Works by Joan Thirsk, Billie Melman, Rohan Amanda Maitzen, Rosemary Mitchell and Miriam Elizabeth Burstein have drawn much attention to women's historical production in the past, particularly suggesting a revised view of Victorian women as historians.[24] Greg

Kucich and Jane Rendall have looked to the Enlightenment to see how Romanticism and revolution shaped women's historical writing in the late eighteenth and early nineteenth centuries.[25] Daniel R. Woolf has even suggested that a 'female past' might be discerned throughout the early modern period.[26] Gerda Lerner has shown that women's historical writing can be dated back to late antiquity.[27] While all these historians have made valuable and important contributions to our knowledge of women's historiography, to date no single text has drawn together the insights of these works into an overarching discussion of the history of women's historical writing and the development of Women's history.

Women Writing History

It is the purpose of this book to provide a broad survey of the development of women's historical writing from the Renaissance until the end of the twentieth century. Following Bonnie G. Smith, this book will demonstrate the continuities between women's history in the past and the development of women's history in the late twentieth century. Although it would be difficult to prove that women had a characteristic relationship with history, it is possible to trace certain recurrent themes and the development of feminist ideas as they emerge through women's historical writing.

The relationship between the writing of women's history and the development of feminism will be a major theme in this text. Women's engagement with historical writing cannot be understood except in relation to the emergence of feminist consciousness. The study of history alerted women to their unequal status and to assert the moral authority of history in order to achieve women's rights. In a very real sense the writing of history can be seen as a feminist activity, as it involved the insertion of women's subjectivity into an ostensibly masculinist discourse. Like contemporary women's historians, historians of women in the past used their writings to force women into existing historical narratives, to assert women's historical subjectivity and to question masculinist historiography. Moreover, they proved truly innovative in their uses of the medium, exploiting acceptable gender norms to create their own historical subjectivity.

The book is divided into two sections, the first dealing with the masculinist historiographical tradition, the second with women's historiography. Part I will explore masculinist historiography as it has evolved since the Renaissance, particularly focusing on the historical representation of women within this tradition. To understand the place of women in 'men's history' these chapters will trace the development of historical writing through the retrospection of the Renaissance, the upheavals of the Reformation and the revolutions in science and industry between the seventeenth and nineteenth centuries, concluding with the emergence of history as an academic discipline. Chapter 1 will focus on the 'classical inheritance', examining how ancient ideas about femininity, gender relations and the place of women in history hardened into historiographical traditions during the Renaissance. The elision of women from history, the focus on the public sphere, traditions based on ancient ideals have inflected historical writing into the twentieth century. Chapter 2 will show that while women were not entirely absent from the historical record, the traces of womanhood that appear have been shaped by men who were self-consciously reverting to the misogynistic images of women found in the historical texts of ancient Greece and Rome. Moreover, the gender prescriptions of the ancients came to be idealised by male historians, justifying women's exclusion from the public sphere and the sphere of history.

Part II will focus on the ways in which women created historical subjectivity for themselves, in response to and reaction against the negative representation of women in masculinist historical writing. Chapters 3, 4 and 5 will examine the emergence of women's history before the rise of organised feminism in the nineteenth century. Chapter 3 will focus on women writing history from the Renaissance to the French Revolution. This chapter will show how the upheavals of the early modern period allowed women to create a sense of their own historical subjectivity, by subverting genres such as family history and biography. Chapter 4 will explore the impact of the French Revolution on the writing of women's history.

Women writers' experience of the Revolution saw them adopt different techniques in their recording of history, pre-empting many of the innovations of Romantic historiography. The appeal of Romanticism would compel other women to record their experiences of revolutions in Europe throughout the nineteenth century.

Women domesticated their historical interests and style in response to the conservative backlash that arose as the Napoleonic wars raged in Europe. Chapter 5 will focus on the impact of the reaction against Napoleon in terms of women's historical writing, arguing that to maintain the appearance of sexual morality and generic decorum women's interest shifted from history to biography. For women biography functioned as a gendered diminutive of history, as women who engaged in biographical writing stressed its 'private' and 'domestic' qualities. This allowed women biographers a certain historical subjectivity while leaving the gendered prescriptions of the day relatively unchallenged.

Chapter 6 will focus on the ways in which first-wave feminism influenced women's historical writing between the 1850s and the 1950s. The emergence of organised feminism saw women self-consciously adopt historical discourse in the struggle for equal rights. Women's history and feminism became firmly intertwined in this period and would remain so throughout the twentieth century. Chapter 7 will examine the experience of women historians as they took up positions within the academy. The tertiary education of women was one of the victories of first-wave feminism and the academy now attracted women students and employed women historians. The chapter will analyse how gender shaped their experience of these pioneering women and whether feminist consciousness informed women's historical writing as it emerged out of the academy.

Chapters 8 and 9 will examine the impact of women's liberation upon the writing of women's history. Chapter 8 will explore the initial effect of women's liberation on the academy, particularly focusing on the ways in which second-wave feminism impacted upon the discipline of history. Women's liberation demonstrated that masculinist interests shaped the role of women in the past and in the present. History as a discursive practice and pedagogy would be profoundly challenged as women historians embraced feminism, leading to the establishment of women's history as a distinct sub-discipline of history. Chapter 9 will examine how debates within feminism shaped 'women's history' as it emerged in the academy in the 1970s and 1980s. During this period women's history and second-wave feminism became mutually dependent. This created a women-centred framework for women's history to emerge, while simultaneously generating methodological problems for historians of women.

The final chapters of the book will examine the debates about difference within feminism and their impact on the writing of women's history. While debates about sexuality, race and class fragmented the women's movement, they also allowed for the development of a more inclusive history of women. Chapter 10 will focus on the place of lesbian history within women's history. The question of sexual differences between women was productive of broader discussions of class and race within women's history. The conclusion will examine how debates about difference came to undercut the very possibility of writing 'women's history' as both the category 'history' and the category 'woman' became fragmented. While second-wave feminism had generated the need for a 'history of women', the emergence of a more diffuse and divergent feminism rendered such a project problematic. Historians of women were forced to recognise that they had adopted essentialist and universalising tendencies they had critiqued in masculinist history. This recognition marked the beginning of a new type of women's history, focused not only on issues of gender but also differences among women produced by race, class and sexuality.

PART I
Men's History

The object of history is, by nature, man. Let us say, rather, men.
Marc Bloch, *Feudal Society*, 1944

CHAPTER 1

The Classical Inheritance

> There is no more significant pointer to the character of a society than the kind of history it writes or fails to write.
>
> E. H. Carr, *What is History*, 1961

The cultural dominance of classical literature during the Renaissance established an exclusively masculinist cast to the study of history. Knowledge of a small corpus of classical texts created a cultural hegemony that regulated elite education and determined entrance into the law, the church and the civil service for 500 years. The 'classical' education saw women largely excluded from intellectual life, based as it was on an ideal of public life drawn from ancient Athens and Rome. This classical ideal was ideologically underpinned by a gendered notion of separate spheres. Not only were women denied the possibility of a classical education, but that very education reinforced the belief that the exclusion of women who from the public sphere was 'morally correct' and 'in accordance with the whole tradition of western civilisation'.[1] From the Renaissance onwards male scholars held a particular scorn for women who usurped the masculine privilege of a classical education and used the historical representation of women in classical texts to argue against the education of women and their entrance into the public sphere.

This chapter will examine how the ideals of the ancient world have shaped modern historiography, particularly in relation to gender. It will argue that gendered prescriptions from the ancient world have hardened into historiographical convention, naturalising the exclusion of women from both the public sphere and the annals of history. It will ask: Why have women been excluded from the masculinist historical tradition? In what ways did ancient historians represent women? How were such ideas taken up by

Renaissance scholars, and has this led to a gendering of historical writing since the Renaissance?

The Classical Heritage

The study of 'the Classics' has been the preserve of 'cultured manhood'. In the medieval period the study of classical texts took place in the entirely masculine and enclosed spaces of European monasteries. During the Renaissance it became the core of elite education designed to prepare men of rank for political and civic roles. Renaissance scholars devoted themselves to the *studia humanitatis*, which included the study of grammar, poetry, rhetoric, history and moral philosophy derived from ancient texts. The term *humanitas* was taken as meaning a combination of instruction (*paideia*) and generosity of spirit (*philanthropia*).[2] This study of mankind, or 'humanism', as it became known, necessarily marginalised women as historical subjects. Although the term 'humanism' appears to be an inclusive one, suggesting a universal focus on all things human, its identification with the study of the classics promoted a gender blindness, that rendered 'invisible all who do not fit the concept of "cultured manhood"'.[3] This gender-blindness would be adopted by the discipline of history that took 'cultured man' as the universal human subject.

A classical education was conceived of as an exclusively masculine endeavour, a lengthy and arduous process, which only the strong would survive. Walter J. Ong has likened it to a primitive initiation ritual, in which boys were 'made to do many things that are hard ... simply because they are hard'.[4] Ancient Rome was the defining point of humanist educational ideology and practice.[5] Humanist teachers believed they were replicating the *educatio* experienced by the male citizens of Rome during the great days of the Roman Republic. This education was supposed to produce 'the man who can really perform his function as a citizen, who is fitted to the demands both of private and public business, who can guide a state by his counsel, ground it in law and correct it by his judicial decisions'.[6] Such an education had come to the Romans from the Greeks, who based their pedagogy around a programme of literature and rhetoric. Greek and Roman teachers maintained that this literary training would provide the young man with 'a secure foundation for full and active life in the service of the community'.[7]

This system of education was not practical, rather it served to establish a class of educated literati who operated the network of power relations of the Renaissance state. Learning Latin was the quintessential element of a classical education. The study of 'dead languages' – Latin, Greek and Hebrew, would remain the critical core of a classical education.[8] This involved detailed readings of Greek or Latin texts, and the composition of prose and verse in these languages. These skills would define a classical education into the twentieth century. The poet T. S. Eliot has suggested that it was important that these languages were 'dead', 'because through their death' they became an 'inheritance'.[9] Renaissance scholars envisaged the relationship between the ancients and moderns as that of father and son.[10]

Renaissance humanism was defined by a conscious return to the literary genres of antiquity. Knowledge of history became critical to the Renaissance scholar wanting to interpret 'their newly recovered literary treasures'.[11] The 'art of history' was central to humanist studies and was linked to the study of grammar, rhetoric and moral philosophy.[12] Renaissance historiography sought to distinguish itself from earlier traditions by its dedication to the 'truth'.[13] The 'rediscovery' of these ancient texts provided the Renaissance historian with valuable new source material, and looking to 'evidence' from these texts allowed him to distance himself from his medieval predecessors. The emergence of a science of philology during this period brought with it a new sense of historical criticism. Renaissance historians came to see themselves as extracting fact from fiction, putting an end to myths and corrupt traditions of the past and creating 'an authentic modern history'.[14] This involved an attack on anachronism, which until this period had been largely overlooked. The shift away from the monastic scholarship brought with it a new sense of historical time, that 'assigned a new importance to the transitory material life of this world'.[15] It was no longer possible to refer to classical or biblical figures as 'knights' or 'nuns', as historians had done in the past. Renaissance scholars avoided anachronism and recognised that the past was genuinely different from the present. This new 'historical sense' was enhanced by developments and discoveries in archaeology and topography.[17] With these changes came a desire to seek only the authentic artefacts of the past and to banish anachronism from historical writing.

The study of history was integral to the success of the classical education, because it allowed scholars to interpret and contextualise ancient texts. While the desire to master classical languages first led Renaissance scholars to the historical writings of the ancients, the study of these historians soon came to be seen as the key to understanding philosophy and political science. The wisdom of ancient historians such as Thucydides and Tacitus became a fundamental guide to ethics and morality. As Thomas Hobbes wrote in the introduction to his translation of Thucydides's *Peloponnesian War* in 1625, the 'principal and proper work of history' was 'to instruct and enable men [sic], by knowledge of actions past, to bear themselves prudently in the present and providently in the future'.[18] The incorporation of ancient ideals into Renaissance scholarship gendered the writing of history, re-establishing historical study as an exercise in masculine pedagogy and depicting the feminine as somehow ahistorical or outside history. Although few historians would follow the Greek historian Thucydides in his elision of women from history, the conscious return to the literary genres of antiquity saw women polarised as historical subjects. This dualistic representation of women saw them caught between hagiography and misogyny, personifying male attitudes and male interests, Madonna or whore, *femme fatale* or saint.

The number of people reading history increased exponentially during this period due to the new industry of printing. The writings of ancient historians were extremely popular with the new readership created by the printing press. Peter Burke has estimated that some two and a half million copies of works written by 'the ancients' circulated throughout Europe between 1450 and 1700.[19] Many of these works appeared in vernacular translations, suggesting an elite and non-elite readership.[20] Burke has argued that most of this readership 'was a captive audience', that is, 'schoolboys and university students'. As his language suggests, the audience was predominantly male.[21]

Humanist historians borrowed their evidence and historical mode from surviving authors of antiquity and adapted them to contemporary conditions and needs. According to Donald R. Kelley, most Renaissance scholars were 'inclined to accept the moral, pedagogical, political and even philosophical benefits of historical studies and to look to history not only for lessons, but also, increasingly, for legitimacy; imitation (*mimesis*) was a constant companion of historical curiosity'.[22] Most Renaissance histories were modelled upon ancient texts. Leonardo Bruni's *History of the People of Florence* (1449), the first humanist history, was patterned in language, style and exterior form on Livy's *History of Rome* and Thucydides's *History of the Peloponnesian War*.[23] Other historians borrowed plots, characters and speeches from ancient writers. '[N]obody would simply be a second Livy or Tacitus'[24]: rather Renaissance historians imitated the literary style of the ancients, often simply substituting modern names for ancient ones.

This imitation went beyond the stylistic. Renaissance scholars looked to history to provide examples 'to inculcate morality in youth and political wisdom in statesmen'.[25] This aspect of historical study became an integral feature of the humanist education. As the French humanist Matthieu Coignet wrote in 1586: 'We do gain more by reading [histories] in our youth; then by whatsoever is either attributed to sence, or the experience of old men, or to such as have been in farre voyages [*sic*].'[26] The view of history as 'philosophy teaching by example' originated in the writings of Dionysius of Halicarnassus (*c.* 100 BCE) but it came to represent the standard view of history during the Renaissance. The study of history provided 'a storehouse of examples for imitation and avoidance in the realms of both private and public life'.[27]

Ancient Historians and the Gendering of History

The valorisation of the moral and political values of the ancient world found in Renaissance scholarship gendered the writing of history. To understand how this retrospection gendered the writing of history it is first necessary to understand how gender featured in the histories of the ancients. Classical learning was deeply imbued with ideas regarding gender relations. During the Renaissance these ideas about women, femininity and masculinity and relations between the sexes went largely uncontested because of their classical origins. Classical ideas about gender relations have not only informed historical analysis but shaped political theory, the law, scientific and medical discourse, art and literature, state policy education, and even popular culture into the modern period.

Classical ideas about gender relations form an entirely masculinist discourse. No authentic historical voice of ancient womanhood survived into the Renaissance. While Tacitus claimed to have based his own *Histories* upon the memoirs of Agrippina the Younger, wife of Claudius and mother of Nero, there remains only a tiny fragment of this text, although it is mentioned in other historical works. There is evidence that a Greek historian, named Pamphilia, lived during the reign of the Emperor Nero. According to Dionysius and Photius, Pamphilia was a learned woman, who was said to have written historical commentaries in thirty-three books. Other ancient sources, however, attribute her work to her husband Socratidas. Evidence of her life exists in tiny fragments, though none of her work is extant.[28]

The historical representation of women coming from antiquity was entirely shaped by male writers and masculine interests. While not all ancient writers were misogynistic, the works of misogynistic writers, particularly Aristotle and Thucydides, became hegemonic during the Renaissance. This created a bias against women that hardened into historical convention as women's absence from history came to be characterised as 'natural' and in keeping with ancient tradition. Such ideas were used to argue against the education of women and so few women were trained to read the ancients. In this climate women scholars risked scorn and suspicion to gain a classical education and could do little to challenge the misogynistic representations they discovered in ancient texts.

The centrality of history to the humanist education saw the re-emergence of the classical ideal of history as masculine pedagogy. The idea that history should teach men to be men was first derived from the writings of the Greek historian Thucydides (c. 460–400 BCE). Histories written following Thucydides 'were unabashedly a preparation for life, especially military and political life'.[29] Thucydides, an Athenian general, wrote his history of the Peloponnesian Wars while in exile. As a participant-observer in the war between Athens and Sparta, he used history to understand the causes of war. The influence of Thucydides during the Renaissance meant that the study of history was seen 'as the key to political science and to making rational and prudent policy'.[30]

The work of the Graeco-Roman historian Polybius (c. 205–123 BCE) defined 'pragmatic history' during this period. Polybius, like Thucydides, was a soldier and politician, who wrote numerous historical works.[31] Polybius saw the task of being an historian as directly related to being a man and he believed that to be an historian, one must have acquired political and military skills.[32] Polybius practised history as if it were a pedagogical tool of masculinity. His main concern was that the budding statesman would take from history important lessons in pragmatism and wisdom.[33] History taught men to embrace an ideal of masculinity defined in terms of courage, self-discipline and steadfast duty.[34] By the end of the sixteenth century Polybius was highly regarded by Europe's intellectual elite, who admired him as much for his eloquence as for his skills as a military tactician.[35]

The lessons Thucydides and Polybius taught men about the role of women in history were critical to the development of history as an essentially masculinist discipline. Women are largely absent in Thucydides's *History of the Peloponnesian War*. One historian has calculated that he mentions women only twenty times.[36] Because of the authority attributed to him by later historians, this absence became a convention of historical writing. While numerous explanations have been put forward for Thucydides's reluctance to include women in his historical narrative, consensus lies around the idea that his silence was because he believed that a woman's name, like her person, should be secluded within the home. The sole evidence for this is his recording of Pericles's funeral oration in 431 BCE, particularly his advice to the widows of the Athenian dead.

> If it is necessary to make some mention of the virtue of the women who will now be widows, I shall define it all in a brief admonition; for great is the glory for you [widows] not to be worse than your existing nature, and of her whose celebrity, whether for virtue or reproach, exists least among males.[37]

Since the translation of Thucydides into Latin by Lorenzo Valla around 1452, reference to this speech has become shorthand for the exclusion of women from historical narratives. The silence surrounding women has influenced historians following the Thucydidean tradition. The elision of women from the historical record, by the refusal to name them, is a practice retained by classical scholars and certain modern historians into the twentieth century.[38] Pericles's funeral oration has come to form deep resonances within European culture. As late as the Second World War, posters with extracts of this speech appeared in advertising slots on London buses.[39] It is impossible to tell what British women made of this, although we do know that Virginia Woolf parodied his advice to women in *A Room of One's Own*.[40]

Not all historians followed Thucydides, and since the first century CE authors of catalog and biographical literature on women have had to contest the notion generated in his work that women should not be mentioned publicly. Plutarch, the Graeco-Roman historian/biographer (c. 46–120 CE), wrote in his essay *The Virtues of Women*:

> Regarding the virtues of women, Clea, I do not hold the same opinion as Thucydides. For he declares that the best woman is she about whom there is least talk regarding either censure or commendation, feeling that the name of the good woman, like her person, ought to be shut indoors and never go out.[41]

Plutarch used the example of virtuous women to inculcate virtue in others. He established the genre of 'women worthies' that would become a vehicle for feminine pedagogy until the end of the nineteenth century. Plutarch understood that Thucydides's historical marginalisation of women replicated the domestic seclusion of Athenian women. This idea would eventually determine the opposition within historical writing between the domestic sphere of women, which was regarded as ahistorical, and the public sphere of men, which was the sphere of history. In addition, this generated a circular logic that naturalised patriarchal gender relations characterised by the ideology of separate spheres, while simultaneously confirming the appropriateness of excluding women from the historical record. Historians following Thucydides would regard the domestic seclusion of women as natural and necessary for the unhindered march of historical progress.

The idea of history defined as masculinist pedagogy meant that historians focused upon those aspects of the past that were critical to the development of cultured manhood. Thus wars, politics, exploration, changes in law and statesmanship were the predominant concern of historical writing. Those areas considered feminine, the private sphere, marriage, motherhood and other aspects of domestic life, were depicted as ahistorical or outside history. Women themselves were regarded as ahistorical as femininity was conflated with 'nature' and the immediacy and intimacy of social life, rendering women impervious to change.[42] This greatly affected the historical representation of women, who were depicted in either hagiographic or misogynistic terms, reinforcing the idea that women were somehow 'timeless', making their role in history purely iconic.

This juxtaposition of good and bad women in history came directly to Renaissance scholars from the 'catalog' literature of the ancients. These 'catalogs' of famous or virtuous women are by far the most common form of 'women's history' produced by men and have been a part of the Western literary tradition since the time of Hesiod and Homer. Catalogs provided biographical sketches of famous and infamous women and were used by men to define femininity and to understand women through historical exempla.[43] The question of women's innate virtue or essential vice would remain a consistent theme within the Western literary tradition. The women featured in these catalogs would fuel this debate.

Although the Greeks initiated this form of biography it was the Romans who developed the two distinct modes of catalog that would characterise this literature. These modes would see women either celebrated for their virtue or representing all that threatened men, the household and the state. The catalog of heroines that first appeared in the Roman poet Virgil's *Aeneid* represents one end of this spectrum. The *Aeneid* was commissioned by the Emperor Augustus around 50 BC. Augustus wanted Virgil to write a national epic demonstrating Roman superiority.[44] Women in the *Aeneid* feature at precise moments of state formation, functioning as a literary device, rather than reflecting any real sense of women as historical subjects. It was as part of the tragic story of Dido and Aeneas that Virgil lists his catalog of seven famous women. Virgil associates these women with confusion, stagnation and alienation, because they represent the tragic past from which Rome must escape to achieve its glorious destiny.[45] Dido herself represents an *exemplum* of passion, as her love for Aenaes transformed her from sovereign ruler to crazed lover. Her dereliction of duty for love placed Dido in opposition to the heroic Aeneas, whose love of Rome transcended his love for her.

In the *Aeneid* Virgil presented femininity in a way that was external and antithetical to the historical. Throughout the text women were identified with private life and were thus positioned outside history. During the Renaissance the *Aeneid* formed part of the founding mythology of Rome. In this context the poem reinforced the idea that historical progress was dependent upon the exclusion of the feminine.[46] Following Virgil, the catalog writing would be used as a didactic device, warning men of the dangerous consequences of elevating private life over public duty. Catalogs joined other historical writings in the exercise of masculine pedagogy, denigrating the domestic while simultaneously celebrating the public. This juxtaposition inflected the genre itself, as women's biographical writing came to be represented as a gendered diminutive of history.

The Romans excelled in producing satirical catalogs that depicted women in grossly misogynistic terms. Best exemplified by the writings of the poet Juvenal (c. 55–140 CE), these texts represented women as the personification of all the sins of the flesh. Although these texts were satirical rather than historical, they used historical figures to justify their most outrageous contentions.[47] Juvenal employed the figures of Messalina and Agrippina to represent the greed, gluttony, luxury and cruelty of the declining Roman Empire. Satirical catalogs warned that women were particularly dangerous to men of learning, remaining popular with male intellectuals into the twentieth century. Messalina and Agrippina would become archetypes of feminine evil in later historical writing.[48]

The rediscovery of the writings of the Roman historians, particularly Livy (59 BCE–17 CE) and Tacitus (c. 55–120 CE) added further authority to this dichotomous representation of women. Although both historians were widely read in the Renaissance, it was the writings of Tacitus that would leave an indelible mark upon historical writing and political theory until the French Revolution.[49] For both historians the writing of Roman history was an exercise in moral and masculine pedagogy. Livy was inspired to write history following the Peace of Actium. With this peace came a desire to return to the values of 'Old Rome', characterised as propriety, courage, self-restraint, discipline, resilience, and respect for patriarchal authority.[50] For Livy, history was an exercise in nostalgia: he wrote so that he might hold up the moral example 'of the early days when Roman society was simple and uncorrupted'.[51]

Women featured prominently in Livy's first five books: the mythical origins of Rome and their presence was shown as integral to the formation of the Roman state. Women in Livy's histories are most relevant when they are being victimised. In Tacitus a different pattern of female representation emerges. While Livy focused predominantly on women as victims, Tacitus was more concerned to demonstrate women's destructive thirst for power. It was women's unnatural lust for power that framed critical moments in state formation in Tacitus's history. Women who usurped male power were not only regarded with scorn, but were portrayed as dangerous to the social order.

Abduction, rape and sexual enslavement were the narrative devices used by Livy to introduce women into his history of Rome. Livy and other Roman writers record that Rome was founded with an act of abduction, known commonly as the rape of the Sabine women.[52] This mass rape, the rape of the Vestal Virgin Rhea Silva by Mars, the rape and suicide of Lucretia and the kidnapping and murder of Virginia all form defining moments of state formation in Livy's history. On one level such sacrifices allowed women a particular significance in the history of Rome, but the way in which Livy reports this is ambiguous. When the Sabine women intervened in the battle between their fathers and their husbands/rapists, Livy records the women as crying: 'Place the blame on us ... we are the cause of the wounds to our men and to our parents.'[53] The rhetoric of blame used by the women served to sustain misogynistic views about rape and absolved Roman men of any guilt. The Renaissance saw a tradition established that referred to such sexual violence as 'rape valid'.[54]

Although women were accorded a certain heroic status in Livy's text, they failed to attain the status of historical subject. Represented as pawns in men's corrupt politics, their historical status is attained by virtue of their victimisation, rather than through any agency of their own. Livy's women never engage in action that generated historical change, rather they served as catalysts for male action. In Livy's account of early Rome women embodied 'the space of the home', forming a boundary, or buffer zone between the domestic realm and the public sphere, the sphere of history.[55] Livy's description of women's role effectively reinforced the importance of their domestic seclusion, rendering women outside history, by eliminating their voice and 'facilitating the perpetuation of male stories about men'.[56]

These stories of female subjugation acted as a 'model for imitation by presenting the deeds of great ancestors for judgment'.[57]

Women function symbolically in the text, forming a causal link in Livy's narrative between female chastity and its destruction and the founding and preservation of Rome. Livy's insistence on sexual violence at critical moments in his history connected the subjugation of women with the survival of Rome. He not only normalised the patriarchal gender order, but wrote that gender order into the structure of Roman history. The lesson men take from Livy's history was that the continued oppression of women was necessary for the good order of the state. If Froma I. Zeitlin is correct in arguing that founding mythologies justify 'retrospectively the identity of a given society', expressing 'what its members want or imagine themselves to be'; then Livy must be seen as responsible for establishing a version of Roman history that conflated masculine identity with brutality and feminine identity with victimisation.[58]

Following Livy, tales of female martyrdom formed archetypes in historical narratives that traced state formation. The martyrdom of virgins offered the greatest opportunity to record the role of women in the early church. In one of the first major texts of Christian history, *Ecclesiastical History*, by Eusebius (c. 264–340), the Bishop of Caesarea, women featured most prominently when he was describing the persecution of Christians by the Romans.[59] According to Erica Matheson, 'the dishonouring of women, the sexual dimension of persecution and women as the sexual objects of men's cruelty, desire and exploitation' were major themes in Eusebius's history.[60] Sexual violence as a motif for discussing women in history formed a continuity between Roman and Christian historiography. Sexual violence in the Christian historiographical tradition functioned so that virgin martyrs attained heroic status, but failed to achieve historical subjectivity. Later Christian historians would maintain and embellish this tradition. Hagiography, the narration of saintly lives, would become the primary vehicle for the representation of women's lives in Christian historical writing. Tales of martyrdom and other acts of female self-mortification particularly reversed the *imago* of Eve. Within the Christian historiographical tradition there is a more elusive meaning to this representation of women. As Marina Warner has observed in her work on the Virgin Mary:

'in the very celebration of the perfect human woman, both humanity and women [are] subtly denigrated'.[61] In the same way, these virtuous victims and saintly virgins presented unattainable moral standards for both Roman and Christian women, rendering all women flawed.

If scholars following Livy adopted the tradition that saw women historically victimised, it was from Tacitus that they gained the vituperative misogynist tradition. While Livy focused on women as passive emblems of civil strife, Tacitus was more concerned to demonstrate women's destructive thirst for power. Women's lust for power framed critical moments in state formation in Tacitus's two major works, the *Annals* and the *Histories*. In Tacitus's histories the women who usurped male power were not only regarded with scorn, but were portrayed as being dangerous to the social order. Tacitus's portrayal of Roman women has been given credence by classicists because he claims to have based much of his evidence on the 'Memoirs' written by Agrippina, mother of Nero, although only a tiny fragment has survived in Tacitus's text.[62]

Cornelius Tacitus was born around 56 CE, and was a politician as well as an historian. His first historical works, *Agricola* and *Germania*, were produced around 98 CE. *Agricola* is an encomiastic text, that is, a panegyric for a great man. (There is no similar term for texts about great women.) *Agricola* was an exercise in masculine pedagogy, providing Roman men with a sturdy example of civic virtue. *Germania* was an ethnological study of Central Europe. Both were essentially moral tales reflecting traditional republican values. It was *Germania* that proved most influential during the Renaissance. Because of this text both German and British historians claimed Tacitus as Tacitus *noster* (our Tacitus).[63] For early modern Germans, living with religious conflict and peasant uprisings, Tacitus defined and unified German culture and revealed to them 'their institutional, cultural and ethnic ancestry'.[64] Britons, recovering from civil war and threatened with invasion from Catholic France, used Tacitus's *Germania* as 'a non-Roman and anti-Gallic source of constitutional history'.[65] Tacitus's politics proved ideologically amebic as both republicans and monarchists throughout Europe found solace in Tacitus.

The gender relations Tacitus depicts among the ancient Germans framed his conception of ideal male/female relations and inflected the representation of women in his history of Julio-Claudian Rome. For Tacitus, part of Germany's potential threat to Rome lay in its strict marriage codes and punishment of female vice. Tacitus favourably reported that German wives were totally controlled by their husbands. Control of female chastity was essential to this form of marriage. German women were barred from banquets and other spectacles that might threaten their modesty.[66] They were domestically secluded, unlike the women of Rome Tacitus would later depict. More significantly, Tacitus defined German women's principal role as 'serving their husband's preeminent interest – war making'. As Sandra R. Joshel has observed: '[W]ives under male control contribute to the *virtus* (manliness, courage) that makes the Germans formidable in war; they make men toughened warriors.'[67]

Tacitus's portrait of German women stands in stark contrast to his depiction of the women of the Julio-Claudian family in the *Annals* and *Histories*. These two studies portray the lives of the Roman emperors from 14 to 96 CE and it is from these texts that much knowledge of Roman women has been gleaned. The *Annals* cover the lives of the emperors, Augustus, Tiberius, Caligula, Claudius and Nero; the *Histories* deals with the period following the death of Nero. More than any other historian, Tacitus used the juxtaposition of good and bad women to structure moral meaning and to serve as masculine pedagogy in his texts. As in Livy's history, women play a critical role in the works of Tacitus, but whereas Livy stressed the importance of women at crucial moments of state formation, Tacitus signals their role in the decline of the Rome. Women's unnatural love of power was held by Tacitus to be the cause of Rome's degeneration. The women who were treated most viciously by Tacitus are those who attempt to thwart male power, or at least overstep accepted feminine roles. Francesca Santoro L'Hoir has argued that since a major theme of the *Annals* was the fall of the house of Caesar, Tacitus was signalling that women's usurpation of power was 'symptomatic of a more serious malady: the appropriation of male *imperium*, both military and civic ... [that would] enervate and finally consume the state'.[68] Unlike German women, who lived strictly under the control of their men, enhancing their virility, Roman women sought to usurp male power, acting as an emasculating force both within the home and the state.

In both the *Annals* and the *Histories* Tacitus's approval and disapproval of women functioned to naturalise certain forms of gender relations which were tied to the rise and fall of Rome. When women were praised in Tacitus it was because they were archetypes of republican virtue; they were apolitical, chaste, maternal and self-sacrificing.[69] Tacitus deemed such virtues necessary for the good working of the state. When women were scorned it was because they represented the opposite of these virtues and became an enervating force, sapping male *imperium* and generating the fall of Rome.[70]

Negative representation of women who breached the boundaries of the domestic to assert themselves in the public sphere was in keeping with the ancient tradition, *stasis* dating from Homer, which connected women with civil war. By the fifth century BCE, the connection was so well established that the Athenian playwright Aristophanes could parody it in his *Thesmophoriazousae*. 'Of course, everyone vies in condemning the tribe of women', his heroine complained. 'That we are a scourge upon humanity and that everything is our fault: quarrels, discord, ominous civil war, sorrow.'[71] It was Thucydides's discussion of *stasis* during the Peloponnesian War that forever conflated femininity with civil strife. In Corcyra and in Platea, Thucydides reported that women intervened in civil strife by coming out on to their rooftops and hurling tiles and other domestic missiles at their enemies.

Thucydides was loath to mention women and so these two incidents are unusual in the text. Thomas E. J. Wiedemann has argued that Thucydides only records women's active intervention, when 'the event in question is somehow odd' or outside the 'rational patterns of explanation'.[72] Thucydides merged contemporary ideas

The Classical Inheritance

about pathological femininity into his historical explanation, rendering civil strife a feminine enterprise.[73] The feminisation of civil strife relates back directly to the ideology of separate spheres. Whereas men as citizens would place their duty to the state above family ties, women were first 'daughters, sisters or mothers' who would 'protect blood at all costs'.[74] This tendency to protect familial relations was seen to make women unreliable allies in any ideological struggle.

Certain historians have suggested that this reading of the *Peloponnesian Wars* presupposes too great a subtlety on Thucydides's part.[75] Whether Thucydides meant to represent women as emblematic of the irrational forces in history or not, the notion that women were a potential threat to the social order was generated within the Thucydidean tradition. Polybius would strengthen this idea in his work, depicting women, particularly of the aristocracy, as a potential 'force of disorder' within the state. This was critical in Polybius's work, as he maintained that it was one of the most important duties of the statesman to protect civil society from 'the forces of disorder and chaos'.[76] Arthur Eckstein has shown that Polybius believed that women by their nature were 'typically frenzied' and 'hyperemotional'.[77] His worst scorn was released upon effeminate men, as men who behaved with the 'irrational passion of a woman' represented an opposition to Polybius's ideology of manliness. Reversals of the gender order would, according to Polybius, only result in social chaos. These ideas were in keeping with notions of women's irrational and volatile nature derived from Aristotelian medicine and philosophy. Polybius presented gender disorder as emblematic of broader social disorder, using women as a historiographical device to represent this disorder. The connection between women, irrationality and social chaos drawn from ancient sources informed discussion of women's social and political role until the mid-twentieth century.

Following Thucydides and Polybius, historians depicted women as the source of civil strife to educate men in the necessity of maintaining patriarchal gender relations. Polybius recommended marriage both as a way of controlling women and imposing 'limits on the behaviour of males'.[78] Polybius's ideal of marriage involved total separation of both spheres. The best wives were those who were chaste, maternal, dignified, silent in the presence of men and uninvolved in politics. The connection between women and *stasis* would become a deep-seated historiographical convention. Women were usually held responsible for the outbreak of civil strife, represented as a reactive, irrational and emotional force, rather than as rational agents of historical change. The authority of the ancients during the Renaissance suggested that male control of women was necessary for the good order of the home and state. Narratives of successful nation-states came to be framed around the ideal of women's complete submission to men. Cautionary tales of unsuccessful nation-states suggested in turn that the rise of powerful women led to the emasculation of the body politic.

With the adoption of the Thucydidean tradition, historians since the Renaissance tacitly rejected the other historical tradition bequeathed to them by the Greeks, that of Herodotus. Herodotus was born in Halicarnassus c.484 BCE. Around the middle of the fifth century BCE he wrote a narrative of the conflict between the Greek states and the Persians that had recently ceased. Although Herodotus is sometimes referred to as the 'father of history', during the Renaissance he was better known as the 'father of lies'. He derived his founding-father status largely from the fact that he is credited with abandoning the 'study of myth' for the 'study of fact'. Renaissance scholars weary of anachronism and wary of fabulous tales viewed Herodotus's *Histories* with great scepticism. His text has long been subject to criticism for its inconsistency, factual errors and fantasy. Renaissance scholars accepted the opinions of Roman authors Cicero and Quintillian, who praised Herodotus's style, but questioned his veracity.[79]

Herodotus offered Renaissance historians another way of thinking about women historically. Herodotus made women central to the narrative of his *Histories*, referring to them some 375 times in the extant text.[80] Women in Herodotus display 'full partnership with men in establishing and maintaining the social order'.[81]

His treatment of women makes Herodotus unique among surviving classical authors, as he treated women as individuals and rarely resorted to limiting stereotypes.[82] Herodotus rejected the *cherchez-la-femme* view that inflected historical writing following Thucydides.[83] The tales of rape and abduction that initiated the feud between the Greeks and the Persians were, for Herodotus, not worthy of belief. Unlike the Roman historians who regarded these stories as crucial moments in state formation, Herodotus dismissed the story of Helen of Troy as mythical and thus 'baseless and in violation of his conception of history'.[84]

Herodotus made the status of women in society an important index of civilisation. The centrality of the status of women to Herodotus's narrative clearly influenced his depiction of gender relations throughout the text. He regarded marriage as a critical political institution, an institution over which women had some degree of power. Reproduction of children was treated seriously in the *Histories,* as necessary for the survival of a society, particularly a society in crisis. In this context Herodotus described women going to some lengths to ensure cultural survival.

Herodotus's work was not free from misogynistic representations of women. Recent work on the *Histories* has shown that he was prone to depict female rulers as more brutal than men. He also resorted to coarse humour when discussing women's sexual virtue.[85] This was very much in keeping with contemporary attitudes to women. This evidence clearly questions what some historians have referred to as the 'female flavour' of Herodotus' work, but it does not diminish the fact that he displayed far greater interest in women than the historians who followed him.

CHAPTER 2

'All Histories Are Against You': Women and the History Men

> Men have had every advantage of us in telling their own story. Education has been theirs in so much higher a degree; the pen has been in their hands. I will not allow a book to prove anything.
>
> Jane Austen, *Persuasion*, 1818

Although classical learning formed an integral part of the intellectual heritage of the West, its authority did not go completely unchallenged, nor has its influence remained static since the Renaissance. The Reformation, the Enlightenment and the revolutions in science and industry that convulsed Europe between the sixteenth and nineteenth centuries produced a climate of continuous intellectual tumult. The discovery of the 'New World', the rise of Protestantism and capitalism and the weakening of absolutist states all shaped a new sense of history. Innovation in science saw it challenge other knowledge systems and fundamentally alter the way in which the world was viewed. Between the sixteenth and eighteenth centuries history moved away from its classical designation as an 'art' to become during the Enlightenment a 'science'. Seeking the prestige and certainties offered by science, historians adopted its language and methodologies.

In spite of these dramatic changes the historical representation of women by male historians remained strangely static. Although classical certainties were challenged throughout the period, classically informed notions of femininity, gender relations and the role of women in history remained largely intact. This changelessness merely reinforced deep-seated beliefs that women could not achieve historical subjectivity, as they were 'the Sex'. Women were believed to be closer to nature and were associated with the private sphere and hence the immediacy of domestic life. Individual women who achieved historical subjectivity in male-authored texts were women who acted 'above their sex'. As the feminist writer Mary Astell astutely observed, such women were really 'men in petticoats' allowed into the realms of history because they had overcome their femininity to become virile women or *femmes forte*.[1]

This chapter will focus on the ways in which women were historically represented in masculinist history until the modern era. It will ask whether ancient ideas about women continued to flourish within history. How did ancient ideas about separate spheres and the domestic seclusion of women shape the writing of history? Did the representation of women within the masculinist tradition change over time or are women seen as 'changeless', aligned with nature and thus outside history?

Reforming History

The catalyst for the Reformation lay in the rejection of 'the pagan implications of classicism' and any notion that Catholics retained of ancient virtue.[2] This generated a revolution in historical writing that saw historians embrace new materials, and develop new narrative forms and different critiques of sources. This was not merely productive of new trends in historiography. It marked a clash of distinct historical traditions.[3] As intellectual debate and civil war raged, history was not simply used as propaganda but became 'the characteristic mode of thought in which Protestants and Catholics expressed their differences'.[4] Sectarianism transformed the study of history from a leisurely pursuit into a major scholarly industry. It gave rise to alternative accounts of historical events, as historians threatened each other's credibility with opposing theories and differing interpretation. Protestant states led Europe in introducing history to the university, with the first chair of history being established at the University of Mainz in 1504. This sense of conflicting history was intensified with the invention of the printing press and the spread of literacy.[5] History was essential to Protestants seeking to re-evaluate ancient Christianity. The church was no longer viewed as a timeless institution: rather, the contemporary church was unfavourably contrasted with its earlier purity. Renaissance concern with anachronism became a 'basic premise of Reformation thought'.[6]

While sixteenth-century Protestant reformers attacked the authority of the Catholic Church in every other respect, they never truly cast aside the classical learning that had constituted ecclesiastical authority.[7] Reformation historians remained committed to the Renaissance emphasis on 'pure' sources and the rigours of classical scholarship, while simultaneously criticising the 'papist' allegiance to all things Roman. These contradictions informed the historical treatment of women during this period, especially in regard to female authority. Protestant historians particularly retained the wisdom of the ancients in regard to what they considered illegitimate displays of feminine authority. Historians throughout this period characterised female interference in politics as the source of all social ills. This was also due to opposition to Catholicism, which framed the Church's degeneration in terms of a feminising effect. The hated figures of Catherine de' Medici in France and Mary Tudor in England provoked righteous anger from their Protestant subjects because of what they considered their illegitimate wielding of power.[8]

Ironically, in this area Protestant historians competed with the hated monastic tradition in developing misogynistic representation of women rulers. Throughout the early modern period historians gave disproportionate and negative attention to women rulers. Women exercising power were represented as 'violating all principles of feminine subordination and social order, particularly in their betrayal of male relatives and allies, they inevitably plunged their families and subjects into ruin'.[9] In Britain Boadicea was frequently invoked to show the dangers of female rule, as much for her insubordination to masculine authority as her resistance to Roman rule. Tacitus had first represented the British 'queen' Boadicea as an irresponsible usurper of male privilege, whose illegitimate use of power wreaked havoc on her family and plunged her people into subjugation. Jodi Mikalachki has observed that British historians used the example of women rulers to demonstrate that female power inevitably led to the indulgence of the basest appetites, the throwing off of proper authority and the inversion of class and gender order.[10] In such histories the queens of ancient Britain – Boadicea, Cordeilla and Cartismandua – represented the ahistorical and uncivilised past from which Britain must escape to achieve nationhood.[11] As in the works of ancient historians, particularly that of Tacitus and Livy, 'new' histories of Britain made a forceful connection between sexual difference and sexual hierarchy on the one hand and political order and historical subjectivity on the other. If historical progress was to be made, women must be excluded not only from the political sphere but from the realms of history.

While this representation clearly derived from the classical tradition it was also shaped by the sexual politics of the Reformation. Lyndal Roper has suggested that the Reformation 'both as a religious credo and a social movement must be understood as a theology of gender'.[12] Traditionally the impact of Protestantism during the Reformation has been depicted as improving the status of women. As Roper has demonstrated, 'the heritage of the Reformation for women was deeply ambiguous'.[13] Protestant political theory on the question of sovereign authority was framed in a gendered language that implied political harmony via the maintenance of sexual difference.[14] In a sense this domesticated absolutist claims, by making sovereign authority only proper in the home where the husband's authority over his wife could be asserted. Reformation figures such as Martin Luther and John Knox insisted upon women's incorporation into the household under total submission to their husbands, prefiguring in theological terms the rise of fraternal patriarchy described by seventeenth-century political theorists.[15] Both Catholics and Protestants exploited gender-inflected metaphors in their quest to gain political and religious supremacy. Patriarchal gender relations as they evolved out of the Reformation saw women totally subordinated to their male kin, in theory if not in practice.

The Historical Defence of Women

By far the most common form of women's history written by men during the early modern period were treatises written in 'defence' of womanhood. Stemming from the tradition of catalog literature, these defences functioned partly to restore women to history, but also establish the excellence of women by referring to examples from history and making humanist arguments for their education.[16] Written in the humanist tradition, such texts were more often rhetorical than historical, and while women were praised, they were 'ultimately contained by most arguments'.[17] Underpinning this rhetorical strategy was a long-standing contradiction in the historical representation of women, as only virile women or *femmes forte* were represented in these texts. In this way humanist scholars inserted women into the masculinist field of history by essentially denying their femininity.

The first example of this literature, *De claris mulieribus*, had been written by the Italian humanist Giovanni Boccaccio between 1361 and 1375. Best known as the author of the *Decameron,* Boccaccio used catalogs frequently in his venacular and Latin texts.[18] Boccaccio's text reflected Renaissance interest in the ancient world, dealing predominantly with the lives of pagan women. His work was also influenced by Christian tradition, drawing upon *Adversus Jovinianum* of St Jerome, the only early Christian catalog famous for its invective against women, as well as medieval didactic and moralising works, particularly the *Vitae Sanctorum*.[19] While the monastic tradition saw women celebrated for their virtue, Boccaccio, in the humanist spirit, celebrated women for their intelligence and learning.

Although a number of feminist scholars have demonstrated Boccaccio's ironic purpose, *De claris mulieribus* was the first text to allow women the possibility of attaining 'civic virtue' and has served as a source of exempla confirming the civic virtue of women throughout history.[20] In dedicating the text to the Countess of Altavilla (so chosen because her name Andrea came from the Greek *andres* meaning men), Boccaccio implored women to emulate the deeds of ancient women to 'spur your spirit onto loftier things'.[21] *De claris mulieribus* questioned Aristotelian images of woman which stressed the idea that women were best viewed in 'modes of submission' as well as the Christian notion formed by St Paul that femininity 'was best realised in ... silence and chastity'.[22]

Boccaccio only included women in his history who had acquired 'a manly spirit ... keen intelligence and remarkable fortitude'.[23] These qualities were not naturally feminine, rather, according to Boccaccio, these women acquired manly attributes that allowed them the courage to act counter to tradition and nature.[24] Only by rejecting the feminine could these women acquire historical subjectivity. Certain observers have suggested that Boccaccio was unsuccessful in depicting women as both virile and virtuous. Constance Jordan particularly argues that Boccaccio does not subject women to the same kind of historical judgment he believes is appropriate for men, because he could not truly conceive of a genderless *virtus*. Such a concept would 'undermine the social order' and effectively do 'away with the power of men to determine the nature and welfare of family life'.[25] This failure to allow women historical subjectivity discloses how male historians relied upon the authority of history to 'naturalise' certain forms of gender relations. Following Livy, the only women who achieved masculine *virtus* and historical subjectivity in Boccaccio were women who had come to a pious but unfortunate end.[26]

The first texts to follow Boccaccio, such as Antonio Cornazzano's *De mulieribus admirandis* in 1467 and Vespasiano da Bisticci's *Il Libro delle lode e commendazione delle donne* in 1480, conformed to the Renaissance preoccupation with the 'idea of woman'.[27] These texts displayed ambivalent concern with women's potential for civic virtue.[28] By the end of the fifteenth century catalogs became more complex and discursive, as commentators were less concerned with their biographical content and more concerned with the question of 'what constituted a woman in theological, philosophical and social terms'.[29] Brita Rang has suggested that the women celebrated in these texts 'were not really intended as models to be imitated, but rather as "objects of demonstration", exemplifying potential rather than actual capabilities'.[30] Presented as an unattainable ideal, it became irrelevant whether these texts portrayed mythical or historical figures, as ordinary women were not really expected to emulate them.

By the sixteenth century men were producing formulaic histories of women derived from Boccaccio but adapted to the current trends in religion and politics. The focus in these texts shifted away from idealised virtuous women to the 'learned' woman as exemplar. Texts focusing on 'learned women' reflected the onset of dramatic changes in Europe wrought by religious and political upheaval. Although these texts were not overtly political, the education of women and their civic virtue remained contentious issues. This was especially true in relation to female sovereigns and governors. How women were to be educated and trained for civil life was a question that fascinated humanist scholars, stimulating the *Querelle des Femmes* throughout this period.[31]

The question of female sovereignty was keenly debated throughout the Reformation because the wars of religion and the consolidation of nation-states had given rise to an unprecedented number of women acting as regents or ruling as queens in their own right. In Britain, where the Salic law was not recognised, there was no legal impediment to female succession. Following the death of Edward VI, the son of Henry VIII, in the mid-sixteenth century, three women laid claim to the English throne in quick succession, while Mary Stuart began her reign in Scotland. Until the reign of Elizabeth in 1558 Tudor Britain was embroiled in political turmoil. In France the regency of Catherine de' Medici, 1547–59, was a period of intense political crisis. Although there were many contributing factors to the political turmoil that engulfed Britain and France, many commentators saw fit to place the blame entirely on the sex of the sovereign.

The same period marked an unprecedented assertion of patriarchal authority from both Reformation and Counter-Reformation theologians and political theorists. Constant parallels were drawn between political and domestic institutions.[32] Reformers like Luther depicted the authority of the husband as 'the glory of God'.[33] Protestant theorists articulated a theology of gender that insisted that the moral ordering of the state was dependent upon the moral ordering of the household.[34] It was believed that the social, economic and moral order of the household represented a miniature cosmos. Parallels were drawn between the macrocosm of state, church and city and the microcosm of the family. The family was described in terms that reflected this relationship as a small commonwealth. Catholics, also, used such metaphors, suggesting that domestic and sovereign authority were seen as essentially comparable. This made the household the model for the commmonwealth, while the commonwealth was created by transferring the natural authority of fathers into the political sphere.[35]

Both Catholic and Protestant political theorists assumed that male government was natural, making the spectacle of female sovereignty unnatural or aberrant. The queen's legitimate and autonomous hold on power left patriarchal political theory in disarray.[36] According to both classical and biblical authority, woman was divinely subordinated to man, so just as she could not assert her authority over her husband, nor could she be the governor of men.[37] Such arguments were further complicated by the marital status of the queen. Should female sovereigns marry, their subordinate role as wives contradicted their authoritative role as queens.[38] Men critical of women's rule argued they were weak and incapable of authority. They predicted all female rule would inevitably lead to political chaos. Those in favour of female rule countered that queens were exceptional women and their role as sovereign meant that they were 'politically male'.[39] Other arguments sidestepped the notion of female inferiority by dividing the queen's body politic from her body natural.

In the uncertain political world of the Reformation historical defences of women served as oblique political criticism or support for a female sovereign. Catalogs of exemplary women gave way to explicit defences of women that used historical examples to support or attack female authority. As Amanda Shepherd has demonstrated, the defenders of women writing during this period were not motivated by feminist concerns, rather they 'were representatives of the political nation who were motivated by self-interest'.[40] Many of these defences had distinct political subtexts. Thomas Elyot's

Defence of Good Women, published in 1540, was among the first English texts to participate in the controversy about women's civic role. Written in the voice of Zenobia, Queen of Palmyra, it has been read as a covert exercise in support of Catherine of Aragon.[41] Lord Henry Howard, Earl of Northampton, borrowed from the writings of Plutarch, Justinian and Herodotus in his *A Dutiful Defence of the lawfull regiment of woman* published in 1590. Written by the Catholic aristocrat to win favour with Elizabeth, he drew upon historical examples of 'good queens', such as Alexandra wife of Alexander the Great, Theodora wife of Justinian and Zenobia, to support his case.[42] Thomas Heywood, author of numerous historical works on women, also wrote to curry favour with Elizabeth. Heywood celebrated *femmes forte*, 'heroic ladies ... derived of masculine spirit'.[43] His viragos were 'worthy' because they emulated men attempting 'brave and martial enterprises', like Elizabeth, who claimed to have the heart and stomach of a king. The reign of Elizabeth would be the occasion for the production of many defences of women. These texts were not only used to flatter the queen but also subtly discredited the French by criticising Salic law and showing the 'practicability of a "gynaecracie" '.[44]

Historical examples were also used to condemn female sovereignty. John Knox, a most vehement critic of female rule, drew upon biblical history in *The First Blast of the Trumpet against the Monstrous Regiment of Women* (1558), to defend his belief that female sovereignty was an aberration. Beginning with Eve, and drawing on other biblical *femmes fatales* like Jezebel, he argued that God had amply demonstrated that female authority inevitably led to chaos. Written specifically to attack Mary Tudor, Knox's work made it difficult for him to ingratiate himself with her half-sister Elizabeth, whose rule ended the persecution of Protestants. Knox eventually refered to Elizabeth as 'England's Deborah', but he refused to accept the legitimacy of female rule, arguing that Elizabeth was an 'exceptional instrument of God's will'.[45] Few Protestant reformers would use examples drawn from secular history, as they believed the truth came only from scripture.

Sixteenth-century wars of religion shaped new directions in relation to men's historical representation of women with the re-emergence of martyrology as a distinct branch of history. Reformation martyrology was shaped by the ever-present fear of civil war. Events like the St Bartholomew's Day massacre in 1574 framed these narratives and meant that all such historical writing had a distinctly political subtext. Religious persecution in the form of martyrdom was framed by a gendered paradigm. While earlier models of martyrology focused on female vulnerability and self-sacrifice, Reformation martyrology consistently focused on the male martyr who was a soldier of Christ, actively embracing martyrdom as a gesture essential for the foundation of the new church. In part this reflected the reality of the persecution. In France, for instance, Huguenot martyrs were overwhelming male.[46] Although many women were subject to ritual abuse, rape and death during these eruptions of sectarian violence, religious martyrdom was almost exclusively represented as the province of men.

Although Eusebius was the model for Protestant martyrologists, Reformation texts rarely replicated his horrific tales of female martyrdom. The treatment of female martyrs by contemporary Protestant historians was intended to be instructional and inspirational, but did not replicate the tradition of *femmes forte* in the secular literature.[47] When female martyrdom was described it was in terms that reflected women as the pious and passive helpmeet to man, as Protestant theology demanded. Such accounts stressed women's bravery in the face of martyrdom as essential proof that God was with the Reformers. Protestant polemicist John Bale wrote of the martyrdom of Anne Askew that 'the strength of God is here made perfyght by weaknesse. When she seemed most feble, than she was most stronge.'[48] This logic informed the representations of female martyrs found in John Foxes's *Acts and Monuments* (1563). In Britain this text was regarded as 'an expression of national faith second only in authority to the Bible'.[49] Foxe would repeat Bale's assessment of Anne Askew in his text, reporting her martyrdom as 'the strength of God in weak vessels'.

Foxe included an unannotated text of Askew's autobiography in the appendix to *Acts and Monuments*. In this text a very different Anne appears, one unbound by the traditional obligation of silence, chastity and obedience. David Loades has observed that Anne's self-representation showed her exploiting 'the traditional pose of silent obedience in order to contradict, indeed to satirise male antagonists for their inadequate comprehension'.[50] In contrast to the male historians who celebrated her demure and weak nature, Askew does not represent herself as a model of submissive womanhood. In concentrating on tales of male martyrs, Reformation martyrologists obscured women's place in the histories of the period. They manipulated tales of female martyrdom to match Protestant polemic about women's preordained role as the weaker vessel, using the gender ideology of the Reformation to frame their historical accounts.

The Science of History

In the wake of the Reformation science came to provide a new standard of knowledge and truth, based on human reason, experiment, observation and mathematics. The laws of science were seen to ensure a sense of certainty and authority in an otherwise unstable world. Connected to the rise of Protestantism as a religion, a work ethic and a knowledge system, science was seen to offer a 'promise of improving the condition of the world, even of restoring it to the condition it had been before Adam's fall'.[51] Those influenced by the revolutionary shifts in understanding generated by science 'sought to extend these approaches to understanding and managing the state and society'.[52]

Until the end of the seventeenth century history had been fundamentally a literary endeavour, deriving its authority from classical and biblical scholarship.[53] Science presented historians with new ways of thinking about, charting and recording historical change. It also allowed new theories of causation in history. Historian had previously relied on providence to explain historical change, which occurred because God had ordained it so. The rise of science challenged these certainties, promoting a more secular understanding of historical change. The influence of Francis Bacon and René Descartes saw historians become more sceptical and more methodical in their approach. Divine explanation for historical change would eventually be dismissed and a more critical attitude developed towards all authority and acceptance of tradition.[54] Historians placed increasing emphasis on the collection of facts and treated source criticism with greater seriousness.

Sir Francis Bacon would be particularly influential in the translation of scientific methods into historiography. As a natural historian Bacon developed an 'experimental philosophy' based around the principles of observation of phenomena, including typical and atypical instances of every event, and the collection of 'facts' to formulate general lessons.[55] In scientific fashion he had classified varieties of history taxonomically, first differentiating between natural and civil history, then dividing the latter into sacred, civil and literary. History had an important place within the Baconian structure of knowledge because it 'represented the empirical foundation on which reason constructed science'.[56] Although often represented as the first modern scientific historian, he was also an historian in the older humanist tradition. In this context he advised young scholars to be 'conversant in Histories', recommending Tacitus, Livy and Thucydides, so they may be instructed 'in matters moral, military and political'.[57] Bacon 'was at once a great exponent of "humanist" history and the theoretician who provided the philosophical basis for "scientific" history'.[58]

By the end of the seventeenth century historians translated Bacon's ideas about the study of natural history into the study of history more generally. This shift towards scientific history developed in a distinctly gendered manner. Those scientists who followed Bacon were not merely interested in observing nature, but in controlling it.[59] The desire to use science in this way clearly lent itself to certain sexualised metaphors that replicated in scientific discourse the rhetoric of masculine dominion and female subservience favoured by Protestant theologians. Nature in this discourse was represented as female. Science was characterised as a masculine philosophy, 'active, virile and generative'.[60] The role of the scientist was likened to that of the husband, who administered the 'right kind of male domination' over an unruly wife.[61]

Scientific understandings of the past came to function in a similarly gendered way. The past, like nature, was represented as female. It was the job of the historian to master the past in the same way the scientist mastered nature. History acquired a male rigour, 'an authoritative forcefulness that contrasted with the unreliability of tales and traditions'.[62] Just as Bacon attacked ancient philosophy as a 'female offspring – passive, weak and expectant', historians informed by science came to challenge the authority of the ancients, implicitly attributing to such histories a 'feminine' and hence fictitious edge. The tools adopted by 'scientific' historians, scepticism and empiricism, were used to diminish the potential fictionality of history and to maintain the rigours of a 'masculine philosophy'.

Hastening the shift of history towards science was a new understanding of time generated by Sir Isaac Newton. Prior to the discovery of his laws, time was a relativistic concept framed entirely by Aristotlean and ecclesiastical understanding. Newton's laws showed that time passed 'independently of the world whose changes it measured'.[63] This new understanding of time necessitated a change in historical understanding. Newton's concept of mathematical time posited that moments of absolute time formed a continuous sequence, like the points on a geometrical line.[64] Following Newton, historians became increasingly concerned with chronology and anachronism.

Enlightened History?

The transition towards a more scientific conception of history was facilitated by the increasing scepticism of the age. Whereas the polemicists of the Reformation had undermined the intellectual authority of Rome, the *philosophes* of the Enlightenment sought to banish all superstition and extend the principles of science to the study of society. As sceptical thought questioned all authority, the study of nature took on an important role. Newton's theories suggested a new scientific understanding of Nature as mathematical and mechanical.[65] 'Science took its character from nature itself, reasoning that as nature was composed solely of matter in motion, it must therefore be neutral'.[66] In the eighteenth century historians came to apply the same intellectual tools to the study of both nature and history: 'their purpose in investigating both was to replace transcendental with empirical causes'.[67] The development of internal criticism of documents came to be the standard practice of 'scientific' historians. This involved authenticating documents and engaging critically with them, reading documents against other sources and questioning the truthfulness of the author. These practices were deemed scientific because it was believed that they allowed the historian to engage in an 'objective' search for the truth.

It was the Italian philosopher Giambattista Vico who first established history as the 'science of man' with the publication of *The New Science* (1725). In this work Vico formulated principles of historical method in much the same way as Bacon had formulated those of science. Vico regarded historical progress as a process whereby human beings built up systems of language, custom, law and government. This process followed a distinctive and uniform pattern: 'first the woods, then the cultivated fields and huts, next little houses and villages, thence cities, and finally academies and philosophers'.[68] Vico's work was largely ignored during his lifetime; however, by the mid-eighteenth century French and British historians developed an idea of philosophical history that harkened back to Vico.

The idea that historical change followed certain patterns or stages became commonplace by the mid-eighteenth century.[69] Enlightenment historians tended to subordinate facts to system.[70] This produced a discourse of 'philosophical history', merging the study of human societies with the study of human nature.[71] Philosophical history, or 'conjectural history', as it was also known, reflected the philosophical age, but was also derived from Enlightenment interest in ethnology. The discovery of America particularly influenced the development of conjectural history. Lacking in specific facts about many aspects of the 'primitive' societies, Enlightenment historians attempted, through philosophic analysis, to trace the origin and development of these societies.[72] Few of those who attempted 'philosophical history' were historians, rather they came to history after establishing their reputations as philosophers, mathematicians or belletrists.[73] Philosophical history eventually formed the disciplines of sociology and anthropology, but in the eighteenth century these influences merged to inform the work of historical writers as diverse as David Hume, Lord Kames, William Robertson, John Millar, Voltaire, Turgot and Condorcet.

Combining elements of natural history and moral philosophy, 'philosophical history' aimed to chart the human development through common stages, studying existing contemporary societies, even the most primitive, and using the evidence of travellers and missionaries rather than focusing on archival documents.[74] These 'scientific' practices were coupled with a sense that historians were attempting to 'bring the methodological authority of the physical sciences to the study of man's past'.[75] Just as natural historians developed certain 'laws' to explain the genetic progress of certain species, historians formulated laws explaining how and why societies progressed towards civilisation. These 'laws' showed how each society moved through a series of 'stages', from a hunting to a pastoral, an agricultural, and finally to a commercial economy. The height of civilisation was the 'Old world' of Europe, which was conceptually opposed to the 'savagery' of the 'New world'.[76]

Unlike earlier historians, who focused only on individual and exceptional women in their histories, philosophical historians used women or rather gender relations as an historical category of analysis. Philosophical historians used the status of women in any given society as a marker of civilisation. As Sylvana Tomaselli has observed, women became 'the barometers on which every aspect of society, its morals, its laws, its customs, its government' was measured.[77] Savage man was said to keep women in a brutalised state and savagery came to be defined in terms of grossly unequal gender relations. Civilisation became measured by the degree of 'equality' allowed women. As Condorcet declared, greater equality between the sexes reflected a 'more sedentary form of life'.[78] Discussion of women in these texts merely reflected the patriarchal relations of Europe as ideal when compared with the brutal state of sexual relations in the 'New world'. Most philosophical historians believed, like Lord Kames, that the story of historical progress was the story of women's progress, 'from their low state in savage tribes, to their elevated state in civilised nations'.[79] Equality in this context did not mean true equality with men, it meant freedom from sexual slavery. Women were 'no longer considered merely as useful objects ... to their masters'.[80] Their influence, however, did not extend beyond the private sphere. The control of sexuality was a central feature of philosophical histories of civilisation. Beliefs about the superiority of monogamous marriage, the preservation of child life and the importance of legitimate inheritance shaped the way in which philosophical historians characterised 'civilisation'. As Robert Wokler has suggested, these histories of civilisation can be read as histories of 'the refinement of attraction into affection, of sex into love'.[81]

New ideas about feminine virtue derived from the culture of sensibility that dominated European bourgeois life in the eighteenth century saw moral purity, benevolence and spirituality increasingly defined as feminine qualities.[82] Philosophical history was both influenced by and contributed to this culture of sensibility. In spite of their rather limited idea of equality between the sexes, most philosophical historians believed in greater education and emancipation for women. Philosophical history made relations between the sexes an important marker of civilisation. Merging moral philosophy with historical analysis, 'enlightened' historians depicted the family as 'the primary transmitter of customs, habits, morals and manners', representing women both as the means and beneficiaries of social progress.[83] The new ideals of feminine virtue that emerged during this period allowed philosophical historians to break the 'conceptual boundaries between public and private spheres' within historiography and 'define a social though not political, role of importance for women'.[84]

The Enlightenment produced the first histories entirely devoted to women. Such texts did not focus on great women in history as earlier historians had, but rather explained women's unequal status in society from an historical perspective. In France, Antoine-Léonard Thomas produced *Essai sur le Charactère des Moeurs et l'Espirit des Femmes dans les différents Siècles* in 1772. In Britain the Scottish physician William Alexander published the *History of Women from the Earliest Antiquity to the Present Time* in 1783 and in Germany Christoph Meiners published a four-part history of women, *Gestichte des weibliches Geschlechts*, between 1788 and 1800. These histories did not subsume women into the category 'man' as later feminist historians have suggested, but instead maintained that women had a separate existence from man and hence a separate history.[85] Informed by Enlightenment rationality, these histories sought to understand women's unequal position in society, and argued for their greater emancipation. Merging Classical ideals, elements of natural history and moral philosophy with new Romantic notions of womanhood, these first historians of 'the Sex' linked the rise of European civilisation with the rise of domestic womanhood. They developed an ideal of European social superiority that was wholly connected to an ideology of separate spheres, creating a paradigm of historical progress that linked the health of any nation-state with the treatment of its women. Following Tacitus, William Alexander depicted the ancient Germans as representing the pinnacle of civilisation because of their treatment of women. Describing the Germans as having provided 'all of Europe with their laws and customs', Alexander claimed that German women were of 'equal and sometimes greater consequence than their men'.[86] Conflating contemporary ideas with ancient history, Alexander claimed this situation arose out 'of a species of Romantic heroism called chivalry', which communicated to German women a sense of dignity and pride, rendering them especially virtuous.[87] Alexander linked the fall of German civilisation with the collapse of chivalry and the decline of the public honour of men. This led to the loss of women's dignity, causing a loss of virtue. German men lost their 'deference for the sex' and 'women lost all the chastity that inspired it'.[88]

Histories of 'the Sex' were written with a female audience in mind. Underpinning the historical narrative was a desire to promote education for women. The *philosophes* greatly approved of history as a study for women and the intellectual climate of the Enlightenment saw educational possibilities for women gradually improve. More enlightened attitudes and better schooling increased literacy levels for women. Historical knowledge was only deemed appropriate when it enlightened women to their true natures and correct duties. It was hoped that an understanding of history would dampen their appetites for romance writing.[89]

The Romantic Reaction

The revolution of 1789 and the events that followed it were so catastrophic that many of the generalisations put forward by eighteenth-century historians were undermined.[90] The Revolution and the Napoleonic wars 'gave rise to questions about the nature of states and the origins of cultural identity, about *differences* between histories rather than their commonality'.[91] The practices of historians underwent radical revision during the early stages of the nineteenth century as part of a larger Romantic reaction to the French Revolution. The turn of events taken by the revolution challenged the certainties of Enlightenment history, necessitating different understanding of historical practice. The classical past, which had been neglected during the Enlightenment, emerged with renewed importance during the nineteenth century. This recourse to antiquity would again alter the way in which women's historical role was perceived.

The Enlightenment had promoted 'a singular sense of the present as a moment of exceptional importance and weight in the history of the world'.[92] Eighteenth-century intellectuals had embraced the modern and, as Michael Bentley has observed, 'seemed transparently pleased to be living in the eighteenth century'.[93] The French Revolution caused European intellectuals to revise this view and to look once again to antiquity to explain current crises in modernity. The past came to be as important to the Victorians as the present had been to the *philosophes* of the Enlightenment.[94] Recourse to the past was part of a wider Romantic reaction to these events. Historians joined artists and poets as part of a Romantic movement dedicated to the search for national origins and identities. Romanticism caused intellectuals to reject Enlightenment rationality, to embrace an ideal shaped by intuition, emotion and sensibility. Reacting against scientific detachment, the Romantics made a religion of nature and immersed themselves in the study of the past. Romanticism generated a new idea of history. Following Vico, German intellectuals such as Leibniz, Lessing and Herder transformed the idea of history, creating a developmental conception of human culture. Known as 'historicism', its essential elements were the ideas of individuality and development.[95] Historicism rejected the certainties offered by philosophical historians. Romantic historians maintained that human nature was not uniform and was constantly undergoing a process of development.[96] Romanticism encouraged historians to reject the Enlightenment view that there were 'constant and universal principles of human nature': instead, history showed how 'human nature differed for different individuals, nations or periods'.[97] The past became 'a peculiar national affair' as historians recognised that each nation experienced a unique historical and cultural development.[98] Looking to the past, tracing the origins of the nation-state, allowed historians to generate a sense of national identity.

While artists and poets tended to focus on the Romantic Middle Ages in this quest for national identity, historians returned to the ancient past. In Germany historians looked to Rome to produce an explicit sense of German nationalism. B. G. Niebuhr, whose work dominated Roman scholarship throughout the nineteenth century, admitted to studying Rome in reaction to the French occupation of Prussia. Stung by this humiliation, Niebuhr wrote that he 'went back to a nation, great, but long passed by, to strengthen my mind and that of my hearers. We [*sic*] felt like Tacitus.'[99] Niebuhr was returning to a pre-Enlightenment tradition that saw Germans look to Rome to define and unify their institutional, cultural and ethnic ancestry.[100] In Britain historians shifted focus away from Rome, with its obvious associations with republicanism, towards Athens. The image of Athenian democracy was initially used by conservatives to expose 'the dangerous turbulence of democracy'.[101] The rise of democracy in contemporary Greece inspired young liberals throughout Europe. Young men, like the poet Byron, went to Greece to experience this at first hand.[102] Such enthusiasm influenced the study of classical Greece.[103] Americans, also, associated their newly democratic state with Athens.[104] In the nineteenth century classical Athens was reinvented by historians to reflect their ideal of the modern liberal state.[105]

Recourse to the classical world affected the ways in which historians represented women's role in history. The idea of the illegitimacy of female power that characterised Roman historians' treatment of women emerged with renewed vigour during the course of the French Revolution. It had not entirely disappeared during the Enlightenment, being kept alive by Jean-Jacques Rousseau, who believed women should be strictly secluded from the realms of politics.[106] Unlike other 'enlightened' men, Rousseau maintained that the entrance of women into the public sphere marked the nadir of the *ancien régime* and was highly critical of the education of women in anything other than domesticity.[107] Rousseau first articulated the ideal of republican motherhood that shaped domestic ideology in France and America throughout the nineteenth century.

During the revolution both Jacobins and Monarchists borrowed images of women from Tacitus and Rousseau to delegitimise women's entrance into the public sphere. French political propagandists were quick to liken the despised Marie Antoinette with Messalina, the promiscuous wife of the Emperor Claudius, and Julia Aggripina, the incestuous mother of Nero.[108] Writers both for and against the Revolution drew on ancient authority to argue against the rights of women and to trivialise their role as historical subjects. Continuities drawn between ancient and revolutionary women undercut the possibility of seeing women as significant historical actors; instead they were characterised as ahistorical agents of reaction. In this sense women came to again serve as historiographical devices indicating social disorder and civil upheaval, rather than as agents of political or social change.

No figure would draw such continuities more dramatically than the British politician Edmund Burke, who wrote the first British study of the Revolution. Two recurring images of womanhood drawn from ancient Rome frame his vehemently anti-revolutionary *Reflections on the Revolution in France* (1790). One image is of the queen, Marie Antoinette. Marie Antoinette was depicted by Burke as vulnerable, sexually innocent and entirely victimised, much like the suicidal Roman matrons found in Livy. While Livy used the tales of Lucretia and Virginia to symbolise the dangers of tyrannical power, Burke inverted this meaning, using the treatment of Marie Antoinette to show the dangers of mob rule. Burke predicted (incorrectly) that, like Lucretia and Virginia, Marie Antoinette would 'in the last extremity... save herself from the last disgrace'.[109] It was, however, the other image of the womanhood conjured up by Burke, that of the women revolutionaries, that would taint the historical representation of women throughout the nineteenth century. Using terms borrowed from classical mythology, Burke described these women as harpies and furies, invoking a sense of sexual as well as political anarchy.[110] For Burke, the political crisis that engulfed France could not be separated from the broader gender crisis symbolised by women's entrance into the public sphere. By usurping the political privileges of men, French women had brought their country to the brink of disaster. Women's trespass into the king's palace and their entrance into the National Assembly were presented by Burke as evidence of France's national decline. Such ideas were in keeping with Polybius and Tacitus, who invariably showed that reversals of gender order led to political crisis.

The idea that gender disorder led to political disorder became a commonplace of counter-revolutionary and revolutionary discourse. Those who supported the revolution and those who opposed it both sought to curtail women's political activities. Although women had been critical to the early success of the Revolution, by the end of 1793 they had been banned from most political activities. When Napoleon assumed power many revolutionary reforms benefiting women, such as the liberalisation of divorce, were rescinded. The ideal of republican motherhood that emerged during this period would further curtail women's political ambitions. Drawn from Roman history and reasserted by Rousseau, republican mothers would find political satisfaction in performing their private duties. As the Napoleonic wars swept through Europe, the Republican mother, like Tacitus's idealised German woman, would serve the cause of war-making by submitting to her husband's control. The idea of republican motherhood subsumed the identity of the female citizen into that of the male citizen. Her image limited the possibility of women engaging in political life and alienated from political authority any women who had gained ascendancy throughout the revolutionary period. The ideal confirmed that women's domestic confinement was necessary for the political and social order. Following the revolution, debates around citizenship, democracy and the development of the nation-state made an emphatic connection between sexual difference, sexual hierarchy and political order.

Women's domestic seclusion would be replicated in their historical marginalisation throughout the nineteenth century and into the twentieth. The domestic sphere, the sphere of women, was again regarded as ahistorical and oppositional to the public sphere, the sphere of men and of history. Like Thucydides, Victorian historians would regard the confinement of women as both natural and necessary for the achievement of historical progress.[111] That is not to say that women were entirely absent from the historical record during the nineteenth century, but rather that both historical writing and the teaching of history served simultaneously to legitimise the exclusion of women and to justify the subordination of women for the good working of society. The study of history endorsed an ideal of public life drawn from the ancient world that defined the public sphere as an exclusively male environment and celebrated women's confiment in the home.[112] The meaning of the domestic seclusion of women in Athens and other ancient societies was one of the few areas of women's history researched by men during the nineteenth century.[113] Underpinning much of this debate was an attempt to justify the exclusion of women from the modern public sphere and to romanticise their continued seclusion in the home.[114] As late as 1925 A.W. Gomme, author of a major study on the status of women in ancient Greece, could write that 'when Theognis said, "I hate a woman who gads about and neglects her home" I think he expressed a sentiment common to most people of all ages'.[115] Such comments naturalised patriarchal gender relations, ensuring women's marginalisation as both political actors and historical subjects.

On the rare occasions when women were recalled as political actors in nineteenth-century histories, it was in ways that showed that disaster inevitably followed their involvement in the public sphere. Thomas Carlyle, the most widely read Victorian historian, would devote a large section of his account of the *French Revolution* (1837) to 'The Insurrection of Women'. Carlyle attributed the cause of women's political insurrection to their roles as mothers, but constituted 'maternity' as an unstable and reactive force, describing women's political actions as driven only by the need to feed their children.[116] Like Burke, Carlyle borrowed from classical mythology, calling revolutionary women *maenads*. *Maenads* comes from the Greek *mainomai*, to rage, suggesting that revolutionary women were simply reactionary.[117] More significantly, the conflation of maternity and *maenad* in Carlyle's text functioned as a warning of the dangers of women's sexuality and reproductive capacities to the public sphere. Jules Michelet, 'the father of French history', in his study *Women of the Revolution* (1854), drew on such theories to explain women's 'innate' political ineptitude. He wrote: 'It is not our fault if nature has made women, if not feeble, at least infirm, subject to periodic illness, creatures of emotion, children of the sidereal world, hence unfitted by their uneven constitutions to undertake the functions of political societies.'[118] Michelet represented women as 'embodiments of the eternal (and non-historical feminine)', forever pairing them with ' "world-historical" men'.[119]

Historical writing in the nineteenth century defined progress in opposition to femininity. The historical narratives of the nation-state that emerged during this period maintained the importance of sexual hierarchy to the political order. The domestic seclusion of women described by Thucydides and Tacitus came to be represented by Victorian historians as women's natural and ideal role. The writing of history and the shaping of the discipline during the nineteenth century was formed around narratives of masculine citizenship, public duty and the exclusion of women. In many ways history became the science of recording how European male elites subjugated others. Colonised and indigenous peoples, women and the proletariat were rarely the subject of history. Men, that is, European male elites, were the subject of history.

The History Men

Women's exclusion from the public sphere was reinforced by practices adopted by historians engaged in creating the new discipline of history within the university. As in ancient times, the study of history in the Victorian academy was seen as critical to the development of manliness. This connection between history and cultured manhood rendered women marginal as historical subjects and limited their potential to become historians. Historical education was deemed necessary to groom [male] individuals for civic leadership and to prepare [men] 'for the noblest kinds of citizenship'.[120] Historical knowledge was believed to inspire in young men 'communal ideals of service in a nation of individuals'.[121] This shift was not a major change in the way historical education had been perceived, rather it marked the shift of these values from the aristocracy to the middle classes. Until the nineteenth century civil service had been heriditary, reserved for the aristocracy. The Napoleonic system put an end to the venality of these offices and saw the creation of a newly rationalised bureaucracy that was merit-based and competitive. Higher education became increasingly devoted to inculcating bourgeois values of economy, political moderation, hard work and manliness.

The idea that knowledge of history was an essential component of bourgeois masculinity united a burgeoning, yet increasingly diverse international historical profession. This transformation was largely due to the work of the German historian Leopold von Ranke. Ranke revolutionised the practice of history by developing a set of principles that stressed the objectivity of historical truth, the priority of facts over concepts, the equivalent uniqueness of all historical events and the centrality of politics to the study of history.[122] He converted the practices and ideals of individual historians 'into a paradigm which could be communicated to an entire profession as its distinctive collective identity'.[123] This revolution was made possible by the fact that Ranke was able to impart both his methods and his principles via his seminar, making the teaching of history critical to the practice of historical writing.

Ranke's use of seminar teaching as the basis of the study of history functioned in ways that explicitly excluded women as both historical subjects and historians. The 'birth of the seminar' saw the study of history at university become an entirely male domain as teaching moved from the public lecture hall, which was open to all, to the seminar room, a private space available only to men. Bonnie G. Smith has documented the way this space was devoted to preparing men for the rigours of detailed archival research in a workshop-like environment.[124] Ranke's influence saw the professional work of historical science, the historian's search for objectivity, become conflated with a masculine quest for identity.[125] Archival research as taught in the seminar came to be articulated in terms denoting masculine and bourgeois values. Young men participating in the history seminar were encouraged to see themselves as part of a 'common brotherhood of professional practitioners' made possible by their shared commitment to archival research and textual analysis.[126] The language of brotherhood and the shared ideals fostered by the seminar gave rise to a proliferation of fraternal history associations in the later half of the century.[127] These groups usually excluded women or only allowed them token participation.[128] The emphasis on the study of archives clearly privileged the history of the public sphere, excluding the feminine and private sphere from historical analysis. As Smith has shown, these exclusions meant the shaping of the discipline and the writing of history were formed around narratives of masculine citizenship and public duty. In the writing of history and in its study in the academy, men were taught that women were not citizens and were thus outside the realm of history.

PART II

Women's History

I learnt history as unquestionably as I did geography, without ever dreaming that there could be more than one view of past events.
    Simone de Beauvoir, *Memoirs of a Dutiful Daughter*, 1959

CHAPTER 3

'Above Their Sex'? Women's History 'before' Feminism

> History can only serve us for Amusement and as a Subject of Discourse.... Some good Examples indeed are to be found in History, tho generally the bad are ten for one... since the Men being the Historians, they seldom condescend to record the great and good Actions of Women; and when they take notice of them, 'tis with this wise Remark, That such Women *acted above their Sex.*
>
> Mary Astell, *The Christian Religion as Profess'd by a Daughter of the Church of England*, 1705

Women have always practised various means of recording history, but these practices have rarely been recognised as history. This chapter will examine the work of women as historical writers from the Renaissance until the French Revolution. It will demonstrate that although lacking in civil rights, with poor educational opportunities and with little access to the materials necessary to write history, a small but significant number of women engaged in the production of history throughout this period. Subverting traditional genres like biography and family history, women inserted themselves into historical narratives and subtly manipulated the gendered expectations of historiography. During this period women historians did not necessarily write about women, nor were they overtly concerned with women's rights, but many of them developed feminist consciousness through their study of history. Women's historical endeavours created an intellectual environment that allowed the development of feminist ideas, and increasingly throughout the seventeenth and eighteenth centuries a sense of women's oppression was acknowledged. If the study of history was seen as essential to develop 'manliness', it served equally to alert women to their unequal status and led to an assertion of history's moral authority in order to achieve women's rights.

This chapter will show how women developed feminist consciousness through their historical endeavours. It will ask: What kinds of history did women produce during this period? How did women acquire historical skills? What factors enabled women to create their own historical subjectivity? How has women's historical vision differed from that of men's? Did the prescriptions of gender inhibit or enhance women's historical production?

History as Feminine Pedagogy

The intellectual culture of the Renaissance necessarily affected men and women differently. As Joan-Kelly Gadol showed in her pathbreaking essay 'Did Women Have a Renaissance?', even elite women were generally excluded from the classical education that formed the 'Renaissance man'.[1] Public life, the desired end of the classical education, meant that it was necessarily inappropriate for women. Women may have been considered suitable for training in devoutness, but they were regarded as poorly suited to intellectual discipline. Only elite women from eccentric humanist families received an education.[2]

Even within these eccentric circles, femininity and classical scholarship were viewed as mutually exclusive. Scholarly women were regarded quizzically as a 'third sex'.[3] At one end of the spectrum this meant that learned women were depicted as virtuous women devoted to a life of celibacy. At the other end of the spectrum such women were represented as monstrous anomalies, destined to pollute the masculine realms of scholarship.[4] Women scholars were the subject of vituperative misogynist attacks, a genre which flourished during this period. Only scholarly women who retained an image of absolute purity succeeded in attaining respect from their male counterparts. Female sexuality was antithetical to female learning and thus only complete celibacy allowed women an unsullied reputation and a glimpse into the world of cultured manhood.

Ironically the ambivalence men felt about female learning meant that they encouraged women to study history. It was assumed that history offered different lessons for men and women. While men studied history to prepare them for public life, history taught women to devote their lives to good works and prayer in domestic seclusion. Leonardo Bruni suggested that history should be prioritised after morality and religion in the education of women.[5] This gendering of historical study did not challenge the representation of women found in masculinist historical texts, rather it confirmed the idea that women were best excluded from the public sphere.

Before Feminism?

The first history of women to be written by a woman during the Renaissance was reflective of humanism's deep ambivalence towards female learning. Christine de Pisan (c. 1364–1431) was the daughter of an Italian physician in the court of the French King Charles V. Her father was concerned with the education of his daughters, and unlike most girls of her age, Christine was educated in Italian, French and Latin. Widowed early in life, she did not remarry but chose to support herself. Studying history, philosophy and poetry, she became one of the most prolific writers of the fifteenth century. Although she wrote many other historical and political tracts including a life of Charles V and the *Book of the Body Politic*, the claim that Christine de Pisan was the first writer of women's history stems from her authorship of the text, *Cité des dames* (1405). The book was dedicated to Marguerite of Burgundy, who married Louis of Guyenne in 1405, and was commissioned by her father John the Fearless. The text was meant to guide his daughter through the hazards of courtly life. Using history to instruct women in the ideals of feminine virtue would become a major impetus for the writing of women's history. The assertion of feminine virtue also underscored much feminist debate into the twentieth century.

Cité des dames is a series of portraits of illustrious women, real and mythical. De Pisan was inspired to write this tract in reaction to popular misogynist catalogs of the period such as Jean de Meun's *Romance of the Rose*.[6] Like Boccaccio's *De claris mulieribus*, *Cité des dames* argued that the virtue of men and women was essentially comparable. De Pisan became the first woman to speak out against misogynistic representations of women and to advocate women's rights, particularly to education. The demand for women's education would be a continuous theme in women's historical writing. Joan Kelly-Gadol has named Christine de Pisan the first feminist, as she began women's participation in the *Querelle des Femmes*.[7] This claim was made eighty years earlier by the medievalist Alice Kemp-Welch, who wrote that de Pisan 'may be regarded not merely as a forerunner of true feminism, but also as one of its greatest champions'.[8] De Pisan has become an enduring symbol of feminine excellence and feminist consciousness.

De Pisan's arguments on behalf of women invoked historical tradition but also broke radically with that tradition.[9] Not only did her text recover women from the obscurity of posterity, but she restored their speech and reinvented male myths about women, rehabilitating the sullied reputation of classical figures like Medea.[10] De Pisan began a tradition of women's historical writing that would continue until the 1970s. Often dismissed as the history of 'women worthies', these acts of recovery have furnished women with role models, assisting in the development of feminist consciousness. They functioned in a subversive way, challenging male versions of the past, celebrating women who questioned male authority and encouraging the idea that women were capable of public roles. Writing the history of 'women worthies' was an important precursor to feminist approaches to women's history.

In *Cité des dames* de Pisan attempted to write a universal history of women. Her use of the city as a governing metaphor for the text enhanced this historical dimension, linking it with St Augustine's *City of God*, the church's most important universal history.[11] Glenda McLeod has suggested that this was an important strategy of the text, associating women with the universal rather than the particular. The city is also a public space opposed to the domestic. This choice of this metaphorical location emphasised de Pisan's argument that women should enter the public sphere and influence practical politics.

Reforming Women

Although certain humanist scholars had championed the education of women, most Renaissance women lacked the learning and the materials required to become an historian. Women were denied the 'public life' which allowed men to travel to collect manuscripts, to observe intrigues and conflicts and to develop the political experience necessary to interpret events of historical significance.[12] The exclusion of women from the public sphere did not necessarily preclude them from writing history, rather these limitations made the women who produced history at this time truly innovative. For women the very act of writing represented an invasion of the public sphere and saw them, in a sense, become public women. To produce history, women had to subvert historical norms, ignoring or reversing the emphasis on the public that shaped masculinist historical discourse. Few women would produce history that resembled masculinist political history, rather they shaped the genre to suit their own particular circumstances, adapting acceptable modes like family history to achieve historical subjectivity.

The tension between the private world of women and the public world of men shaped the historical narratives produced by women throughout this period, and it was only through the manipulation of acceptable feminine ideals that it was possible for women to achieve any sense of historical subjectivity. Religious life and reform allowed a small number of women to produce history during the period between the Renaissance and the Enlightenment. This was particularly true of women who chose to entirely devote their lives to religion as nuns. While nuns lived privately secluded in convents, convents were essentially public institutions. Convents owned land, educated the daughters of the gentry and dispensed charity to the poor and sick. As public institutions they held archives. These records formed the basis of the 'Sister books' that chronicled convent life from the fourteenth century onwards.[13] Historical subjectivity emerged out of the private writings of nuns such as diaries or spiritual autobiographies.[14] Like family history, histories of convent life recorded important events in the community such as professions, as well as more mundane details like deaths. Although these were essentially private writings recounting the spiritual lives of the nuns, they had influence beyond the convent walls as they chronicled the social changes and political upheavals that affected convent life.[15] This would become especially significant during the period of the Reformation and Counter-Reformation.

Convents were unique institutions in that they provided women with the raw materials to produce historical writing and were one of the few sites that fostered female literacy, providing 'a receptive and sympathetic environment for women's writing'.[16] Numerous biographies of 'holy women' were produced as devotional texts throughout the period.[17] Nuns also created hagiographic texts, particularly histories of individual saints.[18] Like later biographical works by women, these histories presented saintly lives for women to emulate. As Isobel Grundy has observed, the historical writing of nuns accounted for 'a history of a whole female culture'.[19]

Religious writings by women exerted a strong influence over ideals of femininity, especially as the role of women became a contentious issue during the Reformation and Counter-Reformation.[20] Although both Protestantism and Catholicism adhered to St Paul's teaching that women should remain silent, the political struggles engendered by religious reform allowed both nuns and secular women a public voice previously denied them.[21] As history was the primary means through which Catholics and Protestants expressed their differences, Protestant and Catholic women drew upon history to argue on behalf of their religion. Writings by nuns and other religious women became important tools in these sectarian struggles.[22] For most women this writing evolved as an extension of their interest in theology. The former abbess of Tournai Marie Dentière (1521–61) wrote numerous religious tracts during the Reformation, including the theological text *Très Utile*, which denounced papal abuses and called for women to have a more active role in the church.[23] She was the author of a religious-political history of the Swiss Reformation, *La guerrre et deslivrance de la ville Genesve* (1536), that described the 'salvation' of the Swiss city of Geneva following the decline of Catholicism. During the Counter-Reformation Catholic nuns wrote histories defending the Pope and documenting Protestant attacks on the church. Apollonia Cabelisin, prioress of St Agnes of Freiburg in Breisgau, wrote a short account of the destruction of her convent by the Swedish army in 1644.[24] Such texts not only recorded the effect of these conflicts on convent life, but they were also vehicles of sectarian polemic.[25]

Other women, less certain of their religious and political position, chose forms of historical writing that were less public. Merging historical narrative with poetic form allowed Anne Dowriche (d. 1638) to contribute to sectarian debate in her tragedy, *The French History* (1589). This verse-narrative detailed the persecution of French Huguenots (Protestants) that culminated in the horrific St Bartholomew's Day massacre in 1574. Dowriche drew on primary sources such as François Hotman's *True and Plain Report of the Furious Outrapes* [sic] of France (1573) and was obviously familiar with humanist models of historical writing.[26] Dowriche did not adopt the role of historian, instead choosing to disguise her public voice with the invention of a male author and 'a godlie French exile' who carried the narrative, bearing witness to the events in France. The transference of her role to a male persona mitigated her presumption, completely disguising 'the knowledge and ability of a woman to write so public a narrative poem'.[27] Merging history with other literary forms enabled women to disguise their political opinions and to deflect criticism for adopting such masculine pursuits.

Women were drawn to the writing of family history as a result of sectarian conflicts. They did not have to venture beyond their private domain to engage in political struggle, as the domestic sphere merged with the harsh realm of war and politics. The conflation of religion and politics in struggles such as the French Wars of Religion in the sixteenth century and English Civil Wars during the seventeenth century allowed women to subvert the genre of family history to develop a new form of writing that was simultaneously religious and domestic, historical and public. Women had practised recording the great deeds of fathers and husbands for the education of sons since late antiquity and were permitted to engage in family history because it focused on private life. Earlier models of family history offered women little space for historical subjectivity. If women had written about themselves in earlier histories, it was 'for proper domestic reasons' like fear of death in childbirth.[28] The social upheavals of the Reformation enabled women to rework the genre of family history to create their own sense of historical subjectivity. From this creation of historical subjectivity emerged nascent feminist ideas and challenges to traditional notions of the political.

Women writing their memoirs, or memoirs of their male kin, subsumed their individuality into the role of perfect Protestant wife.[29] In the sixteenth century Charlotte Arbaleste (d. 1606), wife of the Huguenot polemicist Philippe du Plessis de Mornay, struggled to find her own voice in the history of their family. Referring to Arbaleste, Natalie Zemon Davis observed that 'the wife records, lends her voice to her husband but does not take hold of the material on her own'.[30] Charlotte's self-effacement was doubly strange as she attached her own memoir to that of her husband. This memoir was also filled with details of her husband's life. Arbaleste linked childbearing and child-rearing with the recording of family history.[31] This was in keeping with the ideal of wifely duties espoused by Protestantism. Arbaleste subtly manipulated the ideal of wifely submission and deference. By describing the keeping of family history as one of women's wifely roles she asserted a certain power through this writing. This power enabled women to produce their husbands' lives as their own literary creations.[32] This strategy of modesty became common among early modern women historians.

Sectarian struggles during the Reformation gave rise to confessional history. Participants felt the need to tell of their experiences, justify their political positions and seek consolation for their losses. Women experienced these needs in the same way as men. While men could unselfconsciously engage in confessional history centring around their own lives, women had to use the histories of their male kin to describe their own participation in these conflicts. While few women engaged overtly in expressing the 'self for fame', they came to develop a sense of their own historical subjectivity through family history. Like much writing by women, these texts evinced a paradoxical quality, for while they continued to support domestic life and relations, they also allowed women a public voice.

It was women's knowledge of the private life of their subjects that allowed them to claim unique historical authority. As Margaret Cavendish, the Duchess of Newcastle (c. 1623–73) wrote, the best sort of history was history that 'does not go out of its own circle, but turns on its own axis, and for the most part keeps within the circumference of the truth'.[33] This was in keeping with the tone of all the women who chose to write familial history during this period. This statement reflected the intimate nature between women and their subjects. But the privileging of private knowledge over the celebration of the public persona favoured in political history also marked a radical means of constituting authority in both history and biography. The civil nature of warfare during this period meant that women were closely involved in the machinations of war and witnesses to events that they later described. Ann, Lady Fanshawe, who was involved in the royalist court during the English Civil War, recorded in her memoir that she 'had the perpetuall discourse of losing and gaining of towns and men [sic]'.[34] This proximity allowed women to claim historical authenticity. As Margaret Cavendish wrote in her husband's biography, 'I cannot, though neither actor nor spectator be thought ignorant of the truth of what I write; nor is it consistent with me being a woman, to write of war, that was neither between Medes or Persians … but among my own countrymen.'[35]

The historical writing produced by women during this time retained the structure and religious tone of early family history, while simultaneously challenging the traditional nature of the genre. Events such as the English Civil War (1642–51) allowed women to manipulate their role as wife and helpmeet to describe actions that thrust them into the domain of war and politics. As N. H. Keeble has suggested, 'the prospect of female vulnerability and wifely helplessness is far from being the dominant image' of the women's memoirs of the English Civil War. There 'is also, and perhaps for the first time in narrative texts, the prospect of female indomitability, of women who can act on the public stage independently of men'.[36]

The Life of Colonel Hutchinson, written during the Restoration, provides wonderful evidence of how women transformed family history into political history during this period.[37] Lucy Hutchinson (c. 1620–75), the wife of the English regicide John Hutchinson, wrote a vindication of his life following his death in prison. This text has long been regarded as the testament of a dutiful wife for a much-loved husband. In the nineteenth century, Lucy was held up as a 'heroine of domestic life' and her claim to be her husband's 'shadow' was often repeated for Victorian wives to emulate. But as Stevie Davies has argued, 'a less obedient and more high-handed shadow would be hard to find'.[38] While the text is written entirely in the third person and Lucy appears to distance herself from the action, much of the narration revolves around her heroics. She uncovers assassination plots, negotiates with the army, acts as the governor of Nottingham and wilfully disobeys her husband to save his life. As Davies and other commentators have noticed, though Hutchinson framed her position in the text around a notion of women's submission to the patriarchal order, all evidence points to her ignoring such constraints. The very act of putting pen to paper could be construed as an act of 'gross impropriety', judged by Hutchinson's own standards. 'For Lucy Hutchinson to write at all', Keeble asserts, 'was thus to emerge from the shadow of John Hutchinson by laying implicit claims to the prerogatives of the masculine gender. It was an insubordinate, immodest and unfeminine act'.[39]

The *Memoirs of Ann, Lady Fanshawe* demonstrate a similar flexibility with the accepted norms of femininity. Fanshawe (1625–73), a royalist widow, wrote a memoir of her husband Sir Richard, published after her death. Although on the opposite side of the conflict, Fanshawe, like Hutchinson, maintained the importance of patriarchal order and believed that wives should be 'submissive, dutiful and retiring'.[40] Her narrative betrays an incapacity to sustain this role. She engaged very successfully in the harsh masculine realm of civil war; escaping capture, forging passports, even fighting off pirates disguised as a cabin boy. For Fanshawe it was her belief that husband and wife were 'one flesh' that allowed her narrative licence; to separate their lives was impossible.[41] It was her commitment to patriarchal sexual ideology that allowed Fanshawe to recount this adventurous life. Although seventeenth-century women could not engage in autobiography as propaganda for posterity in ways that commemorated and justified their own public deeds, they could and did subvert the biographies of their husbands to fulfil the same function.[42]

Women on all sides of the conflict exploited accepted feminine norms to attain an unacceptable public/political voice. The adoption of a tone of womanly submission was more than a rhetorical device. Vituperative propaganda against women's participation in the public sphere had been a feature of English political life since the reign of Mary Tudor. Women's participation in politics was seen as emblematic of the more general social disorder occasioned by sectarian conflict. The Restoration brought with it an exaggerated desire to return to the 'natural order'. The ambivalent position of women during the Restoration is amply illustrated by the works of Fanshawe and Hutchinson. For while ostensibly producing commemorative histories that memorialised husbands 'under a restored patriarchal order', they were also focusing upon the marginal, questioning the insistence upon women's silence, challenging traditional definitions of the political and 'affording a story to what should be uneventful'.[43] It may also be true that the memoirs of women who did not pay attention to their duties as loyal and submissive wives would not survive for posterity. Although evidence of this is necessarily scant, it occasionally appears in the form of men reporting their suppression of women's work.[44]

In France the civil war between the Regent Anne of Austria and her aristocracy, known as the Fronde (1648–52), produced a similar outpouring of historical writing by women. French noblewomen played an overtly political and military role in the Fronde, and in its aftermath were keen to ensure that their role in this fracas was not forgotten. Their writings drew on a tradition established by Marguerite de Valois (1553–1615), whose memoirs were published in 1628. These memoirs took several forms, ranging from wholly autobiographical texts to 'fictitious' memoirs of famous women involved in court politics. Although some of these texts blurred the boundaries between fact and fiction, their authors claimed to be writing 'particular' history, which was distinct from the more general accounts written by men.[45] Women who wrote these 'memoirs' and historical 'novels' self-consciously tried to insert into the historical record personalities, events and activities that would otherwise have gone unrecorded.

Unlike their English counterparts, who were careful in their narratives to insist that their actions never overshadowed their male kin's, women of the Fronde wrote semi-autobiographical texts exploring the upheavals of the period largely through their own experience. Women for the first time self-consciously acknowledged that they were not merely writing history, but were responsible for its making. In part this was due to the peculiar nature of the Fronde, a war in which marital alliances and other familial relationships were of critical importance. Women used their power in the private sphere to solidify certain coalitions and thwart those they did not support.[46] This insight allowed women to revise traditionally held views of history and shifted historical focus away from the battlefront and on to the Court. In part this shift related to the distinct class difference between women writers of the English Civil War, who were largely of the gentry, and women writers of the Fronde, who tended to be intimately connected with the French Royal family.[47] Anne-Marie Louise-Henriette d'Orléans, Duchesse de Montpensier (1627–93) and Marie d'Orléans-Longueville, Duchesse de Nemours (1619–79), protected by their immense wealth and 'princely' status, could adopt the position of 'Amazon warrior' with little fear of condemnation. Freedom of self-expression was mostly denied to middle-class women who felt that they must tentatively encroach rather than assault the public realm of war and history-making. Moreover, Catholic women did not feel the need to strictly delineate between history and romance in quite the same way as Protestant women. Protestant writers were inclined to suppress the romantic quality of their histories, because it compromised their 'religious faith and virtuous reputation'.[48] To appear to write 'true' history enabled Protestant women to overcome the silence enjoined upon them by their religion. Allowing any suspicion of 'romance' to appear overtly in these texts rendered their writings idolatrous.[49]

By insisting that the feminine and hence particular realm of 'intrigues, passions, personalities and secret negotiations' was a decisive force in the public political sphere, women writers of the Fronde dissolved the oppositions which framed historical writing and rendered it masculine.[50] Women's favouring of 'particular history' led to accusations that women's historical writing was more concerned with romance and thus less than factual. Unlike histories written by men that focused on the past for moral edification, history written by women was seen to use the past fancifully, to enhance the romantic quality of their writings. It is quite possible women merged the genres of fiction and history not merely to add interest to their writing, but to disguise its political nature and radical intentions. Madeleine de Scudéry (1607–1701), one of the most prolific writers of the seventeenth century, observed in her novel *Artamenes* (1653) that 'the intrigues of war and peace are better many times, laid open and satyriz'd in a Romance, than in a downright History, which being oblig'd to name the persons is often forc'd for several reasons and motives to be too partial and too sparing'.[51] Women who were too forthright about their own part in history risked not only public condemnation for their literary efforts but also imprisonment and exile.[52]

By the eighteenth century prosecution for libel became a strong incentive for women to disguise their historical and political commentary. English writers such as Delarivier Manley (1663–1724), Eliza Haywood (1693–1756) and Lady Mary Wortley Montagu (1689–1762) produced texts they described as 'secret histories', which were thinly disguised satirical attacks on well-known political figures. Delarivier Manley was arrested for seditious libel and imprisoned in the Tower of London in 1709 for her part in the publication of a secret history called *The New Atlantis*, a vituperative attack on Sarah Churchill, the Duchess of Marlborough. In her defence, Manley claimed that she was innocent of libel, as the text was a work of fiction. This ingenious defence not only enabled Manley to protect her sources, but placed the burden of identifying those libelled on to her prosecutors, further damaging their reputation.[53] Disguising her 'secret history' as fiction, Manley subtly manipulated the gendered assumptions that rendered all women's writing fictitious. She successfully pleaded her case.

Lady Mary Wortley Montagu deemed her history so scandalous that she destroyed each chapter after she had written it.[54] The remaining fragment, her 'Account of the Court of King George I', was similar in theme and shape to the secret histories or memoirs produced by women a century earlier, focusing on court intrigues and the illicit romances in a tone that was both anecdotal and morally reflective. By referring to 'Artamenes' in her text, Montagu explicitly connected her account to the historical romances of Madeleine de Scudéry.[55] This mixture of history and romance was viewed critically by later commentators on the text. Her granddaughter Lady Louisa Stuart (1757–1851), editor of Montagu's papers, distanced 'proper' British history from that produced by her grandmother, while tacitly criticising the French. Stuart wrote that court intrigues 'in a government like ours, may influence them but little'.[56] Stuart refused to recognise the historicity of this writing, seeing it as necessarily flawed and fictitious.

Women writers who merged historical narrative with romantic fiction during the sixteenth and seventeenth centuries were important precursors to the Romantic women writers who recorded the events of the French Revolution. Their blurring of history and fiction implied both a criticism of historians who failed to adequately account for the actions of women in the past and a concern about the revision of history that was occurring during their own lifetime. This revision saw women sidelined from discussion of major political events, and largely expunged from the historical record. Following the Fronde, women's innovation in narrative form enabled them to stress the significance of the private world of emotion to the shaping of history. Interiority and self-reflexivity were said to allow for greater moral truth. These writings challenged the 'truth value of the official narrative and its superficial portrayal of power'.[57] By the end of the eighteenth century writers such as Germaine de Staël and Helen Maria Williams self-consciously adopted the novel, because they believed that fictional narratives better allowed for the presentation of moral truths than other forms of historical writing.

Local Heroines

The fear of being rendered invisible or indistinct has been a common theme among women writers since the Renaissance. The writing of memoirs and semi-autobiographical narratives had been one way in which women had attempted to leave some mark on posterity. Such writings revealed how relational women's lives were. The autobiography of Margaret Cavendish, *A True Relation of My Birth, Breeding and Life* (1656), was seen by contemporaries as eccentric, and her quest for fame at odds with accepted feminine norms.[58] Paradoxically, her writing betrayed a tremendous sense of insecurity about her position, her property and her name.[59] Cavendish confessed that she wrote for herself, only so that she would not be taken for another, 'especially if I should die and my Lord marry again'.[60] While her other writings spoke of a desire for fame, she depicted herself in her autobiography as a wife and daughter whose history would otherwise have remained unknown.[61] There is a certain irony in this claim, as the duke's first wife is never named in the biography, appearing only as 'the daughter of William Basset of Blore'.

This ambiguous sense of self was no doubt deeply informed by women's ambivalent legal status and their precarious economic condition. Throughout Europe the legal impediments to women inheriting family wealth and land made women of the gentry especially vulnerable to the whims of their male kin. Their vulnerability and marginalisation sometimes turned women to the study of history, particularly the history of their family home and lands. Evolving as an extension of women's traditional interest in family history, local history was written by women of the gentry, who had long-standing connections with the areas they researched.[62] Women adopted genealogical pursuits to counteract the anomalies in the law that saw women acknowledged as kin for the purpose of inheritance, but ignored them in the written record of descent.[63] Some women, like the resourceful Anne Clifford (1590–1676), Duchess of Dorset and Pembroke, used historical writing to their advantage in such circumstances. Lady Anne's father, Lord Cumberland, had ignored a thirteenth-century entail under which all Clifford estates went to the heirs of the current Lord Clifford, whether they were male or female. Instead of leaving them to Anne, he had named his brother and then nephew as his heir. Clifford spent much of her life researching her family history, presenting brief biographies of all her male and female kin to substantiate her claim to the lands of Westmorland and Skipton.[64] She eventually won back these estates, but only after her uncle and cousin had died.[65]

The writing of local history and collection of local artefacts remained a particular interest of women, who used knowledge of their ancestral lands to counteract their legal disabilities in relation to inheritance and their absence from family history. To retain a sense of connection to the land of their families, women became expert genealogists. Women's historical knowledge was occasionally perceived as a threat to patriarchal authority, as was sometimes intended. Similar impulses led a number of non-elite women to the study of local history. Women were greatly concerned with the preservation of local traditions, folklore and dialects. This was particularly true in the nineteenth century as 'antiquarianism' came to be characterised as a 'quaint' and 'feminine' activity when contrasted with the 'scientific' and 'manly' activity of history.[66] Antiquarianism was related to the acceptable feminine practice of 'collecting'. Women collected folk tales and made glossaries of local languages in much the same way as they collected local produce or souvenirs. While men were able to travel the world making collections from their Grand Tours, women's more restricted lifestyles limited them to being anthropologist-historians of their local district or family lands. A striking example of this is the experience of Sir Joseph and Sarah Sophia Banks (1744–1818). While Sir Joseph Banks travelled the world collecting curiosities, his sister Sarah stayed in Lincolnshire compiling glossaries of the local dialects of their ancestral seat.[67]

As Europe colonised, women were inspired to write about these new and foreign lands. In largely frontier societies, women settlers travelled long distances to make their homes. The research and writing of local history was a way to make sense of these new and unfamiliar environments. Local histories developed out of women's private writings, journals and letters and were not initially destined for publication. It was 'open to any literate woman with some leisure, not merely [those] with elite connections, to notice and record the local and the familial'.[68] Sometimes the domestic environment threw up materials that inspired women to become historians. Deborah Norris Logan (1761–1839) became interested in history when she discovered in her attic the letters her husband's grandfather James Logan had exchanged with William Penn. She transcribed these letters and presented them to the American Philosophical Society. She maintained an interest in history and was made the first female member of the Historical Society of Pennsylvania.[69] In such cases women could engage in the 'manly' task of historical writing, without leaving the womanly seclusion of the home.

The writing of local history was a source of prestige to women, who would otherwise be scolded for literary aspirations.[70] Most of the women Kathryn Kish Sklar found working as historians in eighteenth-century America were local historians, in the sense that their writings developed out of the life in the community to which they were attached.[71] These writings began as personal memoirs, only to become more inclusive texts filled with family and local history. Such writings slyly inserted women into the founding narratives of their countries. While generally excluded from the grand narratives of state formation, women could assert their presence in the not-so-grand narratives of their home towns.

The History Women

The changing nature of patriarchal relations engendered by the political tumult of the seventeenth century was to have a decisive effect on perceptions of femininity and ideals of womanhood in the eighteenth century. Although the impact of Protestantism on women's status in Europe was complex, it did provoke a 'sentimentalisation' of women that did much to encourage feminist ideas until the French Revolution.[72] During the course of the eighteenth century a small number of women, encouraged by improvements in female education and bolstered by the public discussion of women's rights, publicly declared an interest in politics and produced political history that rivalled their male contemporaries.

Enlightenment Britain produced the most famous of all women historians, Catherine Sawbridge Macaulay (1731–91).[73] Macaulay came from a wealthy Kentish family, with strong Whig connections. Her interest in history did not stem from feminist sentiment, but from her political convictions, as she was one of the most outspoken radicals of her day. She wrote a republican history of the English seventeenth century that ran to eight volumes.[74] This text was written to counter David Hume's 'partisan Tory history' of the revolution, and was favourably compared. Unlike Hume, whose work was largely philosophical, Macaulay's *History of England* was based on extensive reading of primary sources.[75] At the height of her fame Horace Walpole described her as 'one of the sights [of London] that all foreigners are carried to see'.[76]

Macaulay's radical politics led her to support the Revolutionary Wars in America (1775–83). An ardent republican, she corresponded frequently with revolutionaries in America, such as James Otis and John Adams. She spent a year in America (1784–85) and was toasted as one of the 'Friends of Liberty' by important political figures, including Martha and George Washington. Through these circles she came to correspond with the American historian Mercy Otis Warren (1728–1814), who would be called the 'Mrs Macaulay of the American Revolution' by her sometime friend John Adams. Warren served a long literary apprenticeship before she completed her *History of the American Revolution*.[77] Begun as a chronicle of the revolutionary period, its publication was withheld by Warren for seventeen years. It is possible that she feared the political consequences of its publication, and, in fact, her friendship with John Adams was tested by its publication. Adams, who had initially encouraged her work, decided after its publication that 'History is not the Provenance of the Ladies'.[78]

While there are certain similarities between Warren's history and Mrs Macaulay's *History of England,* Warren was a participant in the events she described and wrote from the vantage point of one connected by 'nature, friendship, and every social tie, with many of the first patriots and most influential characters' of the revolution.[79] In this way her history recalls the memoirs of women written during the English Civil Wars. The American Revolution, too, relaxed the constrictions gender ideology placed upon women. The particular circumstances of the American Revolution made many domestic tasks like spinning, shopping and educating children 'politically charged as the colonies focused on creating a new American political and cultural identity'.[80] Increasing importance was placed on female duty, defining motherhood in terms of its value to the Republic. In the American context the idea of republican motherhood redefined and secularised traditional Protestant conceptions of pious motherhood, allowing women more scope to exploit their power as mothers to legitimate their literary and cultural authority.

The power invested in the republican mother allowed Warren to move through acceptable feminine genres, the epistolary and the poetic, into 'the male province of history'.[81] Her interest in history was shaped by the maternal. Warren's interest in contemporary history was born both from a grave concern about the state of the young Republic and her frustration at what she saw as the neglect of her family in the new political order.[82] She felt it her duty as both historian and republican mother to expose corruption, puncture complacency and demand improved moral standards in political and private life. Despite her patriotism and activism Warren played down her role in the revolution and failed to make much of the revolutionary actions of other women.[83] Using the role of historian to trivialise her own conduct during the period, Warren argued that 'while those more qualified to write [men] were caught up in the war and later in establishing the new Republic, a woman might interpret events for posterity, lest they be lost to history'.[84] Much of the text was drawn from letters provided by women friends detailing bloodshed, conflagrations and rapes. It is possible, as Bonnie G. Smith has suggested, that Warren's failure to discuss and analyse women's roles in these events stemmed from trauma caused by the revolution in which she lost three sons.[85] It was in keeping with earlier historiographical traditions established by women, who obscured their own heroism so as to elucidate the heroics of their male kin.

Catherine Macaulay followed her enthusiasm for the American Revolution with support for republican politics in France. She visited France in the 1780s and met Turgot, Marmontel and Benjamin Franklin. She was vocal in her support of the French Revolution, writing a vigorous response to Edmund Burke's scathing *Reflections on the Revolution in France.* She viewed both the American and the French revolutions in terms of the possibility of realising the rights of man (and woman) and died in 1791, before these bright hopes could be shattered.

Macaulay's *History* was not a history of women, nor were the rights of women a central theme of her politics. In the year before her death, however, she published a passionate plea for women's education.[86] Bridget Hill has suggested that the criticism Macaulay faced as a woman writing history may have been the catalyst for her adopting a feminist position.[87] From the outset of her career Macaulay suffered the invisibilising effects of femininity. When the first volume of her *History* was reviewed by the *Gentleman's Magazine* she was referred to as 'Dr Macaulay's wife'. Some reviewers even claimed that the doctor had penned the *History*, allowing his wife to take the credit. She was subjected to jibes about her sexuality and was described as having a 'masculine mind'.[88] It was the public outrage at Macaulay's marriage to a man twenty-six years her junior, that sharpened her sense of women's vulnerability. Hill claims that the scorn and public rejection following her marriage to William Graham made Macaulay acutely aware that women were not allowed the same licence as men.[89]

An atmosphere of gleeful triumph erupted amongst Macaulay's critics at the news that she had eloped with Graham. In the bawdy poetry of Grub Street, Macaulay's marriage was treated not merely as a cause for amusement, but was celebrated as a victory of male sexual privilege over female intellect. Such wits tended to imagine that Macaulay's 'submission' to a new husband necessitated a change in political attitude, although it might be suggested that her choice of a much younger man, below her station and in no way equal to her in fame, was a refusal of wifely submission. No doubt the jibes reflected anxiety about this reversal of gender order. In any case, she was subject to misogynist slander regarding the marriage until her death. The same critics engaged in another misogynist outpouring following the publication of William Godwin's biography of his wife Mary Wollstonecraft (1759–97) two decades later. This 'outrage' resurrected the spectre of Macaulay and saw the two women linked, as much by their admiration for the revolution as their mutual slips from respectability.

It is not suprising, then, that in her last work Macaulay turned to the rights and wrongs of women. In *Letters on Education* she wrote poignantly, 'Woman has everything against her.'[90] Despite her pessimism, Macaulay's feminism was both moderate and instrumental. She sought modest changes to women's condition, especially reform of female education. For Macaulay reform was necessary so women would marry rationally.[91] These sentiments were echoed in the letters of Mercy Otis Warren and in the writings of Mary Wollstonecraft, who saw Macaulay as someone to whom she looked for inspiration and support.[92]

Macaulay's claim that women would gladly 'give up indirect influence for rational privileges' framed and fragmented feminist debate throughout the nineteenth century. The examination of the lives of both good and bad women by women historians fuelled much of this discussion. Macaulay died a year after the publication of her *Letters,* and her fame as an historian quickly faded. In the public imagination she was remembered as a female oddity. She was nonetheless an important figure in establishing feminist traditions. Madame Roland, Mercy Otis Warren and Abigail Adams all took inspiration from her work.

It was, however, Mary Wollstonecraft who was most influenced by Macaulay. Like Macaulay, Wollstonecraft was schooled in liberal philosophy and was a supporter of the French Revolution. She too replied to Edmund Burke's *Reflections*. The publication of her *Vindication of the Rights of Man* in 1790 drew Wollstonecraft out of obscurity and into the centre of British debate about the revolution. It was the *Vindication of the Rights of Woman* that became a canonical text for feminism. Written immediately following the publication of the *Rights of Man*, it established Wollstonecraft as an independent author and a 'foremother' of modern feminism.[93] Like Macaulay, Wollstonecraft would have her share of public ignominy, albeit posthumously. The revelations of her biography, her illegitimate child and suicide attempts, saw Wollstonecraft demonised in the anti-Jacobin press.

Perhaps a sense of these commonalities allowed Wollstonecraft to shape her early writings around Macaulay's *Letters*. She borrowed heavily from Macaulay, particularly on the question of women's education. Wollstonecraft wrote of Macaulay that the 'very word respect brings Mrs Macaulay to my remembrance' and that she was 'the woman of the greatest ability that England had ever produced'.[94] At the heart of the *Vindication* was Wollstonecraft's belief that women were rational beings, shackled by their lack of education and the necessity of acquiring a husband. She agreed with contemporary commentators who described women as frivolous and easily led but held that this was not their natural state, rather one foisted upon them by their unnatural education in sentiment. Like Macaulay, her demands for women's rights were modest. She conceived of a 'revolution in female manners' brought about by education for women based on rational principles.[95] Wollstonecraft believed that women should be bound by the same morality as men; she demanded reform of marriage and argued for women's economic independence.[96]

Although Wollstonecraft believed that women should be able to remain unmarried, engage in paid employment and take part in the machinations of politics, she followed Macaulay in placing greatest stress on the need to reform education so that women might be better wives and mothers. It was the 'peculiar destination of women' to be responsible for children, yet Wollstonecraft insisted that unless women were rationally educated they would never 'become sensible mothers'.[97] Like Macaulay she used the example of ancient Greece to turn classically informed ideas about women's inferiority upon their heads.[98] Unlike Macaulay, Wollstonecraft was not entirely convinced of history's power to enlighten and liberate women. At the heart of her critique of history was concern about gender rather than genre. In the *Vindication* she wrote:

> What does history disclose but marks of inferiority, and how few women have emancipated themselves from the galling yoke of sovereign man? ... I have been led to imagine that the extraordinary women who have rushed in eccentrical directions out of the orbit prescribed to their sex, were male spirits, confined by mistake in female frames.[99]

Echoing Mary Astell's pessimism, Wollstonecraft argued that history was merely the record of women's subjugation and misery. The French Revolution altered Wollstonecraft's perception of history, briefly giving her cause for optimism in its libratory potential.

CHAPTER 4

History's Romantic Heroines: Women's History and Revolutionary Feminism

> Thus toward the end of eighteenth century a change came about which, if I were rewriting history, I should describe more fully and think of greater importance than the Crusades or the Wars of the Roses. The middle class woman began to write.
> Virginia Woolf, *A Room of One's Own*, 1929

This chapter will explore the ways in which women came to understand historically the French Revolution. Initially the revolution offered women many possibilities. A new language of equality encouraged women to believe they were witnessing a dramatic shift in relation to gender and genre. This shift necessitated a new historical perspective on the role of women. In revolutionary propaganda historical representations of women were fiercely contested. This chapter will examine how women came to use history to demand citizenship rights and how women as participant-observers developed new historical forms to depict their experiences. Writers like Mary Wollstonecraft and Germaine de Staël (1766–1817) described themselves as not merely recorders of history, but as makers of history. This dual role allowed women to take historical writing in new directions.

The chapter will also examine the backlash women writers experienced in the wake of the revolution and how anti-revolutionary sentiment shaped women's writing of history into the next century. The innovations women used in their attempts to accommodate historical writing within accepted ideals of femininity did much to propel the Romantic imagination. While Romanticism has sometimes been described as a masculinist movement,[1] I shall suggest that many of the literary innovations attributed to Romantic writers like Byron and Shelley were developed by Wollstonecraft, de Staël and Helen Maria Williams (1761–1827). This chapter will ask: What was the impact of revolutionary feminism on women's historical writing? Did the revolution encourage women's historical writing or retard its development in the nineteenth century? Did the revolution allow women to write political history, or did it allow them to create distinctly feminine forms of historical writing?

The Salon

To understand why the French Revolution presented women with an opportunity to engage in both the making of history and as makers of history, it is first necessary to consider the role women played in 'the Republic of Letters' prior to 1789. Throughout the eighteenth century, elite French women found themselves in an anomalous position. While they had lost many of the political powers they had held in previous centuries, they gained considerable political privileges through the institution of the salon and the intellectual culture it generated.[2] The salon emerged in France during the seventeenth century as an alternative to court society, allowing the haute bourgeoisie to mix with the aristocracy. It served as a school of *civilité*, encouraging social mobility and extending the reaches of polite society beyond the court system. Even in the seventeenth century women held tremendous power in the salons, for although the salon was a domestic space, it was also a public stage. The French referred to the salon as *le monde* (the world), a term suggestive of its public nature.[3] Salons were run by women 'and the tone and aims of the gatherings were set by the presence of ladies as much by the intermingling of writers and patrons'.[4]

Initially women of the salons, like aristocratic women at court, served primarily to influence matters of taste and pleasure.[5] During the eighteenth century, the nature of the salon changed dramatically, as did the role women played within them. Salons became 'centres of enlightenment'. Their purpose was to attract the intellectual elite and to encourage the spread of enlightened culture. Whereas seventeenth-century salons enabled the bourgeoisie to ingratiate themselves with the nobility, the Enlightenment salon critiqued the nobility and encouraged reward based on merit.[6] For many women the salon provided the education that had been denied them due to their sex. Eighteenth-century *salonnières* were 'self-educated and educating women who reshaped the social forms of the day to their own social, intellectual and educational needs'.[7] As the salon became a 'working space' for the manufacture of intellectual culture, women as *salonnières* were actively involved in discussions of literature, art, philosophy and politics. At a time when women's opinions were meant to be limited to domestic interests, *salonnières* actively engaged in the production of public opinion.[8] This did not necessarily meet with male approval, and men such as Rousseau were highly critical of women's participation in this institution.

The eclectic nature of the education women received in the salon caused women to be polymathic in their interests. Many of the women who wrote history in France during this period often worked in other quite diverse genres.[9] As Bonnie G. Smith has observed, this 'interdisciplinary quality' characterised the work of women historians throughout the next century.[10] During the revolution the salon became a quasi-political institution. No longer merely sites where politics were discussed, salons became places where political decisions and legislation were made. The salon remained an important space for women to discuss politics and interpret political change in the nineteenth century. Salon culture allowed women an overt interest in politics and consequently political history. While Britain produced only one political historian in the eighteenth century, France saw a number of women engage in the writing of political history. Some, like Marguerite de Lussan (1689–1758), published traditional political histories, focusing on royalty and court society.[11] Others, like Marie-Charlotte-Pauline de Lézardière (1754–1835), were influenced by the development of the philosophical history of the Enlightenment. Lézardière produced a voluminous study of the evolution of French laws and political institutions, which was published during the revolution[12] and republished in the 1840s under the sponsorship of the eminent historian François Guizot.[13]

Initially the revolution provided women with greater opportunity to act both as historians and as agents of historical change. Women writers found themselves in a privileged position. Encouraged by the Declaration of the Rights of Man, women were able to articulate critiques of patriarchal culture and demand the 'fraternal' ideals of liberty and equality. Writers, both male and female, republican and monarchist, saw the revolution as potentially threatening to patriarchal authority. Women's entrance into the public sphere as revolutionaries, pamphleteers and political theorists led many observers to believe that they were witnessing a major historical shift in gender and genre. While women writers characterised this shift as a part of a broader 'feminisation' of culture engendered by the revolution, male writers, following Edmund Burke, predicted social and political chaos would follow from this reversal of gender order. Eventually women writers who had supported the revolution were vilified by both royalist and republican men, who saw their act of writing as an assault on masculine authority.

Revolutionary Feminism

During the French Revolution those women who supported it used the example of history to celebrate women's entrance into the public sphere, to illustrate women's potential heroism and to demonstrate their capacities as administrators. Earlier historical representation of heroic women had stressed their exceptional nature, maintaining that these women were special because of their 'manly' virtue. The revolution demonstrated that all women had the potential to become 'exceptional' through their participation in the male realm of politics. This enabled a shift in the historical representation of women, allowing feminist propagandists to suggest that heroism was as natural to women as it was to men.

The heroic representations of womanhood had been prefigured in the work of the woman dubbed France's 'first *historienne*', Louise de Kéralio (Roberts) (1752–1822), in her two major historical works

Histoire d'Elisabeth and *Collection des meilleurs ouvrages français composés par des le femmes*.[14] De Kéralio had begun her career as a translator and novelist. Her fourteen-volume *Collection des meilleurs ouvrages français composés par des le femmes* was written in the tradition of the *femmes forte* and presented a literary history of women in France since Héloïse, through a series of sketches of exceptional women. Such histories had been the province of male intellectuals seeking to determine whether women were innately virtuous or evil. Around the time of the Fronde several texts appeared that used the figure of the *femme forte* to challenge historical accounts written by men and to give prominence to the muffled historical voices of women. Madeleine de Scudéry's *Les Femmes illustres* (1642) used figures like Cleopatra, Agrippina and Sappho to insert the feminine viewpoint into history.[15] Following in a similar vein, de Kéralio produced an alternative history of French literature, a narrative that questioned the masculinist canon, demonstrating the deficiencies of previous histories that had neglected the contributions of women.[16]

Histoire d'Elisabeth, published two years before the revolution, was for de Kéralio a 'more innovative and ... monumental project' in which she established the reign of Elizabeth Tudor as the 'linchpin in the history of English constitutional law'.[17] In this text the idea of female sovereignty was no longer shaped in relation to the Renaissance genre of *femmes forte*; she transformed it 'into the Enlightenment idiom of a critical history of the law'.[18] At the height of the revolution de Kéralio anonymously published another history of queens, *Les Crimes des reines de la France*. Unlike her earlier works, which had challenged many of the masculinist assumptions that shaped historical writing, *Les Crimes* drew upon the ancient tradition that despised female authority, focusing only upon the evil done by queens such as Frédégonde, Brunehaut and Catherine de' Medici. Following Tacitus, de Keralio used the symbol of the 'bad queen' to oppose the monarchy.[19] This attack on women rulers was part of a broader anti-monarchical movement stemming from the revolution, and the principal object of its venom was Marie Antoinette. Political assaults on Marie Antoinette were a feature of French life in the ten years preceding the revolution.[20] Most attacks were focused on accusations of sexual immorality and featured pornographic depictions of these alleged exploits. It was not uncommon for the queen to be likened to Messalina in this porno-propaganda. Her execution, following accusations of incest, saw her dubbed 'the new Agrippina' by the Revolutionary Criminal Tribunal.[21]

Louise de Kéralio claimed in *Les Crimes* that a woman who 'becomes queen changes sex'.[22] The idea that women wielding illegitimate power became viragos or 'she-men' was a commonplace of masculinist historiography, which characterised the rise of such a creature as inevitably leading to the feminisation of the state and its male citizens, social dislocation and chaos. Sara Maza has demonstrated that the overarching lesson of de Keralio's text was that 'if absolute power corrupts, absolute female power does so with a vengeance'.[23] Yet even in her representation of Marie Antoinette there is evidence of subtle manipulation of masculinist ideas about women and sovereignty. In the years preceding the revolution de Kéralio had suggested that Elizabeth had overcome her femininity to attain greatness as a sovereign. When writing on Marie Antoinette, she adopted the same critical tone in which she described Mary Stuart: the woman 'possessed all the graces and charms of her sex' which 'marred her virtues as a sovereign'.[24] Marie Antoinette had used the traditional and 'weak' weapons of woman to seize power in France: 'the dangerous art of seducing and betraying, perfidious and intoxicating caresses, feigned tears, affected despair, insinuating prayers'.[25] The French queen was represented in *Les Crimes* as the 'evil twin of the *femme forte*'.[26] It is not her virility but rather her femininity that is represented as dangerous. As Carla Hesse has astutely observed, de Kéralio's histories 'expose the limits of the *femme forte* as a model for female and feminist identity. *Les Crimes* records the cruelty of the political culture of absolutism toward women who found themselves in public roles.'[27]

De Kéralio's shift towards the masculinist historical tradition may have been the result of her unsuccessful foray into political journalism at the beginning of the revolution. In 1789 she had been the editor of two radical newspapers, *Mercure National* and *Révolutions de l'Europe*. Her participation in political journalism was initially supported by revolutionary men. Radical publicist Jacques-Pierre Brissot praised her journalistic efforts, writing that her new journal 'breathes pure patriotism and contains the most rigid and sound political principles'.[28] This support was short-lived. De Kéralio stopped publishing her journals after she was characterised as a *phénomène politique* and an *amazone* in the radical press.[29] *Les Crimes* was published under a male pseudonym. This did not prevent her from being accused of being both unwomanly and 'dominated by uterine furies'.[30]

This sense that the revolution 'masculinised' women is found throughout literary representations of the revolution. Initially women had used such representations in their favour. In the feminist propaganda produced by revolutionary women *femmes forte* were represented as 'virile womanhood', women who could lead armies, engage in the masculine work of politics and administer kingdoms. A speech made to the Parisian Society of Revolutionary Republican Women by 'La femme Monic' brilliantly illustrates the ways in which such models were deployed to legitimise feminist claims to all the rights and duties of citizenship: 'To whom did Rome owe her liberty and the Republic? To two women. Who were those who gave the final lessons in courage to the Spartans? Mothers and wives .... If women are suited for combat, they are no less suited for government.'[31]

As the bloodletting of the Terror was increasingly associated with frenzied female behaviour, models of virile womanhood took on unfavourable connotations. Many observers were horrified by women's participation in violence that characterised this period.[32] Heroic models of womanhood were upturned, to become violent and uncontrollable *bacchae* or furies. These representations were culturally over-determined, as historians since ancient times had represented women's participation in politics as always and everywhere leading to chaos.[33] Many of the women who employed heroic language to describe the capacity of women did not survive the Terror, and those who did were politically marginalised.

Foreign Correspondence

Foreign women visiting France during the revolution saw the potential that revolutionary politics offered women, and assumed, like their French counterparts, that the Declaration of the Rights of Man would be followed by a Declaration of the Rights of Woman. Some of these visitors became actively involved in revolutionary politics. Others came to watch from the sidelines but found themselves caught up in the revolutionary fervour. English feminist Mary Wollstonecraft and Welsh poet Helen Maria Williams came to see for themselves the working of the revolution, and during their stay both became participant-observers. Their writings on the revolution caused a sensation in Britain. Both were indelibly marked by their experiences in France.

Drawn from similar radical and dissenting circles, Wollstonecraft and Williams in their life and work followed similar trajectories. Both initially were enthusiastic supporters of the revolution. Williams went to France in 1790 at the invitation of Augustin du Fossé, an aristocrat whose father had disapproved of his marriage and used a *lettre de cachet* to have his son imprisoned.[34] She threw herself enthusiastically into revolutionary activities and participated in the political salons that sprang up around Paris. She published the first volume of her *Letters from France* in 1790 and subsequent volumes in 1792 and 1796. Wollstonecraft was one of the revolution's most vocal supporters in Britain, publishing a critique of Burke's *Reflections* within four weeks of its appearance. She did not arrive in France until December 1792, shortly before the execution of the king. Wollstonecraft had reviewed *Letters from France* before her departure and was encouraged to see the revolution for herself.[35] Williams befriended Wollstonecraft on her arrival in France, and when Williams opened her own salon Wollstonecraft was a regular visitor.[36] Both Williams and Wollstonecraft viewed the revolution as potentially liberating for women and believed that it presented the opportunity for a 'feminisation of culture'.[37] Both were constrained by the limitations placed on women by the revolution and fell victim to anti-revolutionary sentiment in Britain.

Williams's *Letters from France* merged the genres of romance and travel writing with family history and letter writing, creating a new historical form that was in keeping with her ideal of the revolution as a force for the feminisation of culture.[38] The history of the revolution presented in Williams's *Letters* was shaped around the narratives allowed women, particularly those stressing domestic affections. They were presented in language and structure similar to the novel of sentiment. Williams did not 'novelise' the revolution, rather she disguised her historical account of the French Revolution in another feminine form, the epistle. Letter writing was considered an appropriate feminine genre as letters were informal, spontaneous, private and domestic.[39] Like family history, letter writing bridged the public and private, allowing women to 'record desires that might have been otherwise silenced by social codes', insulating the 'feminine persona from masculine politics'.[40] Moreover, letter writing was a genre that required little formal education and was encouraged in women 'as an accomplishment rather than an art'.[41]

Williams was by no means the first woman writer to use the epistolary form to produce history. Catherine Macaulay published *History in Letters* in 1778 and it is likely that this text influenced Williams. As the title of Macaulay's text suggests, she connected letter writing with history, using this form to present a series of arguments relating to British political history.[42] It was, however, the least successful of all Macaulay's work. It was tepidly reviewed and did not sell well. Critics have pointed out that the reason for its lack of success was that Macaulay failed to exploit the immediacy and familiarity of tone required of letter writing, rendering the text unpalatable with a popular audience.[43] It lacked the detailed archival research that characterised her earlier works, making it unpopular with readers of 'serious' history.

Both Margaret Kirkham and Devoney Looser have observed that the historical nature of Macaulay's work made her less popular with women readers who were more interested in the romance offered by fiction.[44] Kirkham suggests that as an historian Macaulay was less suited to develop Enlightenment feminism than novelists such as Jane Austen. Williams was concerned to depict the revolution as a force for the 'feminisation' of culture. She recognised the need to merge fiction with historical writing and romance with reportage to snare a female readership. Drawing on the story of Augustin du Fossé, Williams made the revolution accessible to a sentimental readership, while representing love of liberty as an essentially feminine sensibility. The du Fossé story had all the hallmarks of romantic fiction. It was borrowed by the poet Wordsworth in the *Prelude* and pirated for sale in sensational novellas.[45] Anne K. Mellor has argued that the history of the du Fossés became for Williams 'the narrative of the *ancien régime* itself'.[46] In Williams's rendering of the tale the du Fossés were represented as a couple who overcome adversity caused by aristocratic vice to form a relationship founded 'on mutual esteem … extensive knowledge of each other's character and temperament that promised the highest domestic happiness'.[47]

The romantic nature of *Letters from France* masked its more radical intentions. Although Williams declared the text to be apolitical, recent analysis has suggested that the *Letters* can be read as a covert attack on Burke.[48] Matthew Bray has argued that Williams's declaration that she lacked political interest should be read merely as one of the many 'clichés required of women writers to avoid charges of impropriety'.[49] The text, he suggests, was highly political, in keeping with the major ideals of British radicalism and dissent. Unlike any other text of the period, William's *Letters* refute Burke's analysis of the revolution using the opposition between the sublime and the beautiful he had established in earlier works.[50] It is possible to see a nascent feminism in her work. Williams's text self-consciously referred to women's 'invisible' political machinations, describing women patriots as acting 'in human affairs like those secret springs in mechanism, by which, though invisible, great movements are regulated'.[51] Williams was among the first observers to praise the participation of women in the revolution, suggesting that the revolution originated in 'feminine sympathy and humanity'.[52]

Although the first edition of her *Letters from France* was favourably received in England, Williams was subject to harsh criticism when she refused to condemn the revolution during the Terror. She returned to France in 1791 and her salon became an important meeting place for expatriate British radicals. Her overt political support of the revolution created a furore in Britain and she was vilified in the anti-Jacobin press. No longer was she celebrated as 'an amiable young poet esteemed for her feminine sensibility'.[53] Instead, journals like the *Gentleman's Magazine* complained that she 'debased her sex, her heart ... and her talents in recording such a tissue of horror and villainy'.[54] News that she was living openly with John Hurford Stone generated further accusations against her and created an image of the 'radical woman writer as traitorous, ideological whore'.[55] Initially Williams bore the brunt of this, but in time it affected all British women who had offered support to the revolution.[56] Like Wollstonecraft, Williams would be subject to misogynistic jibes throughout the Napoleonic period.

This was a curious reversal of fortune for both Williams and Wollstonecraft. Both women had written texts wary of 'passion' and had committed themselves to the feminist idea 'that women must think as well as feel ... [and] avoid the pitfalls of sexual desire'.[57] In the liberated atmosphere of revolutionary Paris, however, both women adopted revised positions on sexual passion. Williams established a relationship with Stone, a married man, with whom she spent the rest of her life. Stone came to prominence in 1794 when his brother William's correspondence was seized and both men found themselves on trial for treason.[58] Although William was found not guilty of treason, the impression that John was a 'seditious and wicked traitor' remained.[59] The scandal involved Williams, whose reputation was further sullied. She wrote other editions of her *Letters* under the threat of the Traitorous Correspondence Bill (1793). Williams's life in France, too, was difficult. She was arrested and spent six months in prison. However, this did not diminish her enthusiasm for the revolution: when Napoleon came to power she ardently gave him her support.[60] Her admiration for him did not survive the Napoleonic wars, and in 1816 she published the last series of letters from France. Her *Narrative of Events which have taken place in France* chronicled both the downfall of Napoleon and her own gradual disillusionment with France. Williams, who had once so enthusiastically embraced the revolution, welcomed the restoration of the Bourbon monarchy in this last work.[61]

Wollstonecraft, too, engaged in a 'republican marriage' with Gilbert Imlay, an American entrepreneur and supporter of the revolution. For Wollstonecraft the commencement of her sexual affair with Imlay marked a decisive shift away from the commitment to platonic affection she had made both in her life and work. While Wollstonecraft clearly had political reasons for visiting Paris, she had escaped there to recover from her torturous relationship with the artist Henry Fuseli. Wollstonecraft had hoped to establish a 'revolutionary' relationship based on 'rational desire' with the married Fuseli that reflected her 'politicized, professional middle-class morality'.[62] The failure of their friendship may have influenced her to change her ideas about sexual passion, but this change of heart also needs to be understood as part of her response to the revolution. In her relationship with Imlay Wollstonecraft found it possible to combine 'domesticity, professionalism and egalitarian erotic love'.[63] This 'revolutionary domesticity' allowed her to rethink her position. She now believed that sexual passion was 'natural and right for women'.[64] With Imlay Wollstonecraft could, for the first time, live what she had written, demonstrating practically that reason and passion were not necessarily oppositional and that politics could shape sexual relations.[65]

Reason and passion were deeply gendered ideals, and if Wollstonecraft was successful in combining these elements in life, she was less successful in doing so in the work she produced during this time. Wollstonecraft had initially begun a series of letters on the revolution in February 1793, but only one letter was ever produced. This project appears to have been curtailed by her depression due to the plight of the French under the Jacobins.[66] Her *Historical and Moral View of the Origin and Progress of the French Revolution* (1794) was written while she was pregnant and in better spirits. In this text Wollstonecraft combined disparate elements and in so doing reshaped generic and gendered boundaries. She wished her text to be less immediate and personal than Helen Maria Williams's 'feminine' *Letters from France*, and but not dry and empirical like masculine accounts of the revolution she had read.[67] The gendered nature of the genre boundaries she sought to transcend created tensions within the text. She wanted the text to appear 'philosophical' in the sense that it should be 'detached, historical and analytical', yet this conflicted with her desire that the text reflect her personal experience of the revolution.[68] Wollstonecraft's *Historical and Moral View* shifted the focus of philosophical history away from the past and on to the present and in so doing created an analysis of the revolution as 'history in the making'.[69] There is a certain irony to Wollstonecraft's claim that she used the 'cool eye of observation' to contemplate the stupendous events of the revolution, as her text concludes with the return of Louis XVI from Versailles, months before her arrival in Paris. Ending her account at this point prevented Wollstonecraft from recalling her own troubling experiences of the revolution, although she wrote lengthy descriptions of these scenes in letters to England.

This refusal to touch upon the personal sprang no doubt from Wollstonecraft's desire to avoid 'the erroneous inferences of sensibility' and to contemplate the revolution through the 'enlightened sentiments of masculine and improved philosophy'.[70] Her use of philosophical history to contemplate the conditions in France was fraught with tension as she struggled with doubts about the turn in which the revolution had taken.[71] Although *Historical and Moral View* is replete with the sense that European society and political institutions were moving towards a state of perfection, Wollstonecraft was less than certain of how to interpret the revolution in this context, given the state of France at the time she was writing.[72]

This ambivalence is most obvious in Wollstonecraft's treatment of women in the text. Earlier philosophical historians had paid special attention to the situation of women in their accounts of civilisation. In following their example it would have been appropriate for Wollstonecraft to discuss the place of French women in the revolution. While Wollstonecraft had placed much emphasis on the importance of women's participation in the revolutionary process in the *Vindication*, she was less certain of their role in her *Historical and Moral View of the French Revolution*. She had been stinging in her criticism of Edmund Burke's treatment of market women on their march to Versailles.[73] Writing her history at the height of the Terror, she described the participation of working-class women in revolutionary politics in language close to Burke's in its hyperbole and misogyny. Bridget Hill has observed that this shift in her perspective may have reflected anxiety about class rather than gender.[74] The excesses of the Terror had horrified Wollstonecraft, and she sought to distance in the text her 'good revolution' of 1789 from the 'bad revolution' that emerged in late 1792.

Wollstonecraft's silence on the issue of women engaging in politics may have been due to fears for her own safety. Commentators have recognised the genderless voice of the author of this text, in stark contrast to the obviously feminine narrative voice in earlier works, and have explained this shift in terms of the political climate at the time.[75] She had been urged by Williams to burn the manuscript so as not to be taken for a British spy and she wrote letters home claiming that she feared for her life should the manuscript be '*found*'.[76] This fear may have led Wollstonecraft to avoid the subject of women's political activities. While she was in Paris, the rudimentary freedoms attained by women in the early days of the revolution were revoked by the Jacobins.[77] Many prominent political women were executed or exiled. To be seen to support women's political activities was clearly dangerous during this stage of the revolution, so in this context Wollstonecraft's silence is unsurprising.

Like William's *Letters*, Wollstonecraft's *Historical and Moral View* was initially well received. In the year of its publication it was the subject of a number of positive reviews, all of which stressed the philosophical nature of her historical endeavour as well as her shrewdness as a political observer.[78] Only one review in the newly formed Tory journal the *British Critic* was unfavourable, accusing Wollstonecraft of plagiarism and taking exception to what was described as her 'tinsel and tawdriness of style'.[79] This obviously gendered criticism was the first of many attacks that Wollstonecraft endured. Following travels in Scandinavia, she returned to England in 1795, depressed by both her personal and political experiences in

France. Deserted by Imlay, she attempted suicide shortly after her return. This desertion, however, allowed her to receive the attentions of other men, and in March 1797 a pregnant Wollstonecraft married the radical philosopher William Godwin. Wollstonecraft died following the birth of her daughter Mary in September 1797.

In the year of his wife's death, Godwin mused that

> [T]he writer of romance is to be considered as the writer of real history; while he who was formerly called the historian, must be contented to step down into the place of his rival with this disadvantage, that he is a romance writer, without the arduous, the enthusiastic, and the sublime license of imagination.[80]

This essay, which was not published until 1988, has been seen as an attempt to negate the emerging conservative monopoly on Romanticism and align it more closely with radical and progressive causes.[81] Such sentiment served as a rehearsal for his defence of Wollstonecraft in the *Memoirs*. Both Wollstonecraft's and Williams's writings merged elements of these oppositional discourses, and in so doing pre-empted attempts by male Romantics to 'hybridise the more conventional genres of historiography and the historical novel'.[82]

Neither women successfully 'novelised' the revolution and both were found guilty in the anti-Jacobin press of the 'triple violation of sexual morality and generic decorum as well as national political loyalty'.[83] In Britain fear of 'public women' like Wollstonecraft and Williams inflected all post-revolutionary writing, conflating the idea of 'public women' in the sense of prostitutes with those women who had sought a role in the public sphere. These women were characterised as hyperemotional, frenzied and immoral, consequently denying them legitimacy as political agents and historical subjects. The publication of Wollstonecraft's *Memoirs* in 1798 confirmed her status as a 'Republican harpy'. The *Anti-Jacobin Review* used the memoir as ' "proof" that the inevitable result of liberalism and free thinking was moral collapse'.[84] Even her death in childbirth was reported as providential, 'standing in for the sexual fall she had experienced but refused to acknowledge in her life'.[85] Reactionary anti-revolutionary rhetoric came to be defined as patriotic, and supporters of the revolution risked prosecution for sedition.[86] All women who had publicly supported the revolution found themselves vilified in the conservative press.

Such vehement sentiments had a distinct effect on women's writing, severely inhibiting the nascent feminism of the revolutionary period. By the turn of the century an exasperated William Godwin claimed that 'not even a petty novel for boarding school misses now ventures to aspire favour unless it contains some expression of dislike or abhorrence for the new philosophy'.[87] In the bleak years of the Napoelonic wars British women writers scarcely dared risk the opprobrium that support of the revolution had provoked. Those who did avoided the risk of upsetting 'generic decorum' by using the 'feminine' genre, the novel.[88] By and large writers like Maria Edgeworth (1767–1849), Lady Sydney Owenson Morgan (1776–1859) and Jane Porter (1776–1850) used their novels to tacitly challenge the 'post-Revolutionary aversion to women in the public sphere' and depict the domestic sphere as a new historical site that was critical to shaping politics, national identity and destiny.[89]

Romantic Revolutionaries

It was the Swiss aristocrat Germaine de Staël who brought forth the true marriage between historical writing and romantic fiction. The daughter of Jacques Necker, director-general of finance for Louis XVI, de Staël played a significant role in the politics of the revolution. Through her salon she was at the heart of Parisian political and literary culture. One of her greatest achievements was 'the creation of an exciting intellectual atmosphere for the development and exchange of ideas'.[90] It was through her salon that de Staël wielded immense political influence at this time. The first republican constitution was debated in her drawing room. Napoleon so feared her political influence that he had her banished from Paris for most of his reign.[91]

De Staël is best remembered for her novel *Corinne, or Italy*, published in 1807. *Corinne* has been described as the first novel of genius and the first text in which a woman was allowed to live for herself.

The text was frequently read as an autobiography of the author rather than a fictional biography. The moral portrait of Corinne created by de Staël merged with her own struggles seizing the Romantic imagination of the period. For almost the entire nineteenth century de Staël represented a model of feminine genius that inspired women to become writers and feminists. Not only did women adopt a Staëlean posture for themselves, they also had their fictional protagonists take after her.[92] With *Corinne* she created the concept of the female role model, as Madelyn Gutwirth has observed: '[N]o modern heroine existed that even suggested what she had it in mind to portray: feminine genius.' De Staël had to invent the feminine genius while simultaneously 'endow[ing] it with the density of a tradition'.[93] *Corinne* became a touchstone for Victorian women who felt their intellect trivialised and their talents wasted.

It is possible to read *Corinne* as a 'secret history' of the French Revolution. During the sixteenth and seventeenth centuries French women created a new genre of writing that was ostensibly fictional yet mimicked the writing of history.[94] At the heart of this writing was a wish to advance the 'secret motivations for history', the intrigues, passions and personalities which shaped the course of the past.[95] Women writers attempted to bring to history a moral truth they believed to be lacking in the more general histories of the past. De Staël was the inheritor of these traditions. Rejecting the elitism of masculinist historical traditions, she saw the novelisation of history as a means of popularising an understanding of the past. Like her predecessors, de Staël believed that the novel allowed women to create history that was self-reflective, focusing on the interior world of love, emotion and intrigue. In *Delphine,* a novel de Staël published in 1803, she made this point explicitly in the Preface: 'History informs us only of the general characteristics of events but it cannot enable us to penetrate personal feelings that, by influencing the will of some, determine the fate of all.'

The revolution was the subtext of de Staël's fiction. It inspired her creation of character, the settings for her novels and their narrative structure.[96] Certain historians have suggested de Staël's recourse to fiction was due to her relegation 'to the sidelines of history', where she was condemned to watch helplessly as men co-opted the revolution and determined the destiny of France. In this context it is possible to see the character Corinne as an allegory of the Republic.[97] De Staël's novel *Corinne* embodies the nascent bourgeois system of values that based superiority on merit and talent.[98] These values were celebrated in the writings of Williams and Wollstonecraft as the values of the 'good' and 'feminine' revolution of 1789.[99] Although de Staël trivialised the political implications of her 'harmless book', Napoleon was reported to be enraged by its content, but he could do nothing to lessen its acclaim.[100]

De Staël also wrote a more conventionally historical account of the revolution, *Considérations sur les principaux événements de la Révolution*, published in 1818, which sold 60,000 copies in its first edition.[101] This text, like many historical works by women, began as a vindication of her father, a hero of the Third Estate who was forced into exile during the Terror. Just as earlier writers used familial history to assert their own historical subjectivity, de Staël too filled her father's history with examples of her own political actions, but she felt no compunction to disguise her political ambitions. As Charlotte Hogsett has observed: '[A]lthough Staël's respect for her father was considerable, the reader of the *Considérations* has reason to suspect that the daughter would have liked to have taken over her father's responsibilities, and perhaps believed she would have discharged them better.'[102]

Although her novel *Corinne* saw de Staël celebrated throughout Europe, it was her literary history of Germany, *De l'Allemagne*, which most influenced the development of Romantic historiography. In this text de Staël merged a number of genres to create what John Isbell has called an 'anthropology *avant la lettre*, the history of a vanishing society – the new century's science and art ... [and an] all inclusive manifesto'.[103] *De l'Allemagne* created the idea of nation and nationality, and in so doing offered Europe an alternative to Napoleonic hegemony, a 'Europe of the imagination'.[104] *Blackwood's Magazine* claimed that de Staël had created 'the art of analysing the spirit of nations and the springs which move them'.[105] These ideas were sure to rankle in Napoleonic Europe. French troops pulped the first edition of the text in 1810; however, it went through some twenty-five editions in France before 1883.[106]

De l'Allemagne established de Staël's literary reputation amongst her male peers. Her novels *Corinne* and *Delphine* had categorised her as a woman of genius, but a woman nonetheless. Her erotic life was constantly entangled with criticism of her novels.[107] *De l'Allemagne*, however, saw her credited with masculine understanding, allowing her to transcend both the generic boundaries and moral codes expected of 'lady novelists'. Sir James Mackintosh, editor of the prestigious *Edinburgh Review*, wrote that *De l'Allemagne* was a book 'unequalled among the works of women; ... [and] is not surpassed by many among those of men'.[108] On both sides of the Atlantic key figures of Romanticism — Byron, Emerson, Pushkin and Leopardi — cited *De l'Allemagne* as the formative text.

In *De l'Allemagne* de Staël implored her readers to reject the sterile classicism of the Enlightenment and to look to their national pasts for inspiration. Paralleling discussion of historicism in Germany, she critiqued classicism for its universalism and its timelessness, arguing like Herder and Ranke for relativity in historical understanding. De Staël's historical vision both reflected and shaped German historiography as it emerged in the nineteenth century. Both were formed in violent opposition to Napoleon, and de Staël shared the desire of German historians to feel the past 'as it really was'. Although she did not have the same obsessive interest in archival materials as Ranke and his followers, her enthusiasm for monuments of the past was derived from similar sensibilities.

De Staël's text was responsible for representing German philosophy and literature positively to the English-speaking world. Before its publication German letters and culture had been the subject of ridicule in Great Britain and America.[109] In America especially de Staël's text paved the way for the enthusiastic reception of the historiographical ideas of Ranke and his followers. The high praise de Staël offered German universities inspired the first wave of American intellectuals to pursue their academic training there.[110] Historians Edward Everett, George Ticknor and George Bancroft embraced her nationalism and committed themselves to developing a particularly American national culture. Bancroft, who became known as the 'father of American historiography', was profoundly affected by de Staël, even writing his own literary history of Germany in tribute.[111] It was through Bancroft that de Staël's two most fervent American admirers, Lydia Maria Child (1802–80) and Margaret Fuller (1810–50), became acquainted with *Corinne* and her creator.[112]

The Staëlian Legacy

Europe's return to revolution throughout the nineteenth century provided women with the opportunity to emulate their Romantic heroines. On the Continent a number of women wrote histories of the political crises surrounding them. In France salon culture remained an important vehicle for women's historical voice. Aristocratic women such as Marie d'Agoult (1805–76), Hortense Allart (1801–79) and the Princess Cristina Belgiojoso (1808–71) were *salonnieres*, deeply involved in the politics of the post-Napoleonic period. Marie d'Agoult wrote a history of the revolution of 1848, an event that she experienced 'as fully as an upper-class woman could'.[113] Maintaining no particular party sympathies, she considered herself to be the only unbiased historian to write on the subject. She also produced a history of the Dutch Republic, biographies of Mary Stuart and Joan of Arc and philosophical essays on liberty and morality. D'Agoult was a committed republican and feminist. Her salon became a centre of radical political activity prior to the revolution of 1848. Attended by Eastern European radicals such as Adam Mickiewicz and Georg Herwegh, her salon was an important source of primary materials for her histories.[114] It may have served as a source of inspiration for other women. Emma Herwegh, wife of Georg, wrote a history of the German Democratic Legion in Paris.[115] The salons of d'Agoult and Christina Belgiojoso were visited by historians such as de Tocqueville, Thierry, Michelet and Mignet, who read their work and exchanged criticisms.[116] D'Agoult's historical understanding was deeply informed by the writings of Quinet and Michelet, especially their ideas about the centrality of the common people to the revolutionary process.[117] The failure of the 1848 revolutions did not diminish d'Agoult's enthusiasm for republicanism, although she rejected Romanticism, to return to history and politics informed by the Enlightenment.[118]

D'Agoult's friend Hortense Allart was less of a *salonnière* and more politically conservative than both D'Agoult and Belgiojoso.[119] Her historical understanding was more in keeping with de Staël's. She produced one of the first literary biographies of de Staël and wrote several historical novels before engaging in more conventionally historical writing. In a letter to d'Agoult in 1853 Allart criticised the sterile historical production of men, claiming that women wrote better because they were excluded from the academy and hence were more natural and spontaneous in their style.[120] Such claims were reminiscent of defences of Romantic fiction espoused by de Staël and her predecessor Madeleine de Scudéry. Allart, d'Agoult and Belgiojoso all emulated de Staël's commitment to feminine genius and her failure to observe convention. Like her, their feminism evolved out of their own experience of the limitations imposed by society on women who aspired to genius. Throughout the nineteenth century d'Agoult was more (in)famous for her elopement with the composer Franz Liszt than her historical writing. She critiqued the legal inferiority of women and the indissolubility of marriage in her 1847 *Essai sur la liberté considérée comme principe et fin de l'activité humaine*. Allart, too, ignored the sexual mores of her day by taking a number of lovers, including writers René de Chateaubriand and Edward Bulwer-Lytton.

The Italian Princess Cristina Belgiojoso was more morally conventional than her French counterparts, but more politically radical. Having left her husband, the Prince Emilio di Belgiojoso, on account of his constant womanising, the Princess moved to Paris where she established her salon. Belgiojoso became intensely nationalistic, devoting her life to the cause of Italian unification. She established educational programmes for peasants on her lands, believing that through education and relief from poverty the lower orders would become nationalistic.[121] She became a Risorgimento heroine in 1848, writing numerous pamphlets protesting the suppression of Italian states, running hospital services in Rome and leading a battalion of volunteers from Naples to Milan. She published three volumes on the history of modern Italy (1849), a theological history of early Catholicism (1842–43) and a translation of Vico's *New Science* (1844), as well as an historical novel *Emina* (1856).

The translation of de Staël's *Corinne* into English inspired a number of American women writers. Margaret Fuller claimed that de Staël's intellect made 'the obscurist school house in New England warmer and lighter to the little rugged girls who are gathered together on its wooden benches'.[122] Fuller emulated de Staël throughout her life, earning herself the title the 'Yankee Corinne'.[123] Her major work *Woman in the Nineteenth Century* owes much to de Staël's influence. Visiting the Continent in 1846, she became involved in the Italian struggle for democracy, nursing with the Princess Belgiojoso in Rome, and sending dispatches to the *New York Tribune*. Fuller's writing continued the Romantic tradition of 'hybridising' more conventional genres and creating a style that moved beyond the boundaries of conventional journalism 'to take on elements of history, the sermon, the political manifesto, the historical romance, and ... the diary'.[124] She wrote a history of the Italian Revolution, but the manuscript was lost when she died at sea returning from Europe.

De Staël's work did not meet with the same enthusiasm among British women writers. Although she admired Britain's political institutions, de Staël had found the intellectual and social climate there depressing. In *Corinne* she described England 'as a domestic trap, filled with nice, but silly and empty people whose lives are the horror of sameness and emotional dreariness'.[125] British women writers such as Harriet Martineau (1802–76) did produce political histories at this time, but they reflected a more conservative agenda.[126] Domesticity became the major theme among Victorian women writers. Initially the concern with domesticity suppressed discussion of the rights of woman. Just as women's political role had been restricted to their domestic role, performing private duties as wives and mothers, women's historical role was now shaped by her domestic duties. A theme of domestic heroism pervaded the histories of great women, combining bourgeois and evangelical notions of femininity with a highly romanticised version of feminism. Adopting a view of womanhood that celebrated domestic seclusion allowed women intellectuals of the period to retain a place in the public sphere and engage in that most masculine and public of discourses: history.

CHAPTER 5

'Heroines of Domestic Life': Women's History and Female Biography

> Although history is one of the most useful studies which a woman can pursue, her powers of mind are hardly fitted to enter this field for the sake of instructing others.... And this point we strenuously maintain, that it is not that woman is, in ordinary cases, deficient in judgment, and she is carried away by their power. She feels keenly, and then decides promptly, instead of calmly weighing facts and deciding upon evidence. The very reasons which make the study of history beneficial to her, are the reasons dissuasive from her ever attempting to be an historian.
> M. A. Stodart, *Female Writers: Thoughts on their Proper Sphere and on their Powers of Usefulness*, 1843

By the mid-nineteenth century there were so many women engaged in historical writing they were becoming the subject of hostile reviews bemoaning their abundance.[1] J. M. Kemble wrote in *Fraser's Magazine* in 1885: 'we [men] must plead to a great dislike for the growing tendency among women to become writers of history'.[2] Underpinning this hostility was concern that women were 'feminising' history, at a time when it was reasserting its manliness through professionalisation. In spite of criticism, women engaged enthusiastically with historical writing throughout the nineteenth century, although the types of history women wrote were somewhat constrained by gender prescriptions stressing women's essential domesticity.

The writing of biographies and biographical collections proved the most popular medium for women historians during this period. The beginning of the nineteenth century saw collections of female biographies and individual biographies of great women proliferate. The writing of the lives of great women has been the most common way in which women have engaged in the production of history. Unkindly referred to as the history of 'women worthies', this writing has been largely neglected by historians. Yet these histories have provided a record of female activity in the past and strong role models, and were often written to plead for the rights of women.[3] Histories of 'women worthies' served as important precursors to feminist approaches to women's history.

This chapter asks how biographies written by Victorian women were shaped by the gender prescriptions of the day. Were women historians creating a complementary or counter-discourse through biography? In what ways did Victorian women historians challenge traditional historical paradigms? Did women's historical writing at this time encourage or discourage feminism?

Domestic Woman

As the Napoleonic wars ravaged Europe, an ideal of domesticated womanhood emerged that stood in stark contrast to the revolutionary feminism of writers such as de Staël and Wollstonecraft. This ideal of domestic womanhood was seen to rectify the damage engendered by both the feminist writings of the revolutionary period and the misogynistic outpourings that followed them. This conservative backlash was not unique to Europe. In America anti-feminist sentiment developed after the publication of Godwin's *Memoirs* of Mary Wollstonecraft.[4] In both America and Europe this 'cult of true womanhood' was largely incompatible with the virtues of self-reliance and critical thought that had framed Enlightenment feminism.

This emphasis on women's domestic role shaped the ways in which women were perceived historically and the ways they could engage in historical production. There was a growing tendency throughout this period to delegitimise women as historical subjects precisely through an emphasis on their domestic role.[5] As Billie Melman has observed, not only did this limit perceptions of women's activities as potentially historical, it encouraged the belief that women were devoid of historical imagination.[6] Faced with such constraints women did not retreat from historical production, rather they responded in ways that domesticated historical writing, by historicising the domestic sphere and by adopting biography as their preferred historical form.

By the nineteenth century biography was a thoroughly gendered genre. Male writers used biography as history, a pedagogical tool of masculinity, celebrating the great deeds of great men. Biographical writing by men, about men, demonstrated how through the force of character and the power of personality men could move nations.[7] Male historians self-consciously promoted ideals of male heroism through biography. This heroism was constructed in terms that corresponded with accepted ideals of bourgeois masculinity. Texts such as Samuel Smiles's best-selling text *Self-Help* (1858) featured short exemplary lives of successful industrialists for middle-class men to study and emulate.

Female biography, like conduct manuals and domestic fiction, functioned as a 'textual means for engendering bourgeois subjectivity', presenting lives of 'great women' to serve as role models for middle class 'ladies'.[8] The adoption of biography was in keeping with the tradition of women's memoirs dating back to the sixteenth and seventeenth centuries. The writing of 'memoirs' by women formed 'a particular history' that was distinct from the 'general history' written by men.[9] Many Victorian women engaged in the writing of 'female biography' as a corrective, a way of recovering those lost to history and as a means of asserting women's historical subjectivity at a time when this very idea was under attack. It would be wrong to suggest that such writings were explicitly feminist. While Victorian women used historical memoirs to rescue great women from obscurity, they shaped the idea of women's historical agency around the ideology of separate spheres. Female biographers did not make feminist critiques of history, rather they tried to 'feminise' history, by insisting that history had to be amended to acknowledge the feminine and the domestic.

Women's historical production during the nineteenth century was fraught with contradictory impulses. On the one hand the model of domestic womanhood found celebrated in the biographies of great women and historical novels of the period romanticised the declining status of women. The panic that manifested itself around revolutionary women confirmed misogynist fears about the necessity of women's exclusion from politics. While few women writers engaged in the pornographic hyperbole that characterised male writers on this subject, many rejected revolutionary feminism's insistence that women had a role in the public sphere. Conservative women writers reasserted the pre-Enlightenment notion that women needed to rely only on their moral authority to indirectly influence men. They defined the domestic sphere as the God-ordained place of women and appeared to denounce women's interest in politics. The revival of religion and the emergence of Romanticism in the early nineteenth century did much to bolster such ideas. In the early nineteenth century a feminist ideology emerged that focused upon the idea of woman as moral guardian, with much emphasis placed on her spirituality, her purity and innocence. Such ideas were derived from prescriptions of femininity that had emerged during the Restoration period. Like the period immediately following the French Revolution, the Restoration marked a time when men felt the insistent need for social and gender order.[10] Prescriptive literature written by men emerged during this period, which promised women personal fulfilment through self-negation and self-sacrifice.[11]

This created 'a pattern of female domestic heroism' in women's writing that stressed the virtues of feminine activity, strength, fortitude, self-denial and purity.[12] Whereas earlier models of female biography focused on women with manly qualities, like military prowess or learning, the genre as it developed in the nineteenth century celebrated the 'feminine virtues'. A theme of domestic heroism pervaded all the histories of great women written in the nineteenth century, combining bourgeois and evangelical notions of femininity with a highly romanticised version of feminism. Ironically adopting a view of womanhood that celebrated domestic seclusion allowed women intellectuals of the period to retain a place in the public sphere through their historical writing. Literary critics have tended to see women who spoke publicly against the rights of woman as 'case studies in complicity', 'daddy's girls' seduced by masculine literary discourse.[13] Yet what was at stake were contesting notions of feminine power. While revolutionary feminists such as Wollstonecraft fashioned the rights of woman alongside the rights of man, more conservative women writers saw women's power in terms of moral influence, which they feared the discourse of equality would erase. As women such as Wollstonecraft were pilloried for their public political stand, others realised that the gendered division between the public sphere and the private sphere allowed them a degree of empowerment within their own particular domain.[14] While women's writing produced in this context eschewed any suggestion of being 'feminist' or political, they nevertheless celebrated women's transcendence of the private sphere and allowed women a patriotic, if not political voice.

Domestic Heroism

This ideal of 'domestic heroism' was best exemplified in the writings of evangelical author Hannah More (1745–1833), although numerous women on both sides of the Atlantic wrote on this theme. More began her literary career as a dramatist, but in mid-life her interests shifted to the reform of education, particularly the education of working-class children. By the end of the eighteenth century she had established an international reputation as the great evangelist of education.[15] Her 'improving' poetry and pamphlets sold over two million copies in her lifetime. It was her novel *Coelebs in Search of a Wife* for which she is best remembered. In this text we find More's most formed discussion of the God-ordained place of women. The heroine Lucilla represented More's ideal of perfect wifehood, being passive, obedient, and satisfied with influence and her capacity to inspire male virtue, or in More's words, 'to study household good, and good works in her husband to promote'.[16] A devotee of the 'cult of true womanhood', More epitomised the new discourse on women that emphasised the power of feminine influence over rational privileges. Describing women as 'the procelain [*sic*] clay of human kind', she argued their 'greater delicacy' implied 'greater fragility'. This weakness in women she defined as both 'natural and moral', arguing that this necessitated 'a superior degree of caution, retirement and reserve' in women.[17] Very much a public woman, More championed domestic seclusion, dismissing all discussion of women's rights.[18]

More did not write women's history, probably because she believed, along with Thucydides, that it was the greatest commendation for women 'not to be talked of one way or the other'. She paraphrased his version of Pericles's Oration in the frontispiece of her *Essays designed for Young Ladies*, encouraging women to 'aspire only to those virtues that are peculiar to your sex; follow your natural modesty'.[19] More had fixed ideas regarding history's moral authority. In *Strictures on Education* she 'made clear that the fundamental purpose of history was the inculcation of religious values'.[20] While she did not celebrate the lives of 'great women', she saw fit to advise them, and in *Hints towards forming the character of a young princess* she wrote at length about the benefits of history. *Hints* offered the insights of More's earlier works on women's education coupled with specific regal advice for the Charlotte Augusta, Princess of Wales, for whom the text was written.

What More meant by history was the study of great men. In *Hints* she laid down the rudiments for its study, making clear that history evolved through the study of the lives of men of 'distinguished eminence'.[21] It was not More's primary concern that Charlotte be acquainted with historical methodology. It was the moral lessons of history she considered critical to her education. Drawing on the precedent of Charlotte's predecessor Elizabeth Tudor, More maintained that knowledge of history was particularly beneficial to the princess as a female sovereign. Elizabeth's knowledge of the Classics and her facility with languages had been widely celebrated. More's opinion of Elizabeth is illustrative of the tensions she felt between her overarching belief in female inferiority and her royal duties. More's lesson to Charlotte was that great women had a certain licence as queens, but that this licence rendered their femininity problematic. As she wrote: 'If we look at the woman, we shall see much to blame; if at the sovereign, we shall see almost every thing to admire'.[22]

It was More's hope that Charlotte could be both a good queen and a domesticated wife. While the book proved extremely popular with More's evangelical readers, the princess found it tedious and difficult. In a letter to her father she wrote: 'The bishop [the Bishop of Exeter to whom More dedicated her book] is here, and reads with me for an hour or two every day from Mrs Hannah More's *Hints . . .* this is I believe what makes me finde the hours so longe.'[23] The princess proved in some respects to be one of More's worst students. She shared her father's preference for Jane Austen, approving most of her romantic heroines, particularly Marianne Dashwood, with whom she strongly identified.[24]

Although More's success inspired several generations of conservative women writers to emulate her celebration of the domestic, few followed her in their treatment of history. While More focused her historical interest on the lives of great men, most women engaging in historical discourse during the nineteenth century concentrated on the lives of great women.

Female Biography

Mary Hays (1760–1843), in both her work and life, is an important transitional figure in women's historiography. As biographer of Macaulay and friend of Wollstonecraft, Hays was caught between the revolutionary feminism that evolved out of the Enlightenment and the more conservative domestic feminism that developed in reaction to the French Revolution. In this context it is significant that she published the first and perhaps most important collection of women's lives, *Female Biography, or Memoirs of Illustrious and Celebrated Women, of all Ages and Countries* in 1802. Hays spent much of her early career eulogising Wollstonecraft. In the year following the reception of the *Vindication*, she wrote a response to this text, *Letters and Essays, Moral and Miscellaneous*. Her 'Appeal to the Men of Great Britain on Behalf of Women' (1798) followed Wollstonecraft in denouncing the double standard of morality, but showed Hays to be more timid in her feminism than her mentor. She ignored Wollstonecraft's insight that independence was fundamental to self-respect and insisted that women should give up their education if it interfered with their duties 'as daughter, sister, wife or mother'.[25] In this text Hays laid down many of the ideas she developed more partially in *Female Biography*.[26]

Her connection with Wollstonecraft was more than merely literary. Like Wollstonecraft, her life had been marred by a series of unfortunate romantic attachments. Following advice from William Godwin she turned to writing in her grief, producing the novel *Emma Courtney* (1796), loosely based on her unrequited love for the mathematican William Frend. *Emma Courtney* defies an easy feminist analysis. While it displayed feminist concern to show women as sexual beings, not merely as objects of male desire, the power of such an argument was undercut by its painfully autobiographical nature and its tendency towards 'excessive emotionalism'.[27] The ambiguous position of the novel on these questions related to Hays's diminishing enthusiasm for the 'amorous culture' of English radicalism.[28] The publication of *Emma Courtney* saw Hays ridiculed as an 'outspoken usurper of the male prerogative of love' and parodied as a 'philosophess' and Godwinian, whose novel 'undermine[d] religion'.[29] She was the subject of an unflattering caricature in Elizabeth Hamilton's *Memoirs of Modern Philosophers*. In this text Hays was depicted as Bridgetina Botherim, an ignorant and ugly metaphysician who spends her life annoying men with Godwinian declarations of love. Botherim, who asserts that she never read anything but 'novels and metaphysics', is sharply contrasted to Harriet Orwell, the novel's 'domestic heroine', who performed household duties while her aunt read Hume's *History of England*.

Although Elizabeth Hamilton (1758–1816) satirised Mary Hays's literary ambitions, she too published a biographical text, an 'historical novel', the *Memoirs of Agrippina* in 1804. Ostensibly a life of Agrippina the Elder, wife of the great Roman hero Germanicus, this text was a manifesto of domestic heroism. Predating Hannah More's domestic classic *Coelebs in Search of a Wife* by some five years, Hamilton established a particularly British ideal of republican motherhood in her description of the Roman matron. 'Taught to place her glory in the faithful discharge of the domestic and maternal', Hamilton wrote of the idealised Roman wife that 'her country was no less dear to her than to her husband; but the same spirit of patriotism which impelled him to exert his valour in the field, or his wisdom in the senate, animated her mind in the instruction of her children, and the regulation of her family.'[30] As Jane Rendall has argued, Hamilton was 'reviewing through her historical writing the ways in which British women could participate in the shaping of national character'.[31] Unlike Hays, Hamilton asserted a higher moral purpose in her writing. Openly advocating patriotism rather than politics, she maintained that woman's highest national task was to be a dutiful wife and a happy mother. Her description of this ideal Roman matron came to define the domestic heroine, whose dignity, patriotism and national spirit was strictly circumscribed by the private sphere.

Mary Hay's *Female Biography* marked a shift in perspective that was attributable to the failure of the revolution and the public humiliation she suffered as an associate of Wollstonecraft and Godwin. Deflecting the glare of this criticism, Hays turned to biography to celebrate 'those women whose endowments, or whose conduct have reflected lustre upon the sex', and presented detailed portraits of eminent women. Hays was concerned to create a new type of female biography, a history that spoke to women and taught them their rights and duties. Women's education was her primary concern. She claimed to 'have at heart the happiness of [her] sex' and aimed at 'their advancement on the grand scale of rational and social existence'. Like Macaulay and Wollstonecraft she was greatly concerned that women 'were content with the destination of the slaves of an Eastern harem'. She argued that their lack of education led them to be 'degraded' with 'follies and vices'.[32] Such ideas were tempered by the domesticated feminism of More, as she argued that rationally educating women merely added 'to the graces and gentleness of her own sex' and formed 'the most perfect combination of human excellence'.[33] Following More, Hays maintained that women's influence was best used in the domestic rather than the public sphere.

The combined influence of Macaulay, Wollstonecraft and More resulted in competing ideals of femininity and feminism in the text.

While Hays was keen to display the principles she had adopted from Wollstonecraft's philosophy, she also framed much of her discussion in the language of domestic heroism. The women most admired by Hays were those who represented both 'rational womanhood' and 'domestic heroism'. But while she celebrated the benefits of education for women, she also questioned their role in the public sphere.[34] The women who received most praise from Hays were models of Roman republican virtue such as Calpurnia, Antonia and Agrippina the Elder. Her descriptions of such women illustrate her conception of feminine virtue, encompassing the values of both Wollstonecraft and More.

In *Female Biography*, Hays moved beyond the polemical and hagiographic depictions that characterised earlier biographical works.[35] She chose to show 'great women' as flawed characters subject to human frailty, rather than merely exemplary human beings. Within this schema it was her subject's flaws that made them exemplary. Unlike earlier collections of female biography written by men, which focused on the saintly or the demonic in women, she attempted character sketches that were layered and textured. Women in Hays's text were neither simply good or evil, but rather capable of both. By representing fragmented subjectivity in her biographical sketches Hays pre-empted Lytton Strachey's 'modernisation' of the genre by over a century.[36]

History as Domestic Science

Most female biography written following Hays tended to focus upon women who were only good. Such texts represented virtuous domesticated women, not as women acting 'above their sex' but rather as emblems of the cult of true womanhood. The domestic heroine was a product of eighteenth-century literature. Sturdy heroines such as Richardson's *Pamela* provided middle-class women with the idea that woman could become the 'exemplar of all virtue – public as well as private'.[37] Nancy Armstrong has argued that 'middle-class authority rested largely upon the authority that novels attributed to women'.[38] The novel functioned as a site where femininity was redefined to challenge the structures of class. Underpinning tales of courtship and marriage was the desire to 'contest the reigning notion of kinship relations that attaches most power and privilege to certain family lines', resulting in the exaltation 'of the domestic woman over and above her aristocratic counterpart'. Novels such as Richardson's *Pamela* were narratives in which a 'woman's virtue alone overcomes sexual aggression and transforms male desire into middle-class love, the stuff modern families are made of'.[39]

The effect of fiction, particularly the popular novels of sentiment upon the virtue of women, was often questioned. Since the appearance of the novel, it had been associated with seduction. In the wake of the French Revolution both the reading and writing of fiction by women came to be viewed in the popular imagination as potentially subversive. As the culture of 'respectability' took hold, the 'free flow of passion and fantasy' that had characterised the eighteenth-century novel was now seen 'as symbolic of the threat to the existing order of things'.[40] Novels, particularly those with French authors, were the subject of much critical hostility. At the heart of such criticism were concerns about the effects of genre on gender relations. Fiction was held responsible for all manner of moral transgressions: '[N]ovels of sensibility were denounced for ... allowing to free an outlet to the emotions: gothic romances were condemned for making readers "impatient with the sober facts of history"; love stories were thought to make vice attractive and virtue dull.' Even domestic novels were condemned 'for arousing too high expectations in young maidens for potential husbands'.[41]

The move by women towards biography can be attributed to the need to produce texts that were both commercially successful and respectable. As novel writing became less respectable it also became less lucrative. Biographical writings by women, particularly those depicting the lives of royal women, were enormous publishing successes during the nineteenth century. Agnes Strickland (1796–1874), author of numerous biographies of queens and princesses, was one of the period's best-selling authors.[42] Such texts were successful because they reinforced rather than challenged accepted gender roles. Women who received most praise in these texts were models of domestic industry and good sense. This led certain writers to fear that female biography might prove too dull to appeal to the reader. As Mrs John Sandford, author of the *Lives of English Female Worthies*, admitted, 'in this light also, we fear that female biography is deficient in interest. Women, even of high excellence, do not possess that individuality which characterises the illustrious amongst men.'[43] Such fears proved ungrounded, for while biographers insisted the subjects fulfil home duties before venturing into new fields, readers tended to focus on their subject's heroism rather than their domesticity.[44] Although the intention of much female biography was to nurture feminine rather than feminist ideals, such texts did not necessarily encourage 'quiescence'; rather as Martha Vicinus has suggested, they aroused in their readers 'an imaginative affinity with active public heroines'.[45]

Women seeking to be taken more seriously as writers used the medium of biography to establish respectable reputations for themselves. A number of women turned to biography after writing novels. Rejection of novel writing was often framed in a language of rescue and redemption. Writing of Elizabeth Ogilvy Benger's (1778–1821) shift from novelist to historian, her friend and fellow-biographer Lucy Aikin (1781–1864) wrote: 'No judicious person, however could peruse either work without perceiving that the artist was superior to the work; thus ... she prudently turned her attention from fictitious narrative to biography and criticism; rising in her later works to the department of history.'[46] There was an element of self-protection at work here. Women writers were the subject of male vitriol throughout this period.[47] Male reviewers often forgot the sentimental civility they owed women when faced with the woman writer. As Hannah Adams (1775–1831), one of the first women historians of America, complained in her *Memoirs*: literary women were exempted 'from the common allowances claimed by the species'.[48]

The professionalisation of history within the academy saw women historical writers come to be regarded as 'amateurs'. This designation did not reflect their economic position as writers, as many women developed lucrative careers as biographers.[49] Their 'amateur' status was meant to reflect their lack of scientific rigour. Those areas explored by women came increasingly to be regarded as picturesque and antiquarian, rather than scientific and methodological. Moreover, their economic success was seen at odds with the historicity of their texts, as it was perceived that women writers wrote to please 'market demand' rather than to reflect historical accuracy.[50] While amateur history was not the sole domain of women, female amateurs rarely received the professional recognition granted men such as Edward Augustus Freeman and William Stubbs, who took up Chairs at Oxford in the 1880s after decades of scholarship produced from their homes.[51]

Women who chose to write history at this time were subject to much critical attention. Those wishing to avoid this harsh critique devised ways to use the moral authority of history without the new demands of methodological rigour. Biography proved the ideal medium for the domestification of history, and came to be constituted as a gendered diminutive of history. While history was characterised as a thoroughly manly endeavour, biography was conceived as 'a private female, sort of history'.[52] This act of self-depreciation allowed women to avoid harsh male criticism, because it was suggested that biography did not require the same level of masculine restraint, rationality and pedagogical authority that history demanded. As M. A. Stodart, author of numerous works on female duty, observed: 'Although history is one of the most useful studies which a woman can pursue, her powers of mind are hardly fitted to enter this field ... the humbler walk of Biography is less unfitted to feminine power.'[53] Even as biographers Stodart maintained that 'ladies' were less suited than men to make astute judgements of character and were 'thus prone to veil the defects of their heroes and heroines and give us a partial and distorted portraiture'.[54]

The very act of writing biography was configured in ways that stressed its appropriateness as a form of women's writing, private, domestic and morally influential. Certain women claimed that they wrote biography rather than history for fear of appearing 'unladylike'.[55] The anonymous author of *Memoirs of Eminent British Ladies* confessed to writing that text 'in the privacy of retirement' so as to underscore her message that feminine virtue must be equated with domesticity.[56] Modesty and obscurity were to be expected from women historians, even when they attempted their autobiography. Hannah Adams, who published her *Memoirs* only to support an ailing sister, received much praise from her editors for her 'modesty and unobtrusiveness' which was said to reflect her character. Adams was an innovative and imaginative historian of religion, yet her editors suggested that she should be remembered for 'her warm affection, her glow of gratitude and her childlike simplicity'.[57] She herself replicated these sentiments in her text, which was part providential history, part testimony of gratitude to patrons, part memoir of a saintly life. Adams eschewed any sense that she wrote for her own sake and rather treated her career as a writer as if it were a blight on her life.

Biography offered an ideal medium for domestication as it could be linked to an ideal of moral efficacy. As Miriam Elizabeth Burstein has shown, Victorian women historians judged the quality of women's history by its moral effects rather than its scholarly credentials.[58] As writers of biography women would not appear to be competing with professional male historians, rather they were engaged in the traditionally feminine role of spreading moral influence. The emphasis on the study of exemplary lives functioned as a form of feminine pedagogy, as women's biographical writings reinforced and reinscribed accepted gender roles. It was this insistence on the moral quality of women's historical production that allowed them to begin to critique masculinist historiography. Initially the argument was made that the public virtues privileged in masculinist accounts of the past were inappropriate when analysing the private and domestic lives of women. Rather than being apologetic about this failure, female biographers asserted that history itself was deeply flawed, because it focused on the great rather than the good. Female biography allowed women to reconceptualise the idea of historical progress, which came to be inextricably bound to 'woman's mission' as a moral and civilising force.

The domestification of history through female biography allowed women to insulate themselves from the criticism usually reserved for women writers. History, unlike the feminised discourse of fiction, was the voice of moral authority and could serve as rational amusement. Such ideas reversed the usual defence women used when choosing romance over history. Elizabeth Hamilton compared the two genres, claiming a deeper moral purpose for biography. She confessed: 'in sitting down to pursue the memoirs of a fellow being, in whose past existence we have assurance, in whose eternal existence we have hope, the expectation of amusement is chastened by the solemnity of ideas attached to the truth'. Unlike romances, which were thought to inflame the passions, Hamilton argued that biography was likely to produce emotions that were 'less vivid' but more morally influential.[59]

Women's choice of biography over other historical genres was often making a virtue out of necessity. Both the romantic quality of women's memoirs and their interiority may have been due to the fact that women were not allowed the same access to archival documents as men. There is evidence that men deliberately denied women access to such collections. In 1834 Sir John Russell, Britain's Home Secretary, refused to allow the Strickland sisters, Agnes and Elizabeth (1794–1875), use of any papers in the State Paper Office, inhibiting their prodigious production of regal history. Only after Queen Victoria intervened were they allowed access to state archives.[60] Later Agnes wrote suggestively that women's access to the public record challenged the misogynistic representations of women found in masculinist history.[61]

University libraries proved equally difficult for women to access, with some such as the Bodleian at Oxford only permitting lady visitors during the vacations.[62] The limitations of women's education may have hindered their research, as few women had the linguistic skills necessary to read ancient manuscripts. In any case their very choice of subject matter usually obviated the necessity of work in public archives, because few women left detailed public records. Women who worked in libraries and archives were sometimes caricatured by male reviewers as old, blue-stockinged spinsters with dishevelled hair and horn-rimmed spectacles. It is possible that women felt intimidated while working in archives and other collections. In *A Room of One's Own*, Virginia Woolf painfully evoked the sense of alienation she felt when attempting to enter that bastion of male privilege, an Oxbridge college. Women historians may have felt a similar sense of bemusement.

Feminising History

In the early part of the nineteenth century biographies tended to be devoted to scriptural heroines or female saints. Hagiographic texts functioned as devotional texts as well as educating women in their spiritual and moral duties. More so than other studies of great women, biographies of biblical and saintly women prescribed and reinforced society's ideals of femininity. The accession of Queen Victoria to the throne in the 1830s saw a shift from religious to regal role models. Victoria did much herself to promote historical interest in queens past, as she was an avid reader of biographies. She became a favourite subject of later Victorian biographers, as she combined both royal stature and the virtues of a good bourgeois wife.[63]

The shift from religious to regal role models in female biography led almost imperceptibly to a revisionist challenge to masculinist historical writing and to post-revolutionary prescriptions of femininity. Initially this began as a critique of traditional historians' tendency to obscure or exclude women from their accounts of the past. Female biography that focused on women who had public as well as private lives potentially allowed some discussion of women's role beyond the domestic sphere. Biographers of royal women, such as the Strickland sisters, Anna Jameson (1794–1860) and Hannah Lawrence, emphasized their contribution to European culture, their scholarship and learning and most importantly the political and moral influence they exerted over their male kin and subjects.[64]

By mid-century conditions engendered by revolution and civil war created a subtle shift in women's biographical writing. While the lives of royal women remained popular, biographies of ordinary women who led extraordinary lives came into their own.[65] Collections of female biography tended to focus upon heroines of domestic life. In Britain it was the heroic women of the English Civil Wars who were celebrated, particularly women who defended their homes and their families, like Lucy Hutchinson, Lady Arundell and Brilliana Harley; in America it was the heroines of the American revolution such as Mercy Otis Warren, Abigail Adams and Hannah Lee Corbin; in Europe it was always Madame de Staël. These collections served nationalist agendas by introducing notable women into the national canon and by highlighting women's role in particularly significant moments in the national mythology.

This interest in women reflected the way in which women writers were gendering the notion of patriotism. In this context women's love of country was seen as an extension of their love of home, their patriotic duties an extension of their domestic and familial duties. Women's homebound state was said to enhance their patriotism.[66] This idea emerged most strongly in the 'national tales' invented by writers such as Sydney Owenson, Lady Morgan (1783–1859) and Maria Edgeworth (1767–1849).[67] Deriving their influence from Madame de Staël, national tales were hybrid texts that merged romantic fiction with history and political polemic. While de Staël, protected by her wealth and aristocratic status, could overtly engage with politics, especially sexual politics, in her novels *Corinne* and *Delphine,* bourgeois writers like Morgan and Edgeworth were more constrained. Renaming political interest 'patriotism', their national tales reinscribed the sexual status quo, always ending with a reaffirmation of domestic virtues rather than female emancipation.[68]

Using the language of patriotism allowed women writers to disguise or romanticise the political actions of their subjects. Patriotism became a gendered diminutive of politics, reflecting a belief in women's emotional and moral superiority rather than a discourse of women's rights. As Lady Morgan opined in her aptly titled *Patriotic Sketches*, 'politics can never be a woman's science, but patriotism must naturally be a woman's sentiment'.[69] As nationalist sentiment grew more animated, patriotism became a major theme of women's historical writing. By asserting an ideal of women's patriotic duty rather than their political rights, biographers of great women allowed women a positive and unique role in the nationalist mythology.

This new historical role created by female biography was reinforced by a desire to 'feminise' history. The political upheavals engendered by revolutions and civil wars were seen to provide women with the extraordinary opportunity to apply the virtues of the domestic realm to the public sphere. To understand the influence of extraordinary women, female biographers further conflated the idea of historical progress with women's civilising mission. History written by men was rendered essentially flawed because it dealt with politics rather than patriotism, rationality rather than emotion, man's understanding of the world rather than God's divine plan. Women, because of their moral superiority and civilising influence, came to see themselves as bearers of the new historical age, one in which the feminine and domestic virtues transcended those of the masculine and public realm.

This feminine understanding of historical progress was reinforced by the matriarchal theory emerging from the work of Charles Darwin and Johann Jacob Bachofen.[70] Borrowing from male theorists of sexual difference, certain women historians formed an essentialist analysis of women's role that accounted for their historical invisibility in their innate physical and moral differences from men. As Nina Baym has suggested, such historical accounts assumed 'that because men were endowed with greater physical strength in the past, they had dominated the past'.[71] Men's dominance had been reinforced in the historical record because of women's innate altruism, their maternal self-negation. Far from denying women a historical role in the present, these maternalist accounts reinforced the idea of a new historical age for women, as masculine brutishness declined as an historical force to be replaced by feminine spirituality and morality.

Such ideas presented a 'womanist' rather than a feminist perspective. Certain advocates of this feminised version of history were rabidly anti-feminist. Following Hannah More, they argued that feminist demands for equal rights threatened women's moral superiority and moral influence. Their feminisation of history inadvertently promoted a nascent feminism, because the historical narratives they created challenged masculinist assumptions about the past. Literary historians have pointed out there is a certain disjuncture between the anti-feminist rhetoric of writers like Elizabeth Fries Lummis Ellet (1812–77) and Sarah Josepha Hale (1788–1879) in their biographical accounts of women and the historical role they envisaged for women.[72] Female biography that 'feminised' history also insisted upon women's historical subjectivity and allowed women a different, but equal place in the national mythology. This disjuncture is clearly evidenced in the introduction to Elizabeth Ellet's ground-breaking text the *Daughters of the American Revolution* (1848). Writing of women's patriotism, she declared history an unsuitable vehicle, as it dealt with the head not the heart. Her biographical writing captured 'individual instances of magnanimity, fortitude, self-sacrifice and heroism' for which America 'was not less indebted for national freedom, than to the swords of the patriots who poured out their blood'.[73]

Although Ellet highlights the feminine virtues of self-negation, she simultaneously accords women an equal role in the making of American history. As Scott E. Caspar has commented: 'In offering American women a past in which women had gained influence through patriotism, domestic ability and intellect', Ellet also promoted the ideal of an 'educated womanhood whose influence – like their foremothers' influence during the Revolution, and like Ellet's herself in telling their stories – would extend beyond a passive "cult of true womanhood".'[74] This observation not only reflects the ambivalently feminist influence of female biography but also the paradoxical position of a public author celebrating domestic womanhood. Whether feminist or anti-feminist, women who published served as role models for women seeking a voice in the public sphere and were thus instrumental in encouraging the growing discourse of women's rights.

It would be wrong therefore to only read these texts as quaint records of feminine worthiness. Collections of female biography formed important sites where ideas about the construction of gender were quietly contested and misogynistic assumptions about women's role in history were steadfastly refuted. Female biographers borrowed the moral authority of history to serve as a pedagogical tool of both femininity and feminism. Writers of 'great woman' history were not only reacting against the images of virile womanhood produced during the French Revolution, they were also replying to all misogynistic representations of womanhood that had flourished in the past. Male writers had used the example of history and nature to 'prove the non-existence of a woman worthy of the name "exception" '.[75] In producing 'heroines of domestic life' women historians were challenging misogynist representations while simultaneously demonstrating a transgressive desire to domesticate the boundaries of traditional history.

Eventually female biography came to represent an overtly feminist agenda, albeit one shaped by the constraints of first-wave feminism. Unlike Enlightenment feminists, who formed their arguments to parallel the 'rights of man', Victorian feminists retained an ideology of separate spheres in keeping with the celebration of domestic heroism. First-wave feminists argued that their public campaigns were necessary to protect the domestic interests of women. Women needed the same civil rights as men, not so they could compete with them within the public sphere, but so as to assert the significance of the domestic within the political realm.

With the rise of first-wave feminism the subject matter of female biography became those women who insisted that women's moral influence must reach beyond the private sphere. Reforming women like Elizabeth Fry, Mary Carpenter and Florence Nightingale and Abolitionists such as Lucretia Mott and the Grimke sisters became popular figures in these biographical works. Each wave of feminist protest during the nineteenth and early twentieth century brought with it new heroines to celebrate. By the end of the century even those women who had flaunted convention in their attempts to improve women's rights such as Mary Wollstonecraft and Margaret Fuller became the subject of favourable biographies. Biographical writing may appear to have supported a more conservative feminism as it emerged out of the eighteenth century, but as shall be shown in the next chapter, it had laid the foundation for a more radical feminism as it popularised such ideals amongst an ever-growing female readership.

Chapter 6

Women's History and the 'Woman Question'

> The impression conveyed by our text books is that this world has been made by men and for men and the ideals they are putting forth are coloured by masculine thoughts .... Our text books on civics do not show the slightest appreciation of the significance of the 'woman's movement'.
> Paula Steinman, *The History of Womanhood Suffrage*, 1909

The question of women's status in society came to provide the basis of a number of historical works by women in the latter half of the nineteenth century. The struggle for the higher education of women and the demand for womanhood suffrage and other campaigns of first-wave feminism informed much historical writing on women. Inspired by the 'spirit of historical inquiry' that characterised the Victorian age, women concerned about their declining civil status and their exclusion from higher education turned to the past to understand their present condition. This chapter will explore certain aspects of the 'woman question', as it was called, particularly focusing on how it created new interest in women as an historical category. While women mobilised into feminist organisations they looked to the past to detail their oppression and to supplement their arguments for education, social purity, marital equality and suffrage. As the demands of first-wave feminism grew, women's historical writing came to be framed in light of explicitly feminist arguments. Unlike earlier histories that saw women progress historically towards equality with men, histories of women informed by feminism focused on women's declining civil status. By the end of the nineteenth century the idea that women were reclaiming rights that had been wrenched away from them became commonplace. Feminist histories of women challenged the celebratory nature of female biography, asserting the importance of the experience of the mass of women over the particular.

This chapter will explore the ways in which women's history and feminist consciousness became intertwined as women campaigned for employment, suffrage, higher education, social purity and marital reform. What led feminists to look towards history? How did history shape an understanding of women's role in Victorian society? How did first-wave feminism shape an understanding of women's role in history? Was an historical knowledge of women's subjection necessary before feminist consciousness could develop and reform begin? How did historians write the history of first-wave feminism? Did the 'woman question' lead historians to ask other historical questions about women's oppression?

Women's History and Feminist Consciousness

In 1931 Mary Ritter Beard (1876–1958) wrote a searing criticism of the 'history' produced by first-wave feminists in the first of one of her many works on women's history, *On Understanding Women*. She argued that feminists had treated history 'as if it had been a blank record of defeat' and had unwittingly contributed to the tradition that 'history had been made by man alone'.[1] The idea that 'feminist history' focused only upon the women's oppression became fairly entrenched and by the 1970s a number of historians drew on Beard to critique what they saw as the replication of this trend among radical feminists.[2] Like much of Beard's writing, her ideas about the impact of first-wave feminism upon women's history functioned polemically.[3] The impact of first-wave feminism on the writing of women's history was much broader than Beard suggested. Women historians influenced by first-wave feminism used history not only to highlight women's oppression, but to challenge the idea that women were only domestic beings; to force the lives of 'great women' into the popular imagination and to record their own struggles to gain greater political equality.

Even before the rise of organised feminism in the nineteenth century, writers interested in sustaining arguments about the improvement of women's status in society looked to history to plead their cause. Margaret Fuller was the first to write explicitly about such issues in her 1845 text *Woman in the Nineteenth Century*. Although predating organised feminism in the United States, Fuller raised many issues in this text that framed feminist discussion in that country for the next seventy years. A recent biographer has suggested that the book 'helped set the tone, if not the precise agenda for the Seneca Falls Convention in 1848' that launched feminism in the United States.[4] While her text was not strictly a history of women in any systematic way, in it Fuller skilfully manipulated history to explore the ways in which women's rights had been subordinated to men's and to undercut masculinist arguments about women's inferiority. Trained by her father in the Classics, she made short work of many of the classically informed myths surrounding womanhood and was critical of the tendency to celebrate only the virtues of a 'few great women'.[5]

It is possible to suggest that Fuller's text is one of the first efforts of feminist historiography. While most women who engaged in female biography sought to distance themselves from 'real' and, one presumes, male historians, creating a rhetoric of distinction and subordination in their texts, Fuller was openly critical of masculinist interpretations of history, forcefully demolishing their gendered assumptions.[6] Fuller used historical examples to show how men placed women upon pedestals while simultaneously depriving them of their economic, legal and political rights.[7] While Fuller did not explicitly call for womanhood suffrage, she pointedly depicted the invidiousness of women's unequal social status, likening it to slavery. After her death, 'Margaret Fuller Clubs' sprang up all over the United States. Elizabeth Cady Stanton (1815–1902) and Susan B. Anthony (1820–1906), two doyennes of the American women's suffrage movement, judged that Fuller 'possessed more influence upon the thought of American woman than any woman previous to her time'.[8]

Like female biography written during this period, these new histories of women functioned in ways that highlighted the importance of women's 'moral influence' as an underlying factor in many historical situations. Such writing evinced the same ethos of separate spheres that underscored Victorian domestic ideology. Drawing on the influence of both Enlightenment philosophical history and domestic feminism, historians of women presented an idea that woman's place in society had slowly improved as Western 'civilisation' progressed. Lydia Maria Child's *History of the Condition of Women in Various Ages and Nations*, published a decade before Fuller's text, is a good example of this type of general history. Beginning with the classical period, Child presented historical progress in terms of the civilising effect of women's moral influence. As an abolitionist Child was concerned to stress the importance of women as moral guardians in her quest against slavery.

Women abolitionists were aware of their highly ambivalent position in American society and drew examples of heroic women from history to support their right to protest. The Grimke sisters announced in abolition meetings: 'What if I am a woman; is not the God of ancient times the God of these modern days? Did he not raise up Deborah to be a mother and a judge in Israel? Did not Queen Esther save the lives of the Jews?'[9] Child took these arguments one step further: conflating historical progress with women's slow evolution towards freedom, she argued that abolition of slavery marked the zenith of women's power to change the course of civilisation.

Feminist universal histories of women explicitly critiqued male historiography, connecting women's historical invisibility with their lack of civil and political rights. These universal histories would represent early attempts to document the history of female agency. As first-wave feminists organised themselves around issues like suffrage, university education and social purity, the work of women historians reflected these concerns and looked to the past for both explanation and resolution.

Before Suffrage

The Seneca Falls Convention of 1848 marked, for the first time since the French Revolution, a public commitment to feminist ideals from middle-class women. The idea for a Convention on women's rights had first been suggested at an international anti-slavery convention held in London in 1840, but it was not until some eight years later that the idea was fully realised. Agitation around the New York legislature's Married Women's Property Act pushed women into action.[10] History was of critical importance to the framing of the Convention. Its organisers recognised that understanding the historical position of women was critical to generating a discourse of women's rights. The Convention was called to discuss the social, civil and religious condition of women as well as their rights and privileges, and culminated in a Declaration of Sentiment drawn up by Elizabeth Cady Stanton. The subjugation of women as an historical fact informed this declaration and strengthened women's resolve to demand more equitable treatment.

The demand for womanhood suffrage became the most contentious and significant outcome of this Convention. In that revolutionary year the radical demands of Seneca Falls met with international enthusiasm. Feminism as it emerged in the mid-nineteenth century was different from that which had evolved during the Enlightenment. While Enlightenment feminism had attacked women's inequality in a philosophical manner, Victorian feminists were more concerned to address the 'woman question' from a legal and political standpoint. Suffrage was one of numerous campaigns engaged upon by Victorian feminists, who maintained an ideology of separate spheres, while simultaneously demanding equal legal and political status.

Although the campaigns for womanhood suffrage began around 1850 it was not until the 1870s that the first histories supporting the campaign were produced. Initially these histories functioned very much as campaign literature and so have often been regarded as historically flawed. The principal complaint has been that such texts have focused primarily on women's subjugation ignoring their vast contribution to society. The massive study of woman's suffrage first produced by feminist campaigners Susan B. Anthony, Matilda Joslyn Gage (1826–98) and Elizabeth Cady Stanton in the 1880s has frequently been the butt of much of this criticism.[11] *The History of Woman Suffrage* had been envisaged at a time when American feminists had experienced several defeats and this perhaps accounts for the pessimistic tone of the earlier volumes.[12] As American feminism had evolved out of agitation around abolition it borrowed from the rhetoric of this campaign, so the focus on women's subjugation and their 'chattel status' is not surprising. Slavery, a peculiarly American phenomenon in the nineteenth century, remained an important motif in histories of the women's movement produced in the United States.

The focus on women's subjugation in the historical writing of American suffragists also reflects the fact that they had accepted the idea of women's total subjection to man as the theoretical foundation of the Seneca Falls Declaration of Sentiments in 1848. Recalling Wollstonecraft, Stanton had written in this Declaration that: 'The history of mankind is a history of repeated injuries and usurpations on the part of man toward woman, having in direct object the establishment of an absolute tyranny over her.'[13] According to Stanton and her colleagues the principal architect of women's oppression was the legal historian William Blackstone, author of the *Commentaries on the Laws of England* (1765). In his chapter entitled 'Of Husband and Wife' Blackstone laid out the legal concept of coverture in the Common Law, that rendered a woman civilly dead upon her marriage.[14]

The idea that the rights of married women were subsumed into their husbands was not Blackstone's alone; it had been articulated in the Common Law since the late sixteenth century. This fact had framed both the political and historical understanding of women's civil status within Victorian feminism. In Britain too this inequity shaped discussion of the 'woman question' as feminism re-emerged in mid-century. The case of Caroline Norton, a young wife whose husband had taken custody of her children and her fortune, dramatised the doctrine contained in Blackstone's *Commentaries*.[15]

Norton used her case to highlight the injustices suffered by women under the Common Law, which not only rendered women civilly dead upon their marriage but denied them any rights in relation to custody of their children. Although Norton herself eschewed any notion of women's rights, her case became a starting point for Victorian feminists intent on reforming the laws relating to women.[16]

First-wave Feminism

If the radical politics of abolition informed the histories of the women's movements published in America, it was the reformist politics of Liberalism that shaped British suffrage history. British suffragists used history to invoke the idea of 'an earlier golden age of freedom' for women, that was derived from the Whig tradition established by Catherine Sawbridge Macaulay.[17] Macaulay had first drawn liberal intellectuals into a discussion of 'ancient rights'. In her voluminous history of Britain she had insisted that Britons had lost the rights of their ancient Saxon constitution with the invasion of William the Conqueror. This assertion sustained Whig political critiques in Great Britain and proved inspirational during the American and French revolutions. Suffragists of Whig and dissenting backgrounds used the same discussion of ancient rights to defend their claim for womanhood suffrage.[18]

Suffragists such as Charlotte Carmichael Stopes (1841–1929), author of *British Freewomen* (1894), and Caroline Ashurst Biggs (1840–89), who wrote the entry on 'Great Britain' in Stanton's *The History of Woman Suffrage* (1886), both argued that women's demand for suffrage in Britain was a demand for the restitution to women of their ancient constitutional rights.[19] As one of the editors of the *Englishwoman's Review* Biggs used that journal to advocate the need for womanhood suffrage. When she died suddenly in 1889 she was replaced as editor by the suffragist Helen Blackburn (1842–1903), who also wrote an historical account of the suffrage struggle, *Woman's Suffrage: A Record of the Movement in the British Isles* (1902). Suffrage journals like *The Suffragette* and *The Common*

Cause were important sites for the conceptualisation of suffrage histories. Many women who wrote in these journals went on to write longer pieces on suffrage history.

Suffragists drawing upon the 'Norman Yoke' theory reinvented historical accounts of the feudal system, adopting woman-centred periodisation and chronology.[20] Within this context Britain's suffragists were not demanding new rights, but rather the restitution of their ancient rights as 'British freewomen'.[21] Stopes too looked to Blackstone and his predecessor Sir Edward Coke as the source of women's disenfranchisement, arguing that their authority had resulted in women's declining civil status, using Lady Anne Clifford as an important example of female protest. While the idea that women had lost rights emerged through these more polemical feminist accounts of history, they also found their way into more scholarly assessments of women's role in the past. Medieval historians like Florence Griswold Buckstaff (d. 1948) published texts that emphasised the early rights of women and their loss of legal rights following the Norman invasion.[22] As late as the 1950s Doris Mary Stenton (1894–1971) made such arguments in the *English Woman in History* (1957).

The development of militancy in Britain generated different historical accounts both of women's long-term subjection and the suffrage campaigns themselves. While the histories produced by moderate suffragists were essentially written in the liberal spirit of the age, militant histories rejected both masculinist politics and masculinist interpretations of the past. The discussion of ancient rights found no place in these new histories, rather they focused on the new and radical present. Texts such as E. Sylvia Pankhurst's (1882–1960) *The Suffragette: A History of the Women's Militant Movement 1905–1910* (1911) began with the emergence of militancy and thus avoided any sense of continuity with earlier campaigns. Militant histories tended to focus on the activities of prominent women such as the Pankhursts, reflecting the autocratic style of leadership favoured by militant groups. A number of militant histories were produced by the Pankhursts, who were unselfconscious in celebrating their own importance within the movement.[23]

Women involved in first-wave feminism were acutely aware of their role as participant-observers in the making of women's history. To this end they preserved their correspondence and created archives.[24] Female biography remained an important aspect of the development of feminist history during this time, as the need for strong role models was very important. In the late nineteenth century female biography had turned towards more radical figures such as Mary Wollstonecraft and Margaret Fuller. During the period of intense suffrage agitation female biography became concerned with proto-feminist figures, particularly female reformers who forced women's concerns upon the public sphere, such as the Grimke sisters and Josephine Butler.[25] Celebrating these women was considered especially critical to the development of feminist consciousness. Some believed that the transcendence of such figures in literature marked the arrival of the women's movement.[26] In the period following the granting of suffrage, biography turned to the leaders of these campaigns, such as Millicent Garrett Fawcett and Elizabeth Cady Stanton.[27] Suffrage histories such as Ray Strachey's *The Cause* were drawn largely from biographical and autobiographical sources.[28] Women who wrote biographies of famous suffragists during this period were acutely aware that they were creating new feminist heroines for future generations.

Women chose autobiography more than any other genre to depict their historical experiences of these campaigns. Throughout the campaigns autobiographical reflections were collected to be included in *Suffrage Annuals and Women's Who's Who* to celebrate achievements and to popularise the cause. After the gaining of suffrage these texts served a more commemorative function. Organisations like the Suffragette Fellowship produced calendars celebrating significant moments in suffrage history.[29] Rolls of Honour memorialising militant women appeared during the 1920s and functioned in the same way as the war memorials which proliferated after the First World War. The production of these texts and archives helped to sustain interest in feminism during the interwar period as the heady days of suffrage agitation receded into history. In the years following the granting of suffrage a number of women wrote memoirs depicting their part in the struggle. In Britain alone over twenty autobiographical accounts were produced by both militant and moderate suffragists.[30] To a certain extent most suffrage histories were quasi-autobiographical, as they were written by participant-observers. The use of memoirs freed women from the constraints of objectivity and the demands of the 'authorised third-person narrative'.[31] Such memoirs were often the vehicle for fierce political polemic as much as personal reminiscences.

Suffrage journals and other writings in support of the vote for women frequently drew on great heroines of the past to promote their cause. Heroic women from the past who had protected other women, or promoted the interests of women and children, were widely celebrated in suffrage art and crafts. Historical figures of women saints, monarchs and warriors were used in the tableaux and pageants mounted by suffragists to show 'the physical, intellectual, creative and ethical strengths of women'.[32] In America first-wave feminists made icons of the heroic women of the American Revolution and the Abolition campaigns. In Europe Germaine de Staël and her alter-ego Corinne remained omnipresent in all feminist writing. In Britain the figure of Boadicea was invoked as an heroic emblem in the struggle for women's rights. Boadicea, who was regarded as a scourge in masculinist history, was portrayed in early feminist literature as a vengeful angel, motivated by her desire to protect her daughters. The use of Boadicea reinforced and reflected the idea that women were only demanding the restitution of women's ancient rights that had been diluted with each wave of conquest. Radical suffragettes, following Emmeline and Christabel Pankhurst, fashioned their own political actions around an ideal of radical femininity informed by the heroic actions of women such as Boadicea.

As suffrage was granted, first-wave feminist organisations commissioned historical studies on the impact of womanhood suffrage upon the community. In 1906 the labour historian Helen Laura (Sumner) Woodbury (1876–1933), as part of the Collegiate Equal Suffrage League, surveyed the impact of womanhood suffrage on the American state of Colorado, which had granted women the vote in 1876. She published the results of her survey, *Equal Suffrage*, in 1909. Although predominantly sociological in its analysis, Woodbury's text provided an extensive history of the granting of suffrage in the United States. Texts such as Woodbury's were used to enhance pro-suffrage arguments, but also served as important historical accounts of the immediate impact of womanhood suffrage. Accounts of successful campaigns and the impact of the granting of suffrage were included in suffrage journals and other campaign literature. Women from the Antipodes, where womanhood suffrage was first granted, were called on to give such accounts. Vida Goldstein (1869–1949), the Australian 'suffragette', addressed large public meetings on this subject in Britain and published accounts of women voting in the colonies.[33] Alice Henry (1857–1943) found herself addressing the annual convention of the National American Suffrage Association in Baltimore on Australian women's suffrage a month after her arrival from Melbourne in 1906. She shared the platform with Susan B. Anthony.[34]

Although suffrage history was the province of 'amateur historians', many women who were academic historians were involved in suffrage agitation. Eileen Power (1889–1940), who became Professor of History at the London School of Economics (LSE), was drawn into the movement by her sister Beryl, an ardent member of the National Union of Women's Suffrage Societies (NUWSS).[35] Power lectured on suffrage and other issues pertaining to women's rights, and she remained committed to feminist ideals throughout her career. Lucy Maynard Salmon (1853–1927), Professor of History at Vassar, also became involved in suffrage agitation in America. For Salmon, the education of women, the history of women and the rights of women were inextricably bound together.[36] In Canada, too, historians such as Isabel Skelton (1877–1956) took up the cause of suffrage, publishing impassioned arguments in its favour.[37] Other women such as Alice Clark (1874–1934) and Frances Collier (1889–1962) came to study history within the academy as a result of their experience of suffrage agitation. For Clark, her experience in suffrage campaigns made her want to understand women's unequal position in society. Clark was awarded a fellowship to study at the London School of Economics in 1913. Her classic text, the *Working*

Life of Women in the Seventeenth Century (1919), was informed by the rhetoric of first-wave feminism and the work of contemporary feminists such as Olive Schreiner. Collier ended militant activities with the Women's Social and Political Union (WSPU) in 1907 because she seriously questioned the practical outcomes of the vote for women. She studied history and political economy at the University of Manchester, publishing a study of the family economy in the cotton industry in 1921.[38] The whole question of women's tertiary education formed a significant undercurrent in many of the histories of womanhood suffrage.

In Britain, North America and in much of continental Europe the war work undertaken by women was rewarded with the vote.[39] The granting of suffrage allowed those involved in the campaigns to analyse them with hindsight. Viewing suffrage campaigns as hard-won victories rather than as ongoing struggles allowed former suffragists to develop a new sense of the past and their relationship to it. While early suffrage histories glossed over dissent and division amongst individual suffragists and various suffrage societies, histories written after the granting of suffrage tended to be more concerned with such issues. Political differences between feminists were further polarised in the wake of victory, particularly in Great Britain, where militant suffragettes and moderate suffragists both claimed responsibility for women gaining the vote. The contested history of the suffrage campaigns became the source of further acrimony between groups such as the Women's Freedom League (WFL) and the National Union of Women's Suffrage Societies (NUWSS). The publication of *The Cause* in 1928, written by Ray Strachey, secretary to Millicent Garrett Fawcett, generated great hostility among the militants. Feeling their integrity as feminists had been attacked and their past actions inaccurately described, the WFL passed a resolution demand-ing that the edition be pulped and rewritten.[40] In America similar dissension arose around particular biographical studies of individual suffragists, such as Elizabeth Cady Stanton and Lucy Stone.[41]

Preservation of the spirit of the woman's movement was a defining feature of the histories published following the granting of suffrage. Former suffragists recognised that this was imperative if women were to become central to the political process. Underscoring this desire to preserve the history of first-wave feminist campaigns was the very real fear that the movement might fall into oblivion if its records were lost.[42] The preservation of the history of the 'women's movement' became itself inextricably linked with 'the cause'.[43] Saving the history of first-wave feminism became itself part of a broader feminist project. Former suffragists recognised that making suffrage history central to political history was essential if women were not to be politically marginal. Inter-war feminists placed great importance on the memory of their foremothers, not only because it served to recuperate women to history, but because it ensured that women would never again be historically invisible. Feminist organisations such as the WFL and the National Union of Women Teachers produced literature celebrating the achievements of women in the suffrage movement to inspire the next generation and to allow inter-war feminists to forge connections with veterans of earlier campaigns. In stark contrast to much masculinist history produced during the inter-war period, histories of suffrage reflected a positive outlook, celebrating the ways in which the vote facilitated women's progress towards equality.[44] These biographical and historical accounts of feminist struggles permitted modern feminists to see important continuities (and discontinuities) with the first-wave feminists. This proved critical to the re-emergence of women's history in the post-war period. As Carol Ellen DuBois has observed, the historical production of first wave feminists 'awaited – even enticed – feminists of the 1960s and 1970s to become historians of women'.[45]

First-wave Feminism and the Social Sciences

Although the struggle to gain womanhood suffrage has tended to dominate accounts of first-wave feminism, Victorian and Edwardian feminists were involved in many and varied causes around education, social purity and marital law reform. Participant-observers wrote historical accounts of all these campaigns.[46] Initially such texts were written to inform women of their secondary status and to encourage them to improve their situation. Increasingly these texts engaged with women's history as they sought to account for the longevity of women's subjection. It was feminist interest in the working conditions of women, both within and outside the home, that produced a proliferation of historical writing, rivalling the historical accounts of womanhood suffrage. Feminist concern with women's working conditions grew out of their philanthropic endeavours. As women took up places in tertiary education, women's philanthropic concerns came to be informed by social sciences such as political economy, sociology and economic history. Armed with these tools, feminists took an increasingly important role in the formation of social policy. They expressed concern about the opportunities available for women to find meaningful work, the apparent decline of the status of women's work and the brutalising effect of industrialisation on women and children. These concerns were later reflected by women historians, who utilised the new sub-disciplines of economic and social history to recover the lost world of women's work.

Women's historical interest in work needs to be contextualised in relation to the emergence of the social sciences in the nineteenth century. The idea of social science first appeared in the wake of the French Revolution as the upper classes of Europe tried to understand the revolutionary behaviour of the lower orders. Initially it took the form of a 'science of the poor' dedicated to bettering society through the education of the working classes and the amelioration of the worst effects of poverty.[47] By the mid-nineteenth century the social sciences were almost exclusively the preserve of the reforming middle classes. What had begun as a rather ad hoc set of philanthropic practices evolved into various quasi-scientific discourses. The work of the social sciences remained intertwined with philanthropy, but merged with a desire to understand the fundamental causes of poverty and to address those causes. To understand the causes of poverty it was necessary to understand the lives of the poor. To do this reformers used 'scientific' tools such as data collection and statistics to create social surveys. Much of this surveying was anthropological and sociological in its emphasis, with researchers living in the field, discovering 'the facts' of the phenomenon they sought to explain.

As Eileen Yeo and others have observed, the development of the social sciences was a highly gendered process that reflected the ideology of separate spheres.[48] Women were drawn to the social sciences for the same reasons they were drawn to philanthropy and feminism. In many ways women's contribution to social science during this period functioned like feminism to domesticate the public sphere, as the traditionally feminine aspects of philanthropy such as visitation evolved into social observation. Many of the earliest texts of social science were written by women merging their interest in feminism and philanthropy with a desire to understand social problems.[49] Women reformers adopted a language of 'social motherhood' to enter the public sphere and seek reform through social science.[50] Similar language was used throughout the campaigns of first-wave feminism. Women involved in feminist causes were well represented in forums such as the National Association for the Promotion of Social Science and the American Social Science Association because they 'provided an unusually welcoming context for women's concerns'.[51] The practices of social science such as surveying and the accumulation of statistics were used by women to argue for equal rights, particularly in relation to higher education and suffrage. Just as first-wave feminism expressed through the rhetoric of separate spheres the need for womanhood suffrage, women drawn to the social sciences argued that it was imperative for women to bring their particular sensibilities to its study.[52]

The Settlement movement proved critically important for women trying to impose their influence upon the social sciences. Initially institutions such as Toynbee Hall, the first Settlement House established in the East End of London in 1884, were envisaged as masculine institutions. By the turn of the century, however, they had become almost exclusively feminine spaces. The domesticity of the Settlement House was productive of an environment conducive to women's social reform and the development of feminist social policy.[53] Settlement Houses became an important link between women reformers in the United States, Britain and her colonies.[54] By the early twentieth century the influx of women into this type of social investigation ensured that it was regarded as a thoroughly feminised discourse. As Denise Riley has observed, the social question became synonymous with a broader anxiety over the domestic conditions of the working class, nutrition, household management, maternal morbidity and infant mortality.[55]

The analysis of social problems as they related to women led social scientists to believe that the key to women's subjection was her economic dependence on men. First-wave feminism had always expressed an interest in women's economic position in society and the brutalising effects of industrialisation. In the early years of the twentieth century the question of women's labour and economic oppression both revitalised and fractured the women's movement. Drawing on their experience of social observation, groups of feminists, philanthropists and social scientists worked together to produce studies of the working life of women. These studies allowed them to better understand the causes of poverty and assisted them in making demands for reform. Initial studies produced by groups such as the Fabian Society's Women's Executive Committee or the National Federation of Settlements focused on the working conditions of women and children such as work hours and the physical impact of factory labour. Analysis of women's working conditions led women social scientists to begin to form radical critiques of the sexual division of labour and the way in which gender shaped industrial practices, pay differences between male and female workers and 'protective' legislation. Their work in this field laid the groundwork for historians of women's labour throughout the twentieth century.

The Social Sciences and Social History

The role of women's history, particularly since the rise of industrialisation, became critical to feminists interested in the economic plight of women. Just as suffragists looked to history to understand women's inequitable political position, social scientists also turned to history to explain women's economic oppression. Women social scientists such as Caroline Dall (1822–1912), co-founder of the American Social Science Association, were among the first to articulate the importance of adding an historical dimension to understanding social problems. For Dall the connection between feminism, social science and history was self-evident, as she wrote in the women's journal *The Una* in 1855: 'Without reading the past clearly, it is impossible to go on to the root of present evils.'[56]

Schooled in first-wave feminism, reformers and social scientists looked to history to explain the longevity of women's subjection and the historical causes of her economic dependence on men. In challenging the idea that domesticity rendered women passive and idle, historians of women's work argued that women's domestic labour was integral to the survival of the pre-industrial family, while also insisting on the historical importance of domestic labour more generally. This idea was not entirely new as it drew on the work of earlier Victorian women, who had explored historically women's cultural productions.[57] The historical accounts of women's work generated within this feminist tradition established the idea of a 'golden age' of women's employment that existed prior to industrialisation. Just as constitutional suffragists had suggested that women's political rights declined following the Norman conquests, historians of women's labour argued that women's rights had declined with the rise of capitalism. This analysis radically undercut the ideology of separate spheres, because it insisted that the household had always been a site of economic production. Women's economic dependence upon men was not the result of their naturally subordinate position, but rather created by the exigencies of capitalism.

The idea that women had been more economically powerful in the past was first tentatively raised by Lucy Toulmin Smith (1838–1911) in 1870. While editing a text written by her father, Smith wrote the following aside in the introduction: 'It is worth noticing who were the persons who composed the guilds. Scarcely five out of five hundred were not formed equally of men and women, which in these times of the discovery of the neglect of ages heaped upon woman, is a noteworthy fact.'[58] It was another twenty-five years before Georgiana Hill made a similar argument about the declining status of women's labour. In *Women in English Life* published in 1896, Hill showed that the Middle Ages allowed women a degree of economic and civil freedom unknown in the nineteenth century. Political exigencies such as war meant that women not only controlled entire households but also that they 'frequently controlled the management of estates, and occasionally held public offices of trust and importance'.[59] Hill concluded that industrialisation 'lifted the middle-class woman out of the purely domestic sphere by lessening her household duties. And so leaving her free for other occupations.'[60]

In the sociological studies of women's working life written during this period the idea that the industrialisation was responsible for women's declining economic status merged with a critique of the brutalising effects of industrialisation on women and children. Fabian women such as Barbara Leigh Hutchins and Mabel Atkinson (b. 1876) used historical examples to argue that marriage had been an 'industrial partnership' before the rise of the factory system. They recognised the importance of reproduction to this partnership, arguing that the labour of motherhood was labour enough. Moreover they suggested women's economic importance within marriage modified 'considerably the harshness of the common law'.[61] These critiques were not unique to Britain, and in the United States Helen Laura Woodbury (Sumner) and Rolla Milton Tyron (b. 1875) both drew similar conclusions about the history of women's economic production in America.[62]

The idea that the Industrial Revolution had generated an apocalyptic decline, causing the economic value of both working men and women to be radically diminished, was popularised during this period by the historians Barbara Hammond (1873–1962) and her husband J. L. Hammond. Barbara Hammond had spent much of her adolescence at Toynbee Hall. Although she did not necessarily embrace the philosophy of that institution in later life, her experience of the effects of searing poverty no doubt inflected her analysis in *The Town Labourer* (1917) and *The Skilled Labourer* (1919).[63] While these ideas were challenged by economic historians such as

Lillian Knowles (1870–1926), Ivy Pinchbeck (b. 1898) and M. Dorothy George (d. 1971) in the inter-war period, they established the importance of women's role in the pre-industrial economy and during the phase of proto-industrialisation, an idea economic historians are only just revisiting.[64]

Economic history as it emerged in the academy mirrored this interest in sociology and political economy and formed connections with the social reform and educational reform movements.[65] Through economic history, many scholars came to be interested in the more social aspects of history. Attempting to understand the evolution of an economy forced historians to consider the structures and changes of a society.[66] To do this it was necessary to focus not merely on elite groups, but on all sections of society who contributed to the economy. Social history as it evolved out of economic history was concerned with the working classes and with social and political movements of the poor. Unlike constitutional and political history, which were self-consciously elitist, economic and social history had 'grass-roots' appeal. Part of this appeal lay in the fact that it was seen as more pragmatic and 'hands-on' than other forms of history. The political and institutional contexts in which economic and social history first thrived were instrumental in forming its populist appeal. They were popular subjects at provincial and civic universities as well as in workers' education and university extension programmes. Economic and social history rendered the past 'less bookish' and brought students 'into closer touch with the men [sic] of by-gone days'.[67]

Women were drawn to the study of economic and social history in large numbers in the period before the First World War. Through their interest in socialist and progressive politics, particular institutions became havens for women scholars interested in the social issues of the day. The connection between the Fabian movement and the LSE meant that it become an important centre for the study of women's work and their role in the economy. By the 1920s and 1930s women associated with the LSE shaped some of the most critical debate in economic and social history during this period.[68] The connection between Hull House and the University of Chicago allowed women social scientists to gain practice at the Settlement and theory at the School of Civics and Philanthropy. Women historians who did not find work in the burgeoning sub-disciplines of economic and social history found themselves part of the growing bureaucracy of the welfare state. In undertaking such work these women combined their feminist and historical interests with their professional concerns. Moreover, their historical and feminist insights helped influence the maternalist aspects of the welfare state during this period. Women who worked as sociologists and social scientists were not so much withdrawing from the writing of women's history, as creating primary sources for future women's historians.

CHAPTER 7

Amateurs or Professionals? Women's History in the Academy

> Women who took the PhD in history hold poorer positions, are more likely to be unemployed, and are less likely to do research than men. Moreover the historical profession awards less recognition to its women members. What the future holds for the woman who seeks the Doctor of Philosophy is as dark as the future always is.
> William Hesseltine and Louis Kaplan, 'Women Doctors of Philosophy in History', *Journal of Higher Education*, 1943

This chapter will explore the experiences of those women who achieved success as academic historians from the end of the nineteenth century until the rise of women's liberation in the 1960s. While the vast majority of women who engaged in historical writing did so outside the academy, a small but growing number of women trained at university and took up places in the newly formed discipline of history. These women had to face numerous obstacles as they slowly worked to gain acceptance within the academy. They dealt with male hostility and were relegated to peripheral standing in the university system. These exclusions allowed women historians to form powerful networks of female scholars and to draw inspiration for their work from this sense of female community. The first forty years of the twentieth century proved particularly fruitful for women historians, with a number of women making significant innovations in the new sub-genres of social and economic history.

In focusing on the experiences of these pioneering women this chapter will examine the forces that led women to become historians during this period. It will ask: What factors contributed to their successes and failures? What part did feminism play in shaping their ideas and their careers? What innovations did women make in the profession? Did their experiences within the academy cause them to write women's history?

Women and Higher Education

One of the most important campaigns of first-wave feminism was the struggle for women to attain access to higher education. Throughout the nineteenth century the demand for equal educational opportunities for women slowly materialised into ladies' colleges and coeducational universities. Eventually, by the mid-twentieth century, women gained full admittance into elite universities such as Oxford, Harvard and the Sorbonne. The study of history became the centrepiece of female higher education during this period. Initially this was due to the domestic nature of feminism in the early nineteenth century which valued history because it 'connect[ed] domestic women to the polity' and brought civic understanding to [the] home'.[1] By the beginning of the twentieth century the rise of 'scientific history', with its democratising principles, was utilised by women educators intent on producing graduates ready to take up their role in the public sphere.[2] Until the 1950s history departments were important sites for displaying the possibilities of female education and the development of nascent feminism.

Although agitation for women's education had begun in the Enlightenment it was not until the 1860s that women really gained access to the university system. This was the result of the bold experiment of Matthew Vassar, founder of the eponymous college for women. Vassar insisted that his newly founded institution provided the same liberal arts curriculum as any male college. Taking Yale as its role model, Vassar College for Women rejected seminary-style teaching with its focus on domestic and teaching skills, to become the first 'real University for women'.[3] Vassar offered women the study of classical languages and was 'unusual only in its emphasis on the fine arts and the natural sciences'.[4] What made Vassar unique was Matthew Vassar's insistence that the college have the same professional faculty as the men's colleges, and advocated professionally trained women faculty, asserting that their example would prove 'the certainty of woman's higher possible future'.[5] Vassar's insistence on professional faculty provided the first possibility for women to gain a toehold in the academy and may have been the incentive for women to gain further professional training, such as acquiring a doctorate.

In the same year Vassar was chartered, the first Ph.D. was conferred by Yale. This had important implications for the study of history within the academy. More than any other discipline, history used the Ph.D. as the short route to professionalisation.[6] The first Americans to hold history Ph.D.s had been trained in Germany: Ephraim Emerton from the University of Leipzig and Herbert Baxter Adams from Heidelberg. Both returned to the United States in 1876 to begin teaching at Johns Hopkins, the first American institution to establish a doctoral programme in history. Johns Hopkins based its doctoral programme around practices of seminar-based teaching, as in Germany. Emphasis was placed on archival research and standardised training in esoteric skills like philology and paleography. Unlike in Germany, where the doctorate was only the first of a series of academic awards, in the United States the Ph.D. became the final step towards professorship. Within a generation most of the elite universities had established Ph.D. programmes in history, the American Historical Association had been established and the journal of that association, *American Historical Review*, began publication.[7] The first woman to receive a doctorate in history was Kate Everest (Levi), who obtained her degree from the University of Wisconsin in 1893.[8] Wisconsin became a major institutional support for women's further education in history.[9]

The beginning of the twentieth century saw American women colleges becoming increasingly committed to producing for women the same education available for men. In part this reflected the changing nature of college life as second- and third-generation graduates became faculty and insisted upon their own vision of women's education. In part this reflected the slow democratisation of elite education in the United States.[10] Most importantly, it showed the impact of first-wave feminism upon the academy. Underpinning educational reform was the desire to increase the independence and capabilities of women. First-wave feminism was viewed ambivalently by the hierarchies of women's colleges, but it was impossible to curb interest in women's advancement. By the turn of the century women's colleges on both sides of the Atlantic were in the vanguard of first-wave feminism. Feminist activism within these institutions ensured that the education of women for domesticity gradually declined as the main objective of women's colleges.

Unlike their predecessors, the generation of educators who took women's colleges into the twentieth century had experienced both the limitations and the freedoms of the coeducation. Mary Woolley (1863–1947), who revolutionised college life at Mount Holyoake, was the first female graduate of Brown University and obtained a Master's degree in history from that institution. M. Carey Thomas (1857–1935), radical founder of Bryn Mawr, had spent much of her early life at Johns Hopkins and had surreptitiously taken classes at that institution. She was one of the first American women to study Classics in Germany, although neither the University of Leipzig or Göttingen examined her for a degree.[11] Her sense of exclusion from these institutions was enhanced by the fact that she was forced to sit behind a black curtain while taking Classics at Johns Hopkins so she would not be 'an unnecessary distraction'.[12] In Germany it was proposed that visiting women students be made to sit in a curtained theatre box apart from the male students. These methods were not only used to evoke a sense of separateness in women and to remind them of the inappropriateness of their course of study. It was also a protective measure to prevent young men from being distracted from their lessons.[13] Women like Thomas and Woolley became committed to shaping women's college life in the image of male colleges such as Harvard and Yale so that women might have the same advantages as men without the slights they had experienced.

From their inception women's colleges created separate intellectual communities for women and provided continuous employment for female academics.[14] The shift to a more 'equal' education clearly benefited both students and faculty alike. At Mount Holyoake, Woolley undertook a series of reforms that rapidly transformed the college from a seminary for teacher training 'into a self-consciously professional faculty'.[15] The Ph.D. was central to Woolley's reform programme. She insisted that faculty required this degree and that they maintained their research interests while on staff. She facilitated this by creating salaried sabbaticals as an essential requirement of faculty. In return she required faculty to publish if they were to advance within the college hierarchy.[16] Vassar, Bryn Mawr and other elite women's colleges followed Mount Holyoake in the move towards adopting the professional standards of the best universities.

These reforms proved particularly beneficial to historians. The study of history as a discipline within the university underwent a professional transformation that in many ways paralleled that which was occurring in women's colleges. The rigours of scientific history demanded the adoption of objective methods of inquiry and intense archival research. History at women's colleges had previously been part of a sentimental education in morals and character. Women historians on faculty saw that the transformation of history into a scientific discipline had the potential to enhance the transformation of women's education. Around the same time the American Historical Association (AHA) was established, women's colleges were taking steps to introduce history as a 'scientific study'. Herbert Baxter Adams, the first President of the AHA, who taught at Smith, did much to ensure that American women's colleges taught history through the detailed analysis of primary sources.[17] Between 1875 and 1885 Smith, Wellesley, Vassar and Bryn Mawr reorganised their schedules, made new appointments and improved library and other research facilities.[18]

Women historians such as Nellie Neilson (1873–1947) and Bertha Putnam (1872–1960) at Mount Holyoake and Lucy Maynard Salmon at Vassar enthusiastically embraced the new research methodologies posed by their male counterparts, while simultaneously rejecting 'the praise of ladies dead and lovely knights' that had characterised earlier historical writing.[19] Both male historians and women's educationalists shared common assumptions about the liberalising and democratising potential the study of history offered.

Perhaps without understanding its full significance, those who supported women's entrance into the historical profession were simultaneously enhancing educated women's potential power in the public sphere.

Initially only two women's colleges in the United States, Radcliffe and Bryn Mawr, awarded doctorates in history, so most women had to undertake postgraduate study at coeducational institutions.[20] Women in coeducational colleges faced many obstacles, not least the indifference and hostility of male faculty. This treatment often encouraged sisterly collaboration between women and made it imperative for women to establish effective networks for themselves and their graduate students. It is possible to discern distinct patterns of graduate study based around these friendships, which developed into informal mentoring systems and eventually blossomed into communities of women historians, not just in the United States but in Great Britain, Europe, Australia and Canada. It was particularly through the experience of separatist education offered by women's colleges that women historians forged their most meaningful and intellectually fulfilling relationships. College provided women, perhaps for the first time, with a sense of both personal and intellectual freedom, that might otherwise have been stifled in domesticity. Before women's acceptance into higher education, their friendships with other women were largely dependent on their familial ties. At college friendships could be forged independently. Many women relished the potential for female companionship that postgraduate study presented.

The European Experience

Europe was slower in advancing the cause of women's education and opposition to women's higher education was both more widespread and more entrenched, as older universities with clerical traditions dominated the intellectual landscape. In the same year Vassar opened, Cambridge University granted women permission to sit for its local examination.[21] This marked the beginning of an eighty-year struggle for women to gain equality of education at that institution. The first women's colleges at Cambridge, Girton and Newnham were established in the early 1870s. By the 1880s women were permitted to attend lectures if chaperoned and to sit for the same examinations as male undergraduates. But they were in no way recognised as members of the university and could not take out degrees or hold any university office.[22]

History was very popular among women at both the Oxford and Cambridge colleges.[23] At Oxford Louisa Creighton (1850–1936), wife of the future Bishop of London and keen 'amateur' historian, had been a central figure in the push to integrate women into Oxford. A number of men she lobbied to form a committee to provide lectures and classes for women were also historians, such as William Stubbs, Thorold Rogers and her husband Mandell Creighton.[24] In part the push for women to study history may have been shaped by gendered assumptions about the discipline. At both universities history was considered an 'easy study involving little more than memory'.[25] Efforts were made throughout the latter half of the nineteenth century to 'stiffen' history up so it appeared as a more 'vigorous' study, but the impression remained that it was 'easy school for rich men'.[26] Many assumed that women studied history because 'it made no demands on their non-existent knowledge of the Classics'.[27] Yet most of the women who established careers in history first read at Girton College. Girton had been established by the formidable Emily Davies, who insisted upon the importance of women reading the same subjects as men, particularly the Classics and mathematics. Girton women such as Eileen Power, Lilian Knowles, Ivy Pinchbeck and Dorothy George were classically educated before coming to Cambridge.

It is more likely that women were attracted to the study of modern history because it was an emerging discipline and thus was more welcoming of newcomers and more open to innovation. As in America, British women saw that the study of history clearly offered them a liberal training in citizenship, enhancing their potential in the public sphere. Through the endeavours of the British Historical

Association young women were trained to accept the importance of history in relation to their citizenship, both at school and at university. By 1921, 91 per cent of members of this association were women.[28] Ironically, in both countries women were educated to citizenship through history, before they became citizens following the First World War. The enthusiasm of supportive male academics enhanced the pattern of 'mutual intellectual debt and scholarly partnership' that the women's colleges fostered.[29] In the United States men such as Herbert Adams, Henry Adams and George E. Howard, through their research and teaching, did much to encourage women into historical scholarship.[30] In Britain, despite the controversy over academic recognition of women, men such as Frederick Maitland, Edward Armstrong and G. G. Coulton were supportive of the work of women colleagues and students.[31] Such scholarly co-operation between the sexes was apparently lacking on the Continent. While studying at the Sorbonne in 1911, Eileen Power wrote to her friend Margery Lois Garrett complaining of the remoteness of her supervisor C. V. Langlois and longing 'for one of [her] kind and interested Cambridge men!'[32]

The newness of the discipline meant that there was potential for women to gain employment when they had finished training. The lowly status of history at Oxford and Cambridge meant that men were more likely to pursue Classics or philosophy to establish academic careers. This resulted in only a small number of suitably qualified graduates in the new discipline enhancing women's employment potential.[33] This was also true outside 'Oxbridge' where the newer civic universities were establishing history departments. In England the London School of Economics (LSE), established in 1896, employed a number of Girton-educated women to teach social and economic history. The LSE established scholarships and bursaries to assist women in continuing their studies. In Ireland, a similar pattern emerged with a number of the first Chairs in History being taken up by women.[34] Modern Irish history was regarded as a novelty and did not have the same prestige as older disciplines. Women professors did much to encourage the scholarship of other women, establishing networks of graduate students and colleagues throughout the world.

It would be wrong to suggest that women experienced the same possibilities as male graduates. Most women historians found that gendered assumptions shaped their educational experience. Women's salaries were rarely the same as men. In the United States, when women became faculty, their positions invariably carried an adjunct or inferior status.[35] In England both Oxford and Cambridge acted in ways that actively obscured women's intellectual achievements and disguised their role within the university. Women's employment was limited to the women's colleges and women were not allowed to participate in the workings or ceremonies of the university, nor were they acknowledged when they received any academic distinctions. Although women were still able to obtain employment as historians in tertiary institutions, many deeply resented these exclusions.

Lack of recognition was only one of many obstacles facing women wanting to become academic historians. In France women undergraduates took their history examinations separately from men as it was believed that women spent their careers teaching in secondary schools.[36] No professorial positions existed for women at the University of Paris or the Collège de France and there were only a limited number of posts that supported woman applicants, however talented.[37] This exclusion reflected the ways in which gender shaped education in France before the First World War. As in Great Britain, there was much opposition to women's higher education in France.[38] As Karen Offen has described, education for girls established by the Third Republic promoted an understanding of sexual difference that prepared young women 'to submit to an "interior life", legally and economically subordinated to their future husbands'.[39] Although historians, particularly Michelet, had championed the need for women's education, this was not translated into the acceptance of women historians in the academy. Michelet's support of women's scholarship and his interest in women as historical subjects were described as his downfall by later generations of French historians.[40] French women who became historians during this period engaged in an intellectual form of coverture, where their work became subsumed into that of their husbands.

Ironically, Germany, the country that was most innovative in regards to modernising the university and the most progressive in its professionalisation of history, was also the country most resistant to the tertiary education of women.[41] Although German women demanded access to university education around the same time as women in Britain (c. 1865), few German women received a tertiary education before the First World War. As in Britain, women were allowed to attend lectures as 'auditors' during the 1860s but they were not allowed to take out degrees. British women in Germany created women's Lyceums, so that women could attend lectures on educational subjects deemed suitable for women.[42] Courses at the Lyceums proved immensely popular and famous professors such as Fredrich Paulsen, Erich Schmidt and Ulrich von Wilamowitz-Moellendorff offered lecture series. Male critics of higher education for women continued to argue that the presence of women within the university was antithetical to the rigorous masculine *Kultur* of German university life. By the end of the 1870s opposition to women's tertiary education had hardened and in 1879 women were explicitly barred from entering university by the government.

Far from being an enlightened influence in regard to women's education, the practice of historical research as taught by Ranke's followers in the German universities seems to have enhanced the desire to exclude women. As Bonnie G. Smith has demonstrated, Ranke's seminars were a male-only preserve, established precisely with the exclusion of women in mind.[43] Moreover, Ranke's pedagogical techniques, revealingly referred to as 'exercises', assumed a language of intellectual exertion, fit only for vigorous young men.[44] The conflation of vigour and rigour sustained the practice of scientific history throughout the nineteenth century, thoroughly enmeshing the newly professionalised discipline with the development of masculinity.[45] German historians were among the most vocal opponents of women's entrance into tertiary education. The legal historian Otto von Gierke declared in the 1890s: 'our universities are men's universities...adapted to the male spirit', thus encapsulating the spirit of German opposition to the feminisation of university culture. Heinrich von Trieschke, German nationalist and successor to Ranke's Chair in Berlin, vociferously attacked the possibility of women attending his classes, claiming that such an experiment was 'insulting to his [male] students'.[46] At the root of Trieschke's opposition was the belief that women sullied the pristine masculine *Kultur* of the German university. Like Gierke, he celebrated the longevity of male supremacy in this arena, stating emphatically: 'For half a millennium German universities have been designed for men, and I will not help destroy them.'[47] Prior to the rise of Nazism and the large-scale exclusion of women from the academy, women only accounted for 9 per cent of the student population.

The Impact of War

The outbreak of war in 1914 presented certain institutional advantages for women historians. The absence of men occasioned by the war proved beneficial, at least professionally, to women studying at university. As male students left for the front, women found themselves in increasingly feminine spaces. According to Vera Brittain, the first two months of the war 'altered Oxford more drastically than six centuries' as the majority of men left their colleges for the front.[48] Cambridge was likewise affected and gained the reputation during the war of being 'a bleak place of women and old men'.[49] French, German and eventually US universities were similarly devastated. While the war continued, women were allowed a degree of liberty and a range of opportunities hitherto regarded as inappropriate. Opponents of women's education were silenced as it became apparent that women could and did engage in the same work as men. At university, women often found that their work received greater attention and their intellectual aspirations were regarded more seriously. The University of Sydney, dubbed the 'women's university' during the war, produced Marjorie Barnard (1897–1987), a university medallist in history. G. A. Wood, Founding Professor of History at Sydney, named Barnard his greatest student.[50] This trend continued after the war, as the number of women students engaged in coeducation increased. Men who had been at the front spent less time at university. Oxford and Cambridge, for instance, introduced short diploma courses for those whose studies had been interrupted by the war. The high death rates occasioned by the war increased the potential of women to gain employment at coeducational institutions and even, though rarely, at men's colleges.

The decade immediately following the war saw the rates of participation for women in all professions increase. Prior to the Great Depression women's employment in the US academy peaked at 32.5 per cent.[51] Some five hundred women earned Ph.D.s in history in the United States between 1920 and 1940.[52] Most of these degrees were attained from coeducational colleges, although few women found employment at such institutions in the inter-war period. A small number of women had attained these prestigious positions while men were absent at the war, though few sustained them in the post-war period. In 1935 a survey revealed that no women historians were employed in men's colleges.[53] More often than not women historians found employment in the women's colleges, where some established distinguished careers. While women's colleges provided friendly environments for women scholars they sometimes hampered their careers. This was particularly true with regard to research. In all but the Ivy League colleges women scholars were viewed primarily as teachers. This meant that they had large teaching loads and little time for scholarship. It was rare during this period for such colleges to offer women's faculty salaried sabbaticals, so it was difficult for historians to spend time researching abroad.

As in the pre-war period, women tended to find themselves largely sidelined from history's professional organisations and rarely took on executive positions.[54] Prizes and fellowships were usually reserved for men.[55] This exclusion, however, allowed women to establish their own historical associations and to carve out women's spaces within those that were male dominated. The original Berkshire women's history group was established in 1929 as a result of women's segregation from the 'smokers' that followed the annual dinners of the American Historical Association (AHA) conferences. Its first conference was held in 1934. In an attempt to foster collegial relations, women historians sponsored breakfasts at the AHA, to promote networking and to exchange ideas on professional activities.

In Britain Oxford and Cambridge moved slowly towards the acceptance of women, with Oxford awarding women degrees in 1918 and Cambridge in 1923. Cambridge resisted, not allowing women full membership of the university until 1948. Helen Maud Cam (1885–1968), one of the most important constitutional historians of the inter-war period, participated in her first academic procession at Cambridge in that year. She was just about to leave Cambridge, after some twenty years, to become the first woman to hold a Chair of History at Harvard. She had received a D.Litt. from Cambridge in 1937, but as with all other degrees offered to Cambridge women it could be received, but not awarded in a graduation ceremony.[56] Cam's first (and last) procession marked the first time women had been allowed to participate in a graduation. As in the United States, even the most important women scholars found themselves restricted to employment at the women's colleges of Britain's elite universities. While women's colleges like Girton were important sites for training women historians, they ensured women students and staff remained marginal figures within the broader university community.

It was in London and the provincial universities that women were more successfully integrated into academic life. The London School of Economics (LSE) proved the most popular place for women historians to train and employed more women historians than any other institution.[57] Lillian Knowles, who joined the LSE in 1897, became the first woman professor in Great Britain. During the 1920s and 1930s the LSE produced a whole generation of women historians, who emerged from its auspices to take up newly formed positions in social and economic history. Ivy Pinchbeck (b. 1898), and Dorothy Marshall, who studied under Knowles, became readers in economic history at Bedford College; Mabel Buer took up a similar position at the University of Reading. Vera Anstey (1889–1976) and Eleanora Carus-Wilson (1897–1977) remained at the LSE itself and became vital members of the newly formed Economic

History Society. The significance of the LSE as a training ground for women historians was not restricted to Great Britain. Sylvia Thrupp (b. 1903), a Canadian medievalist trained at the LSE, earned a Ph.D. and a postdoctoral fellowship before she returned to Canada.

In Britain's former colonies the loss of men occasioned by the war was more sorely felt. This loss, however, enabled women to attain academic positions that had been unobtainable before the war. In Australia, during the inter-war period, two out of three tenured historians in the history department at the University of Melbourne were women. Kathleen Fitzpatrick (1905–90) and Jessie Webb (1880–1944) greatly influenced the shape of the discipline in Australia.[58] In Canada, too, women attained positions in history departments during the inter-war period, although here their acceptance was more grudging. Sylvia Thrupp who went on to become professor at the universities of Chicago and Michigan, and Margaret Ormsby (b. 1909), who studied for her doctorate at Bryn Mawr and became Professor of History at the University of British Columbia, initially found appointments in smaller provincial universities. The conditions for women historians in these institutions were often difficult. Ormsby recalled that when she was appointed to McMaster University in Hamilton she was forced to work from a desk in the women's lavatories, the only space available.[59] Elite universities such as Toronto and McGill seldom appointed women above the level of tutor until after the Second World War.[60]

On the Continent the position of women within the academy remained tenuous during the inter-war period. In Germany women had gained the vote after the First World War and embarked on an uneasy road to emancipation that abruptly ceased with the rise of the Nazis in 1933. During the 1920s, however, German women did begin to participate in academic life. By 1929 university enrolments indicate that women made up just under a fifth of the university student body. The second woman to receive a regular academic post in Germany was the historian Hedwig Hintze (1884–1942), who was appointed to the University of Berlin in 1924. Hintze specialised in political history, focusing particularly on the French Revolution.

She was forced to flee Berlin when the Nazis assumed power.[61] The first woman appointed to teach in an Austrian university was the historian Erna Patzelt (b. 1894), at the University of Vienna in 1925.

In France women historians only seemed to find work within the academy in positions as auxiliaries to powerful male historians. As a result, some of the most gifted women historians of the generation between the wars found themselves either based outside the academy or collaborating with men.[62] Even amongst the Annalistes, the most innovative and important group of historians to emerge in France during this period, women played a peripheral role. Women worked alongside *Annaliste* men in paid and unpaid positions, but they seldom attained public recognition for their efforts. The experience of the wives of the founders of the Annales provides telling evidence of this. Susan Dognon (1897–1985), the wife of Lucien Febvre, held a doctorate in history and geography. She gave up her work to raise their children and to assist him with translation, copy-editing and entertaining fellow scholars in their social circle.[63] Simone Vidal Bloch devoted her life to the work of her husband Marc Bloch, serving as his secretary, editor and research assistant, a role never acknowledged in Bloch's publications.[64] Women's adjunct status was reflected by their lack of representation in the journal *Annales* produced by Bloch and Febvre.

No women served on the board of the Annales before the Second World War and only two contributed essays to the *Annales* during this period, Thérèse Sclafert (1876–1959) and Lucie Varga (1904–41).[65] Thérèse Sclafert was an expert on medieval trade routes, though she spent most of her life teaching at secondary schools and teacher's colleges. She produced two major works, *Le Haut-Dauphiné au Moyen Age* in 1926 and *Cultures en Haute-Provence. Déboisements au pâturages au Moyen Age*, posthumously published in 1959. Lucie Varga had studied in Vienna in the 1920s, producing a thesis on the history of the expression of the Dark Ages.[66] She came to Paris as a refugee and worked with Febvre as his research assistant. At some stage during this collaboration the two became lovers. She published several essays on the nature of totalitarianism and secretly carried messages into Nazi-occupied territories.[67] She planned to work with Febvre on a history of religion, although this collaboration ceased when their affair ended. Varga died of diabetes, brought on by stress and an inadequate diet in the early years of the Second World War.

Women's History in the Academy

Certain historians have suggested that as women became more settled within the academy they tended to write on the same subjects as men.[68] While it is true that some women worked in the fields of constitutional and political history, a great number of them maintained historical interests they had formed in response to first-wave feminism. The great legal struggles between men and women over suffrage, university education, employment opportunities, marital reform and property rights that defined pre-war feminism still informed women's historical writing in the inter-war period. Even as women became more established within the academy much of their historical research was devoted to understanding how women had come to their unequal position in society.

The exigencies of the war had forced many women and children to become economically independent of men. During the course of the war many women had left the industries which had traditionally employed them to undertake 'men's work' for the first time.[69] With some nine million men dead or missing, many families had been left without male breadwinners. Women's work outside the home achieved a significance in the inter-war period unknown since the rise of industrialisation. This did not necessarily translate into acceptance of women's work. Far from liberating women from pre-war gender expectations, the inter-war period was shaped by an attempt to return to the more restrictive domestic ideology of the nineteenth century. While many women felt the push back into the home, there were large numbers for whom this was now impossible.

The war was productive of major shifts in historical writing.[70] The forms of history that proved most popular during the inter-war period were economic and social history. Although more conservative historians continued to write the histories of great men in great wars, other historians responded to the chaos of the war, by 'looking steadfastly backwards to more coherent times'.[71] The new theories and methodologies posed by social and economic history allowed historians to conceive of a richer, more detailed and nuanced idea of the past. The pairing of social history and economic history proved critical to the maintenance of women's history in the inter-war period and served as an impetus for its re-emergence in the period following the Second World War.

The impact of the war complicated the ways in which historians dealt with the question of women's role in the past. Whereas in the pre-war period much of this discussion focused around women's political rights in the inter-war period, women's economic role in the past became a central focus of women's historical research. The key historical questions posed by women historians during this period related to the changes in women's status generated by the slow development of industrial capitalism since the Middle Ages.[72] Women's history focused almost entirely on women's labour, depicting the effect on women's lives of the decline of domestic industry and the rise of the factory system.[73] Social changes, too, particularly those created by the wars of religion, were seen to impact negatively upon women's labour. The aim of research produced during the inter-war period was to better understand how such changes impacted upon women's status in society.

Such questions reflected continuing interest in women's present economic conditions as well as their conditions in the past. The writing of Alice Clark, the first historian to publish on women's work following the First World War, demonstrated clear continuities with the sociological and reformist material produced on women's work by groups such as the Fabian Women's Committee Executive and the Women's Industrial Council. Clark shared similar concerns about the relationship between production and reproduction and their general pessimism about industrialisation. The central thesis of the *Working Life of Women in the Seventeenth Century* is that the Industrial Revolution diminished women's capacity as 'producers' by diminishing the importance of domestic labour.

This idea was rigorously challenged by a number of her colleagues at the LSE during the 1920s and 1930s. Following Lillian Knowles, Ivy Pinchbeck and M. Dorothy George drew differing conclusions about the impact of industrialisation on the lives of women. A committed Tory, Knowles had maintained that the Industrial Revolution brought positive changes to production, and insisted that the factory system was a marked improvement on home-based industry.[74] Both Pinchbeck and George questioned earlier feminist interpretations of the impact of industrialisation on women.[75] Pinchbeck, in *Working Women and the Industrial Revolution* (1930), drew almost opposite conclusions to Clark.[76] While Pinchbeck's study was more systematic and empirical than Clark's, the difference between their conclusions also reflected the shifting concerns of feminism in the post-suffrage period. Pinchbeck's study was informed by her experience of women's war work and her understanding that the vote did not necessarily emancipate women. In the preface to the 1968 reissue of this text Pinchbeck was incredulous about the historical interest in political enfranchisement and the historical neglect of women's employment outside the home.[77] This neglect, however, ensured that Pinchbeck's text has remained the classic study of this period.[78]

History and the Feminine Mystique

While the Depression had seen educational and employment opportunities for women shrink, the Second World War allowed women already in academic positions to gain greater prestige and a number of women to acquire employment as historians for the duration. The professional advantages women gained throughout the war were short-lived. The return to 'normalcy' following the war often resulted in women leaving paid employment or higher education and returning to the home. The 1950s marked a return to the domestic ideology of separate spheres that characterised the Victorian period. The Second World War had seen the state call upon women to become the reserve labour force. When their countries no longer needed them in this capacity, they were encouraged by the state to return to their 'true' roles as wives and mothers. Women's dependence upon men was once again politicised and their entitlement to citizenship framed in terms of motherhood and pronatalism.[79]

The 1950s and 1960s marked the nadir of female employment in tertiary education. Although women had taken over men's jobs *en masse* during the war, they often found that their new employment was only for the duration. In the United States women's employment within the academy had peaked in the 1920s.[80] In Great Britain women continued to work in the margins, with few attaining employment as tenured academics. Even with the growth of universities in the 1950s, women remained grossly under-represented in academic posts. Similar trends occurred in Australia, Canada and throughout Europe. In some countries universities retained marriage bans, though few women found it possible to sustain a career and a family, even when they were permitted to do so. Educational opportunities for women were better than at any other time in the previous century. The 1950s saw the democratisation of higher education on a massive scale. Women attended college and universities in large numbers, 'where they performed to intellectual standards that made no allowances for sex'.[81] While more women were able to attend college or universities, large numbers of them failed to complete degrees, many marrying before graduation.

The failure of women to take up the educational opportunities offered to them in the 1950s was due to the many contradictory influences facing women at this time. Women who lived through the war had experienced a considerable degree of freedom during this period and were unprepared for the restrictive climate of 'excessive femininity' in the 1950s. Consumer culture melded with popular culture in ways that saw women represented as 'sex-bombs', housewives and goddesses of consumption, however, the figure that women were most meant to aspire to was 'the bride'. Interest in the bride reflected changing expectations around marriage and childbirth. In the two generations that followed the First World War, many women had chosen or were forced to forgo or delay marriage. The age at marriage increased throughout the Western world, while birth rates simultaneously declined. The period following the Second World War was dubbed the 'baby boom'. Ages at marriage declined, rates of marriage increased and birth rates improved, albeit briefly, for the first time in several decades. The post-war economic boom meant working-class and middle-class families felt less compunction to limit family growth, while governments attempted to promote post-war stability by introducing maternalist policies designed to benefit 'the average family'.[82]

Given this political atmosphere it is not surprising that the two most important texts of women's history to appear in the immediate post-war period were popular texts not written by women within the academy. Mary Beard and Eleanor Flexner (b. 1908) worked on the periphery of the academic world and both wrote as independent scholars.[83] They did not publish with historians in mind, rather their works popularised the idea of women as important historical agents and insisted on the power of women to generate historical change. Mary Beard's *Woman as Force in History* was published in 1946. Focus on this text has sometimes meant that Beard has been seen as the 'creator' of women's history and an important inspirational figure for women historians in the wake of women's liberation.[84] As recent criticism of her work has shown, Beard was a more transitional figure, marking the space between women's history as it existed before women's liberation and women's history as it emerged out of second-wave feminism. *Woman as Force in History* is quite anti-feminist in its rhetoric, although not perhaps in sentiment.[85] Beard's negative assessment of earlier feminists has inflected the writings of second-wave feminist historians who took their cue from Beard and who followed her critiques when establishing differences between the new women's history and the old. Beard spent little time analysing the important contributions first-wave feminists made to the public sphere, which she saw as only important in men's eyes.[86] Rather her emphasis in this text was on rethinking history to show that women's unique contributions to society were historically significant. Beard also recognised the importance of recording multiple voices and replicating diverse sources, so that the women's words and deeds would not be lost. She spent much of her life creating archives to preserve the work of earlier feminists so that other scholars would have access to their work. While the Centre for Women's Archives she envisaged was forced to close during the war, the materials collected have formed significant sections of the Sophia Smith collection at Smith College and the Schlesinger Library at Radcliffe.[87]

Eleanor Flexner's *Century of Struggle* (1959) was primarily about feminism's contribution to the public sphere. Like Beard, Flexner was not situated in the academy, but rather was a public intellectual active in feminist and other radical politics. Whereas Beard offered a limited analysis and opinion of first-wave feminism, Flexner's history of the movement was expansive. While Flexner does not discuss feminism, the whole focus of the text is about feminism, or rather, the struggle for women's rights, as she called it. Flexner's history, too, was different from other histories of the suffrage movement. According to one reviewer, 'it was the first balanced and scholarly account' of the movement.[88] Flexner was not working within an established tradition, rather she was inventing a new one. *Century of Struggle* broadened discussion of feminism in the United States to include the contributions of African-American women, immigrant women and women of the working class.[89] Flexner's analysis of women's rights was informed by her own experience of radical politics, making her discussion of women's rights more overtly political than earlier 'celebratory' suffrage histories. While Beard's work harkened back to older forms of women's history, it was Flexner's work that set the agenda for the new women's history.

It was Flexner's text too, that influenced the work of Betty Friedan (b. 1921), who published one of the most influential texts of second-wave feminism in 1963.[90] *The Feminine Mystique* reshaped ideas about women, femininity and sexual relations in the United States and in most of the Western world. The book detailed Friedan's study of young American women, based on interviews with young, white, urban middle-class women. Friedan claimed to have discovered a syndrome affecting women, which she called 'the problem with no name'. According to Freidan the 1950s produced particular conditions that generated in women feelings of *ennui*, frustration and disillusionment with their societal role. Friedan characterised the 'problem' as a crisis in feminine expectation. Material chains no longer bound women in the post-war period. All educational, legal and political barriers to women's equality had been removed. The core problem facing women was a problem of identity. Women were being challenged by conflicting discourses around femininity. Friedan said that she had found evidence that threw into question all 'the standards of feminine normality, feminine adjustment, feminine fulfilment and feminine maturity by which women are trying to live'. She warned: '[We] can no longer ignore the voice within women that says "I want something more than my husband, my children and my home."'[91]

Friedan's text struck a note among the women of 'Middle America'. The text became a best-seller, heralding the age of 'women's liberation'. She became a spokesperson for the new movement and in 1966 formed the National Organisation for Women (NOW). Friedan declared that NOW would 'take the actions needed to bring women into mainstream American society' and demand full equality for women.[92] Although she had long-standing ties with the labour movement and other working-class organisations in the United States, Friedan and NOW drew their support largely from apolitical white women of the middle classes. The politics of NOW were reformist rather than revolutionary and Friedan did much to protect her organisation from more radical elements. By the end of the 1960s, however, NOW was only one of many groups demanding equality for women as the era of women's liberation had truly begun.

CHAPTER 8

'Clio's Consciousness Raised'? Women's Liberation and Women's History

> We've heard enough about *his*tory, let's hear about HERSTORY!!!!
> 1970s feminist slogan

This chapter will explore the connections between women's liberation and the development of women's history in the post-war period. Women's liberation was born out of the radical politics of the 1960s. Women's liberation groups rejected masculinist political theory and structures and asserted the superiority of feminine politics, values and beliefs. They challenged many of the discriminatory practices women faced daily and demanded equal pay, equal opportunity employment, better childcare services and the right to abortion.

Women moved into tertiary education in unprecedented numbers during the 1960s, so it is not surprising that much feminist politics emerged from institutions of higher education. Such institutions were undergoing radical change, initiated by an increasingly politicised student body. Since the 1950s universities had undertaken a slow process of democratisation in response to particular post-war conditions. The discipline of history was profoundly affected by these changes. New methodologies and approaches to the study of history appeared. Although initially the new approaches ignored the question of women in history, they eventually proved critical to the emergence of women's history.

This chapter will examine how women's history came to take its place within the academy and the critiques of historical practice engendered by feminism. How did second-wave feminism shape historical writing? Did feminism enable women historians to demand a greater presence within the profession? What institutional support became available to women's historians with the advent of feminism?

The Emergence of Women's Liberation

By the end of the 1960s the groundswell of dissatisfaction that had begun with the publication of Friedan's *Feminine Mystique* had evolved into a fully-fledged mass movement for women's liberation. While Friedan had given a voice to the housebound, middle-class women of suburbia, many other women were critical of her and NOW for being bourgeois, conservative and self-serving. Friedan's reformist politics did not appeal to working-class women, women of colour and women on the left, many of whom had spent much of the 1960s in struggles over civil rights and the Vietnam War. Women involved in radical politics had begun to develop their own critiques of male power.

In the United States the experience of the civil rights movement, New Left politics and the anti-Vietnam War movement radicalised women and convinced them of the need for a separate movement devoted to women's liberation. The civil rights movement, like the Abolition movement of the nineteenth century, politicised the white women who engaged with it and alerted them to inequities in their own lives. While the experience of African-American women was clearly different to that of white women, both groups were deeply affected by the masculinist sexual politics of the civil rights movement. Many African-American women chose to stay within the movement, but a large number of white women left, disgruntled with their treatment. This experience was replicated in the student politics of the New Left and the anti-war movement, which were also notable for their masculinist politics. Women struggled to be heard in groups made up predominantly of men. The anti-war and black power movements often articulated their politics in aggressively masculine tones. Collective identity was formed around masculine and iconic figures such as Che Guevara.[1] Those women brave enough to speak up or seek leadership positions were often met with misogynist jibes and blatant hostility. Many women felt they were left to lick envelopes and make cups of tea.

The year 1968 marked a number of crises throughout the world. In Europe, the Russian army rolled tanks into Czechoslovakia to be met with popular resistance. In France, West Germany, Great Britain and Italy student uprisings erupted, followed by widespread industrial action. The black power and anti-Vietnam War movements also impacted upon Europe, particularly with the assassinations of Martin Luther King, Jr and Robert Kennedy and the escalation of the war in South-east Asia. Although different political pressures framed the European experience of the late 1960s, women involved in radical politics found themselves in the same marginalised position as their US counterparts.[2]

By the beginning of the 1970s women started organising outside the male-dominated parties of the left. North America led the way, with radical women rejecting both the liberal reformist politics of Betty Friedan's NOW and the socialist politics of the New Left. These 'radical feminists' attempted to develop a distinct politics of women's liberation. Gender relations, they argued, needed to be reconfigured in political terms. Harking back to Engels, they saw gender inequality as the quintessential form of social domination and argued that women constituted a sex class.[3] Many radical feminists came to women's liberation disgruntled and disillusioned from time spent as helpmates to New Left men. They sought a different form of politics and liberation from masculine political structures, agendas and theories. In their own practice, women's groups abolished bureaucratic structures, resisted the appointment of leaders and struggled to legitimise the idea of an autonomous movement.

Consciousness raising (CR) in small groups was the preferred means of working out political positions within women's liberation. CR had evolved out of the civil rights movement and Maoism, which informed much student and New Left politics during the 1960s. During the Cultural Revolution in China Maoist revolutionaries had encouraged peasants 'to speak pains to recall pains'.[4] The technique had been modified by American civil rights workers who adopted the slogan 'Tell it like it is'. Women schooled in the civil rights movement were quick to adapt the technique to politicise women by making them aware of their own struggle. Underpinning the rationale of CR was the idea that women, through the articulation of their own experiences, would be able to make revolutionary changes in their own position. CR allowed women to create a collective identity as feminists. Such techniques would later inform certain aspects of the history of women's culture.

Radical feminists adopted a politics of active resistance to male domination. Protests were organised against obvious symbols of men's power. The first 'radical feminist' action involved the storming of the Miss America pageant in 1968. Underlying this action was a belief that such pageants degraded all women, producing regulatory standards of beauty. A 'freedom trash bin' was set up for women in which to dump their girdles and bras, to protest against the way such items forced women into uncomfortable shapes so as to appeal to men. Spurred on by images of draft-card burning, the press created the myth that women 'burnt bras' during this protest. Other means of attacking 'the patriarchy' evolved: a national women's strike was organised demanding twenty-four-hour childcare, abortion on demand and equal employment and educational opportunities.

Similar actions took place all over the world. On the Continent many women first united around the issue of reproductive freedom. In Germany, France and the Netherlands the call for abortion on demand was the impetus for the development of women's liberation.[5] While it was women's sexual oppression that first saw the large-scale political mobilisation of women, radical feminism in Europe remained firmly connected to broader socialist and Marxist politics. Although feminism in Western Europe was influenced by the publication of American texts such as Kate Millet's *Sexual Politics* (1971), it was Simone de Beauvoir's *The Second Sex* (1949) that remained most influential. In Britain women's solidarity was built up around particular instances of industrial action. Following the publication of Juliet Mitchell's book *The Longest Revolution* in 1969, small groups of socialist and Marxist women began meeting all over Britain. As in Europe, feminism in Britain remained firmly entrenched within a leftist tradition. In Australia and Canada the rise of women's liberation was closely connected to the industrial action undertaken by women in demand for equal pay and the radical politics arising out of the anti-war movement.

Radical History?

The academy was the institution most emphatically challenged by radical politics in the 1960s. Until this time universities had remained bastions of elite male privilege. While a slow democratisation of these institutions began in the inter-war period, women remained largely marginalised within the universities. This process of democratisation escalated in the 1960s with the development of an international student's movement. A new generation of students and academics called to end elitist practices in universities. Radical pedagogical techniques were implemented and innovative courses of study offered to create a more egalitarian university system.[6] The heavy-handed responses of police and civil authorities to student protests had a radicalising effect, causing moderate and apolitical students to undertake 'a more deliberate activism'.[7]

The discipline of history was profoundly affected by these changes. The influx of working-class men into the university system through returned soldiers programmes had done much to seriously challenge the elitist assumptions that framed pre-war historical understanding. As other marginalised groups took their places within universities, historians found themselves increasingly open to the question, 'Whose history is this?' In the United States the influx of African-American students in the post-war period clearly raised questions about the place of slavery in the national historiography. In Europe, formerly colonised peoples queried the triumphal tone of imperialist history. In Australia, Canada and Latin America, indigenous peoples started to characterise settlement as invasion and colonisation as dispossession.

These issues could not be dealt with merely in terms of additions to grand narratives. They necessitated new methodologies and approaches. Distinct sub-disciplines of history emerged, such as black history, subaltern and post-colonial studies. Older sub-disciplines such as labour history and social history emerged in this period with renewed purpose and design. During the late 1950s and early 1960s a new type of social history evolved that attempted to develop a more comprehensive history of society. Issues of class and race became critical to the new social history. Social historians framed their work within new paradigms, reshaped by neo-Marxism, the Annaliste tradition and the political theory of Antoni Gramsci. Annalistes were particularly influential in the post-war period, as historians moved further away from grand historical narratives to focus on the minutiae of daily life. Private life was as critical to the Annalistes as the concerns of public life. Essential to this new type of history was an acceptance of new forms of evidence and new ways of reading such material. Iconographic, literary, folkloric and mythical evidence was treated seriously. Drawing on such traditions, the new social historians claimed that the experience of the powerless and inarticulate had long been ignored by historians and sought to give it voice.[8] They tried to turn 'history upside down' or read it 'from below'. This was not, however, to be a history of victims. Questions of agency and resistance formed much of this new work, offering new ways of thinking about the groups most oppressed by society, the working poor, indentured labourers and slaves.

Non-elite educational institutions were particularly important in establishing the new social history as it was popularised through the university extension movement, workers' and continuing education and the newly developing 'open' universities. Ruskin College, Oxford, established as a workers' education college in the nineteenth century, became the focal point of the new social history in Britain, with the development of the History Workshop movement. Established by Raphael Samuel, a tutor at Ruskin in 1967, the first History Workshops saw budding historians join with trade unionists and socialist academics to create a new type of 'democratic and participatory working people's history'.[9] History Workshop was committed to teaching and researching history that encompassed all social groups and human activities.[10] It took history outside the academy, claiming that it was too important to be left to professional historians. Such democratic impulses were sustained by workshops held in pubs. In the United States similar trends developed, and by the end of the 1960s workshops were being established on the east coast. The History Workshop movement extended into Europe, with similar groups established in West Germany, Sweden, Ireland, Italy and Russia.[11]

While the new social history seemed to offer much potential for the study of women's history, initially few social historians examined the role of women within society, except within the context of family history. Men remained the pre-eminent subjects of this new history, although the 'great man in history' was replaced by the 'heroic proletarian'. This, too, marked a shift within the parameters of labour history as well as social history. Whereas older labour historians had focused on the aristocracy of labour, such as trade union organisers or working-class politicians, new social historians tended to look to the ordinary 'heroes' of the working class. This worked in ways that often excluded women. As Anna Davin has pointed out, the focus on men reinforced masculinist values and attitudes.[12] The new labour history treated the sexual division of labour as natural and constant. The terms 'work', 'worker' and 'working-class' were only used to refer to working men. The periodisation used by labour historians continued to rely on male experience.[13]

The political atmosphere generated by the new social history did little to encourage the entrance of historians of women into the field. Just as radical groups had represented politics in terms that were aggressively masculine, radical historians celebrated political victories in the past in ways that focused upon heroic masculine action. Works such as E. P. Thompson's *Making of the English Working Class* embodied this 'New Left purpose'.[14] The new social history was constituted as an act of transgression, where 'groups previously portrayed as victims, or as actors peripheral to the central political narrative, became active agents of their own history'.[15] Thompson, in the *Making of the English Working Class*, framed his text around a male coming-of-age narrative, suggesting it was a 'biography of the English working class from its adolescence until its early manhood'.[16] In a sense the experience of aggressive masculinity was embedded within the new social history. It was first the historical practice of angry young men seeking to challenge the elitist hierarchy of universities. In turn it became the history of angry young men, focusing on 'primitive rebels', slave heroes, revolutionaries and street-fighting men.

New forms of cultural history emerged during this period also. Cultural history had been an elitist practice, consumed by an interest in high culture. The rise of the new social history necessitated new understandings of the history of culture. To gain an understanding of how the poor, the working class, slaves, indentured labourers and other marginalised groups lived it was necessary to study changing social and cultural processes 'over a considerable period of time'.[17] Until the 1960s those interested in the history of popular culture tended to have antiquarian interests in folk customs. New social historians demanded a new cultural history that examined the 'history of culture from below'.[18] This meant that analysis of popular culture became more relevant to an understanding of social history, as popular culture came to be viewed by historians as a site of political resistance.

Women remained marginalised in the new social and cultural histories that emerged during this period. The excessive masculinism of labour history hindered the potential to view women as workers. In this context work meant waged work and the sexual division of labour, and reproduction was not seen as a form of production.[19] By ignoring the domestic sphere as a site of production, labour and social historians reinforced the idea that women were sidelined from historical action. While family history dealt with issues pertaining to women such as fertility patterns and household work, the family was often treated as 'an undifferentiated unit', thus obscuring women's unique role.[20]

Women's Historians and Women's Liberation

Women historians and women training to be historians were subject to the conditions described by Friedan and the attempts at reform that followed in her wake. The expectations that shaped femininity in the 1950s and feminism in the 1960s moulded their lives and their careers as historians. Recent autobiographical work undertaken by historians coming of age in the late 1950s and early 1960s has indicated that women felt considerable tension between their desire to undertake postgraduate study and their expectations of being good wives and mothers.[21] Historians of women, like historians of men, were radicalised by the politics of the 1960s and many embraced the new trends emerging within historiography. Social history offered women greater potential to see themselves as historical subjects, however, the misogyny and gender blindness of radical politics often replicated itself in the historical writing that radical historians produced. Historians of women and women historians sometimes felt the same sense of alienation and trivialisation as the women who had emerged out of radical politics and into women's liberation.

It became apparent that women were not only largely absent in the historical record, they were marginalised in history departments in universities and in professional historical associations. Women's liberation informed much of the discussion about women's place in history and women's role as historians. Many women came to recognise that the marginalisation and alienation they felt as individuals was part of a wider problem of discrimination against women. In the United States the first move to challenge discrimination in the history profession came from Berenice A. Carroll, an historian who was employed in the political science department at the University of Illinois-Urbana. Carroll's career had been impeded by sexual discrimination at several universities where she had taught. Her decision to protest against this discrimination evolved out of her association with women involved in the Chicago Women's Liberation Union.[22] The 1969 Convention of the American Political Science Association had been the scene of considerable fallout over the discriminatory practices of that organisation. Carroll had joined the women protesting these practices and decided to pose 'similar challenges to the members of the historical profession'.[23] She drew up a petition, signed by twenty-two women, who then organised themselves as the Co-ordinating Committee on Women in the Historical Profession and demanded that the American Historical Association establish a permanent Committee on the status of women's employment.

The protest resulted in the AHA establishing a temporary Committee to investigate Carroll's claims. The Committee was chaired by Willie Lee Rose of Johns Hopkins University. In the following year Rose reported to the AHA that women faced discrimination because of their sex. The Committee on the Status of Women in the American Historical Association found that women historians were predominantly based in women's colleges. Some 33 per cent of historians at women's colleges were women, compared to 5.5 per cent at liberal coeducational colleges. Women made up about 1.5 per cent of professorial positions in the top ten graduate schools in history.[24] Rose called upon the AHA to change its own discriminatory practices, to ensure greater representation of women in its programmes and its committees. She asked that the AHA work towards less discriminatory practices within the academy, such as the elimination of nepotism rules, support for flexible part-time employment and maternity leave.[25]

Such demands reiterated many of the demands that were being made by women's liberation at this time and clearly raised the consciousness of women involved in the profession. According to the US historian Linda Kerber, who had heard Rose address the AHA, this knowledge could be life-changing.[26] The Rose Report sent women historians into a flurry of activity aimed at bettering their position within the profession. One of the first actions of the newly militant women historians was the establishment of an international conference on women's history. In the 1920s women historians had responded to the discriminatory practices of the AHA by establishing a social group, known affectionately as the 'Little Berks', which met annually for a weekend of socialising, research and networking. The impetus of women's liberation saw a larger conference grow out of the Little Berks, to become the Berkshire conference on the history of women. The first of these conferences was held at Douglass College, Rutgers University in 1973 and was attended by over 300 participants. For many women the Berks provided an important lifeline, allowing women to network in a male-dominated profession and providing an avenue for their research to be reviewed. By coming together in this way women historians became more aware of their marginalisation in the profession, while simultaneously realising their own power. Linda Kerber has described the Berks as 'a profession specific consciousness raising group'.[27]

This enthusiasm to meet and discuss women's history was matched by an impulse to create and teach it. Women's history courses had been taught in the United States since the 1920s, but with the impetus of women's liberation they proliferated.[28] In other countries women had been experiencing similar degrees of marginalisation within the profession and were heartened by the US experience. The enthusiasm for women's history generated in the United States was infectious and by 1975 many universities were offering courses in women's history. In Canada the first women's history course was established at the University of Toronto in 1971 and was taught by Natalie Zemon Davis and Jill Kerr Conway. Similar courses were offered at Carleton University, the University of Manitoba and York University. In 1975 the Canadian Committee on Women's History was founded, giving women historians an institutional base within the Canadian Historical Association.[29] The first women's history course in France was run by the University of Paris in 1973. The course 'Do women have a history?' was taught by Fabienne Bock, Pauline Schmitt Pantel and Michelle Perrott and, following Annaliste tradition, involved the integration of sociology and anthropology with history.[30] French women's history remained deeply connected to Annaliste history, while challenging its methodology and gender-blindness. Annaliste historians such as Jacques Le Goff, Mona Ozouf and Emmanuel Le Roy Ladurie were called on to help develop women's history and participate in its teaching. Macquarie University was the first campus in Australia to teach women's history, with a course proposal first put forward in 1971.[31] In the next decade most major Australian universities had established women's history courses. In Britain women's history grew alongside the new social history as it emerged through History Workshop. Initially women as a social group and women's activities had been ignored by such historians, however, by the mid-1970s the impact of women's liberation made itself felt. Ruskin College held the first major women's liberation conference in Britain in 1970. History Workshop fostered scholarship on women's history and produced a generation of women historians such as Sally Alexander, Catherine Hall, Carolyn Steedman, Jane Rendall and Barbara Taylor, who radicalised understandings of British history.

In response to overt forms of discrimination women historians all over the world formed their own social and political blocs within the profession. Conferences were devoted to women; women-only social groups and other forms of women-centred activity created broad networks of like-minded colleagues. Women's history also flourished outside the academy. The most radical attempts to write women's history certainly tended to evolve outside institutional frameworks. In part this was to do with the marginalisation of historians working on women. Many researchers in this field found difficulty in attracting tenured positions in the academy. Other women chose to deliberately eschew the 'ivory tower', rejecting it as an intrinsically masculinist institution, to create history outside its boundaries. These historians drew on the earlier traditions of popular historical writing by women, focusing on aspects of women's culture or the lives of exceptional women. Other texts, like Rosalind Miles's *Women's History of the World*, revisited the idea of the feminisation of history.[32]

During the 1970s numerous feminist history periodicals appeared, some within institutions, but most emerging from tiny radical presses. Feminist reading rooms, libraries and archives were established, such as the Fawcett Library in London and the Jessie Street Library in Sydney. Taking their names from feminist icons, such institutions proved vital for research into women's history. Not only did they supply much needed source material, they also created an atmosphere conducive to feminist scholarship. Women produced collections of documents from the archives and surveys of archival material relevant to the writing of women's history.

Women often found it difficult to have their work published by the more prestigious university presses. Smaller presses and presses specifically devoted to publishing feminist literature such as Virago and the Woman's Press emerged and became very successful, promoting women's history to both an academic and non-academic audience.

Clio's Consciousness Raised?

Not only did the women's liberation movement provide women historians with a voice to condemn the inequalities and injustices they had experienced within the profession, it also presented an opportunity for them to view the past in a different way. Women involved in the movement understood that rereading and rewriting history helped them to understand the present position of women; it gave women a sense of the past, by allowing them to view women's struggles and successes at other times and in other places, and it helped establish that patriarchal relations were not natural and inevitable, but contingent and changeable over time.[33]

Women's history, as it evolved out of women's liberation, tended to develop as part of an international movement and within the established methodologies and traditions of individual nationalist histories. In each country affected by the women's movement a variation of women's history developed, reflecting the unique feminist concerns of that country and the current debates within mainstream historiography.[34] Throughout the world historians became aware that women were not only historically marginalised, but that mainstream historiography privileged the public experience of men. Although the new social and cultural histories had given voice to groups traditionally alienated from history, women's presence in such narratives was often obscure, thus undercutting any claims such history had of being 'total' or inclusive.[35]

It became the mission of women's historians to insist on female agency in the 'making of history', to uncover women's participation in major historical events, to write women into received historical categories and to interpret their actions in terms recognisable to political and social historians.[36] Initially historians of women were concerned to correct what they saw as omissions from the historical record. As Judith Allen has suggested, by 'writing the experience of women into existing historical knowledge, these historians [sought] to make it more accurate and more comprehensive'.[37] By the end of the 1970s many countries had produced collections that restored 'women to history and history to women'.[38] It appears to have been almost mandatory for historians of women to begin articles, textbooks and edited collections with a discussion of the recuperative nature of their project. Readers were reminded that women had not previously been the subject of history. The titles of these new texts and articles serve as a barometer of changing emphases in women's history during this period. In the early 1970s books with titles such as *Hidden from History* (1973) intensified the sense of women's historical invisibility. These texts were a testament to what Gerda Lerner has described as historiography's 'general neglect' of women.[39] By the mid-1970s there was a shift towards viewing these absences in stronger, more empowered terms. 'Right-on' titles appeared, which, despite their bravado, continued to use the language of discovery and recovery. The renaming of history, *Herstory* fulfilled a similar purpose, at once asserting that history was a masculinist knowledge system, then reappropriating it with the insertion of a feminine pronoun.[40] While such innovations expressed a new confidence in women's history, it reinforced the sense of women's experience being outside history. The end of the decade saw another shift, dating from the publication of *Becoming Visible*, edited by Renate Bridenthal and Claudia Koonz, in 1977. The sense that women were historically invisible slowly shifted to an assertion that women had been overlooked or misplaced rather than entirely neglected. These tropes of visibility and invisibility constrained the possibilities of women's history by only asserting its recuperative possibilities. While ostensibly invoked to 'shed light' on women's historical experience, they also worked in ways that obscured women's past by attempting to insert women into essentially masculinist narratives. In so doing, 'restorative' histories of women unwittingly sustained ideas about historical writing that privileged masculinist understandings of the past.

Historians of women reacted in ways that attacked the cherished myths of nationalist historiography. This was particularly true in countries that had espoused overtly masculinist foundational myths. In North America, for instance, women's historians led the assault on the mythology of 'the Frontier'. Since the publication of Frederick Jackson Turner's essay 'The Significance of the Frontier in American History' in 1893, the idea of white men's 'conquest of the West' had shaped an increasingly masculinist vision of American historical progress. The experience of the 'Frontier' was described by Turner 'as a liberating, democratic process rather than a geographic place' and this 'process' was said to shape US values and culture.[41] Needless to say, Turner equated the characteristics of white American men with the entire American people. During the twentieth century detractors of Turner's thesis suggested that he had ignored the experience of Native Americans, African-Americans and European migrants on the Frontier. It was not until the 1960s that his failure to include women was considered. The first 'feminist' challenge to Turner's thesis was written by a male historian, David Potter, and published in 1964, a year after *The Feminine Mystique*.[42] With the impetus of women's liberation, feminist reactions to Turner's thesis became more critical of the absence of women in the history of the West.[43] Rejecting the masculinism of Turner's Frontier, numerous texts were published that 'recovered' and 'restored' women to the Frontier, insisting upon the centrality of women to the democratising and liberating processes described by Turner.[44]

Women's history written in reaction to masculinist historiography actually reinforced the supremacy of men as agents of historical change by merely inserting women into the nationalist mythology without seriously challenging it. It became increasingly obvious to those involved in women's history that simply 'adding women and stirring' was hardly adequate.[45] Women's historians recognised that it was important not only to correct omissions from the historical record and to challenge masculinist historical narratives, but that it was critical for women to recognise that 'the very procedures of history' were 'inherently problematic'.[46] The evidence used by historians, the nature of historical investigation, periodisation and even the nature of time itself came to be seen as phallocentric constructs. By deeming such structures phallocentric feminists argued that they not only privileged men, but conflated the experience of both sexes into a 'single so-called human model'.[47] Such criticism only questioned the possibility of writing women-centred history within the boundaries established by the discipline and challenged the very basis of the discipline itself. Women needed a history of their own, that drew on feminist methodologies to challenge the accuracy of previous masculinist accounts of the past.[48]

These critiques moved women's history beyond being compensatory and restorative and forced historians of women to ask whether it was possible to write effectively about women's experience within the structures laid down by 'the founding fathers of academic history'.[49] At the heart of feminist criticism of masculinist historiography was concern about its overt focus on the public sphere. While initially historians had taken a 'women and …' approach to writing women's history (e.g. 'Women and the French Revolution'), it became increasingly apparent that traditional areas of historical study such as war and politics yielded little information about women because they were largely excluded from these fields. Although many historians of women contested the idea that women had been relegated to the domestic sphere, it became imperative for them to argue that the privileging of the public sphere over the private sphere had severely impeded the historical analysis of women. Unlike men's lives, which were usually defined by their impact upon the public sphere, women's lives were 'relational', that is, they were defined primarily by their relationships with men. This meant that women tended not to appear in the public records as their lives were subsumed into that of their male kin.[50]

Because women were rendered 'historically' invisible in this way, women's historians had to develop new ways of locating the experience of women in the past. Women historians examined events and activities relating to private life, that not previously the subject of history. Much of this history stressed the separateness of the world of women from the world of men and focused on events and activities that were exclusively feminine. They reconsidered what historians considered evidence as women did not usually leave the archival records. Historians of women also questioned the privileging of discursive sources, suggesting that what was not in the historical record might be as important as what was in it.[51] Informed by feminism, women's historians questioned the masculinist assumptions of primary and secondary sources in the same way political biases were questioned.

Women's history needed to move away from a focus on male-centred events such as war and politics and to incorporate an historical analysis of the private sphere into the history of war and politics. Historians of women in the 1970s wished to fundamentally alter the way in which historians conceived these activities, to argue that the emphasis upon the public sphere had created an unconscious 'masculinism' within historical writing. Moreover, masculinist accounts of the past, that is, accounts that privileged the views of the white male elites, had become 'general' or universal history, while history that included women or other marginalised groups was seen as 'particular' history. To challenge the masculinism that shaped historical writing it was necessary to demonstrate the historical particularity and specificity of men. Historians of women argued that ideologies of masculinity, disguised as discourses of 'objectivity', 'positivism' and 'empiricism', had determined the boundaries of traditional historical scholarship. Such discourses excluded evidence of women's lives from history and perpetuated phallocentric preoccupations within historiography that inhibited the possibilities of developing a meaningful history of women. To challenge phallocentrism, women's history had to be liberated and to do this historians of women had to embrace feminist theory and methodology.

CHAPTER 9

Liberating Women's History? Feminism and the Reconstruction of History

Woman *is* and *makes* history.
Mary Ritter Beard, *Woman as Force in History*, 1946

This chapter will focus on the complex relationship between the development of feminist theory and the writing of women's history in the 1970s and 1980s. While it came to be accepted that history was a phallocentric discipline, there remained much debate about how feminism should inform women's history. As women's liberation fragmented into various schisms, different feminisms evolved, each with their own specific agenda for women's liberation, and consequently with a different vision of women's role in the past. By the end of the 1970s women's history had become a major vehicle in the struggle for feminist legitimacy, while feminist theory proved critical to historians of women deconstructing masculinist historiography.

This chapter will examine the mutually dependent relationship between feminism and women's history, particularly focusing on how historical discussion has informed feminist debate and vice versa. It will ask: What effect did debates within feminism have on the writing of women's history? What methodological problems did feminism pose to the writing of women's history? What lessons did the history of women offer feminism?

Radical Feminism and the History of Women's Oppression

Underpinning feminism's critique of history was the very real question of women's oppression and its absence from the historical record. Radical feminism as it emerged in the 1970s was ideologically committed to telling a history of women that focused primarily on women's oppression. Radical feminists insisted that women formed a sex class or sex caste, oppressed by a dominant class or caste, men. They argued that the roots of all oppression lay in the oppression of women. Borrowing from Marxist theory, radical feminists maintained that the division of labour by sex 'formed the earliest and most basic cause of oppression, from which all other forms, including racism and classism', sprang.[1]

Such ideas harkened back to the early feminist writings of Simone de Beauvoir, particularly her text *The Second Sex* (1949). Published shortly after the Second World War, *The Second Sex* had presented an incredibly pessimistic analysis of women's oppression. Rejecting Marxist and liberal theories, de Beauvoir argued that women's oppression was entirely unique, cast by her biological destiny and the shape of heterosexual relations that coupled women with their oppressors. De Beauvoir's analysis of the relationship between biology and women's destiny was complicated and ambiguous. She described heterosexual relations as a 'caste system' that rendered men and women in a constant state of war, an idea taken up by radical feminists.[2] Later writers have argued that her analysis made women's oppression seem monolithic.[3] This was not her intention, for while she did ground her analysis of women's oppression in sexuality, she argued that this was not constituted as an irreducible essence. Unlike radical feminists, she rejected the fundamental primacy of sexual difference. According to de Beauvoir, women did not need to be rescued from their biological destiny, rather liberation would come when women no longer embraced the masculinist construction of woman as 'Other'.

In spite of this proviso de Beauvoir's writings established the idea within feminism that women were the ahistorical Other. Repeatedly she referred to women having 'no past history [sic] of their own' and that 'all history has been made by men', creating an essentialist view of women's subjection that saw women excluded from history and allowed them no possibility of historical subjectivity.

De Beauvoir believed that 'anatomy was destiny', linking women's historical invisibility to their sexed body. Through such an analysis radical feminists came to link women's oppression to the female body. Borrowing heavily from de Beauvoir's analysis, radical feminists such as Shulamith Firestone and Robin Morgan produced accounts of women's subjection that conflated women's historical role with their biological destiny. Women's lack of historical subjectivity was characterised as their inability to transcend 'the patriarchy's' co-option of the female body.

Radical feminist theorists created an all-encompassing history of women that focused primarily on the commonality of women's oppression, stressing its longevity across a range of culturally similar sites. They argued that it was this 'shared history' of oppression that would allow women to overcome their differences and to unite in the struggle against patriarchy. It was in the interest of radical feminism to be reductive of diversity, suppressing differences of class, race, sexuality, politics and religion, to stress a common identity of women, formed in opposition to patriarchal oppression.[4] radical feminism presented a somewhat static and essentialist understanding of women's history that made women's oppression and men's patriarchal power seem monolithic. The historical narratives devised by radical feminists refused historicity, by insisting that 'the past must be mapped in a certain way because such a map still applies in and to the present'.[5]

Such monolithic conceptions of women's oppression caused consternation among historians of women. To assert that women's oppression was always and everywhere the same was ahistorical, as it ignored the particular historical contexts that shaped that oppression as well as issues such as class and race that mitigated any analysis of women's oppression. As Beard and later historians of women have shown, women's oppression was contingent and changed over time. Moreover, at certain times it was possible to document that women had been a force in history, challenging male domination and rejecting their inferior status. As many radical feminists contended, the focus on women in history led women's historians to an increased understanding of women's oppression and a sense that although the structures of patriarchal domination changed over time, men's patriarchal control over women remained a constant.

Following Mary Beard's analysis of first-wave feminist history, Gerda Lerner argued that the political agenda of radical feminism was based around the concept that 'all women are oppressed and have been throughout history'.[6] What Lerner and other women's historians rejected in such history was its overt political commitment to an idea of women's oppression.[7] This ideological dependence was seen to place radical feminist history at odds with the appropriate methods of historical scholarship, the rules of evidence and the discipline's discourse of objectivity. Moreover, the idea that patriarchy was omnipresent throughout history seemed to undercut the very possibility of liberation for women.

Victim History?

Radical feminism's insistent focus upon women's oppression generated a sense of 'victim' history, which complicated the relationship between feminist theorists and historians of women. While women's historians refuted the ahistoricity of radical feminist theory, they remained dependent upon it to challenge the overt masculinism of the discipline. Questions of oppression and resistance became critical within historiography more generally. Women's history drew upon insights from other sub-disciplines such as social history, labour history and black history to develop a better understanding of the history of women's subjection and their resistance to the patriarchy.

Since the 1950s angry young men had challenged the discipline's focus on the victors of history and had shifted the focus of social history on to the most marginalised of society. Seeking to read history 'from below', this new history looked to the 'victims' of history. It would be wrong to suggest that its focus was victimisation, rather questions of culture, agency and resistance were essential to its formation. Whereas traditional Marxist historical analysis offered little consideration of the role of the lumpenproletariat in the processes of social transformation, historians of the New Left looked to 'give history a human face'.[8] This shaped the writing of the history of oppression into a history of survival. Social history as it emerged in the post-war period focused upon people's collective control over their experience, with class-consciousness and working-class culture being the ultimate expressions of human agency.[9] Central to this new understanding of history was the sense that oppressed groups 'made' themselves, that they evolved out of their own distinctive culture. As E. P. Thompson wrote, explaining his 'clumsy' title *The Making of the English Working Class*: '*Making*, because it a study of an active process, which owes as much to agency as to conditioning. The working class did not rise like the sun at an appointed time. It was present at its own making.'[10]

Thompson's idea that class formation was predominantly a cultural experience revolutionised British labour history and challenged all accounts of the relationships between oppressed peoples and their oppressors. By arguing that the working class was not simply the by-product of the rise of industrial capitalism, Thompson was breaking with traditional Marxism and suggesting that cultural effects were critical to the development of class-consciousness.[11] In arguing that the working class made itself, Thompson was suggesting that through their own agency the proletariat converted 'a collective experience into a social consciousness which thereby defined and created class itself'.[12] The elements that made up this cultural experience – 'traditions, value-systems, ideas and institutional forms' – became critical to an historical understanding of class and class-consciousness.

Converging with this new history was a language of protest and political authority derived from contemporary social movements of the period, such as black power and anti-imperialist movements, which placed much emphasis on the importance of culture to the development of political identity and consciousness. The black consciousness movement, particularly, stressed the need for an historical awareness of black culture to develop a strong sense of black identity. The convergence of black nationalist sentiment with an analysis of culture and its relationship to class-consciousness and resistance transformed African-American historiography in the late 1960s.[13] Black historians argued that a separate black consciousness and culture, derived from Africa, had always existed in the United States.[14] African-Americans emerged in this new history 'as a people who, far from being lastingly damaged and crippled [by slavery] resisted brutalisation and constructed a rich and vital culture'.[15]

Replicating the macho posturing of New Left politics, historians following Thompson focused their history upon heroic masculine action.[16] The emasculating qualities of victimhood found no place in this discourse. Questions of alienation, hopelessness, alcoholism, interpersonal violence, social fragmentation and other aspects of culture that did not demonstrate a vibrant opposition to the ruling classes were rarely considered. It was taken for granted that a sense of heroic manliness was imperative to the construction of political identity within this context. While women were often missing from such histories, women's historians began to think about issues such as culture, agency and resistance and to develop a cultural approach to the history of women.

The Culture of True Womanhood

The idea that women as a social group formed their own separate culture in the past became an influential theme within women's history by the mid-1970s. Combining elements of radical feminism with Thompson's theories of working-class cultural formation enabled historians of women to create a cultural history of women that accounted for the formation of feminist consciousness in the past. The telling of stories and celebration of women's culture was a definitive feature of second-wave feminism. Feminist practices such as consciousness raising (CR) allowed women to understand the importance of their own stories and to recognise how little they knew of other women's lives. It alerted women to the power of networking. The formation of supportive female networks through CR was not only essential to the success of women's liberation, it challenged prevalent masculinist assumptions that women could not form social organisations.[17] It was only a matter of time before the everyday life of women in the past was scrutinised to cast light on women's experience in the present. Women's liberation encouraged women to bond, to forge identities on their own and to create a woman-centred culture separate from men. The experience of women's bonding in the past became an important ideological tool that reinforced the evolution of a separatist women's culture in the present.

The cultural history of women that evolved out of radical feminism allowed for distinctly feminist readings of women's history. By focusing on areas traditionally eschewed by historians, the domestic sphere and women's private experience of marriage, religion, romantic friendships and family life, historians of women could delineate the distinctive nature of women's rituals, values and beliefs. This was not to subsume women into a straitjacket of domesticity, but rather to insist that the domestic realm and other women's spaces were just as important historically as the public realms of men. This historical interest in women's culture involved a certain rehabilitation of the historical conception of the 'private sphere'.[18] Since Thucydides, male historians had tried to replicate the domestic seclusion of women in their historical writing, not merely excluding women from historical narratives so much as excising the feminine from the study of the past. In so doing they effectively rendered all things associated with women, but especially the domestic sphere, as unsuitable for historical analysis. While the new social history had done much to challenge history's emphasis on the public sphere, the domestic sphere as the proper sphere of women retained a sense of ahistoricity.

With the rise of women's liberation, historians of women made the metaphor of separate spheres central to an understanding of women's experience in the past.[19] Historical works such as Barbara Welter's ground-breaking essay 'The Cult of True Womanhood' and Aileen S. Kraditor's collection, *Up from the Pedestal*, stressed the importance of creating an historical understanding of the domestic sphere, linking women's seclusion in this sphere with their continued oppression.[20] Framed within the shadow of the

Feminine Mystique, these texts did not allow for the possibility that women's domestic life could be anything but restrictive and shallow. The experience of radical feminism transformed the historical understandings of women's lives in the past. Radical feminism encouraged women to celebrate their difference from men and to focus on the unique aspects of their culture, making possible new readings of the domestic sphere.

The study of women's culture did not simply appear in the 1970s. Since the 1920s historians such as Eileen Power, Lucy Maynard Salmon and Mary Beard had described the importance of women's cultural experience in their work. These women argued that it was important to recognise that although women's cultural experience was different from men's, it was no less worthy of historical consideration. Beard particularly maintained that until the separate 'woman's world' was analysed by historians, history would necessarily be partial.[21] In the 1970s the study of women's culture evolved naturally out of the histories of 'women's contribution' inspired by women's liberation.[22] Whereas contribution histories examined women's participation in the public world of politics and work, the new history of women's culture viewed women's experience as largely separate and different from men's. This was done to more fully understand the experience of women in the past, in women's own terms. Much of women's experience had been missed by historians because they framed questions in terms more appropriate to the experience of men. As Gerda Lerner cautioned in 1979, '[T]o rectify this, and to light up areas of historical darkness we must, for a time, focus on a *woman-centred* inquiry, concerning the possibility of the existence of a female culture *within* the general culture shared by men and women.'[23]

Drawing on insights made possible by radical feminism, historians of women, particularly those who focused on philanthropic work, education or moral campaigning, showed that women in the past had formed extensive networks bound by female friendship, but were also committed to political action in opposition to men. This networking demonstrated that the domestic sphere was not necessarily an oppressive institution, rather it formed 'the basis for a subculture among women that formed a source of strength and identity and afforded supportive sisterly relations.'[24] This allowed for the idea that 'gender oppression, the experience of sisterhood and a feminist consciousness' had a 'natural and evolving relationship'.[25] Such ideas were reinforced by theories emerging from feminist sociology and anthropology. The work of anthropologists such as Michelle Zimbalist Rosaldo and Sherry Ortner was tremendously important in forming discussion about the possibilities of exploring women's culture.[26] As Rosaldo argued, it was only through the examination of informal female networks that we might glimpse the 'important structural factors which … give rise to female power'.[27] Reacting against prevalent masculinist assumptions regarding women and social organisation, sociologists such as Jo Freeman argued that women's networks were critical to the emergence of the women's movement.[28] Encouraged by the supportive female networks of women's liberation, women's historians speculated that such networks were responsible for the development of feminist consciousness, a 'sisterhood' in the past.

It was the publication of Carroll Smith-Rosenberg's article 'The Female World of Love and Ritual' in 1975 that first generated this paradigm shift in women's history. Instead of viewing women's exclusion from the public realm as necessarily oppressive, Smith-Rosenberg 'offered a striking re-interpretation of the possibilities of separation'.[29] Her article was framed around the analysis of the correspondence and diaries of American women between 1760 and 1880. Smith-Rosenberg aimed to examine what she called 'the elusive question of female friendship'.[30] Responding to women's liberation's desire to demonstrate evidence of a women-centred culture in the past, Smith-Rosenberg argued that we know so little 'or perhaps have forgotten so much' about the world of female relationships, not because they did not exist but because historians have not chosen to examine them.[31] Smith-Rosenberg used the private documents of 'ordinary' women to set out the elaborate and rich network of female friendship, culture and rituals that existed among this group. She contended that the analysis of these letters and diaries permitted 'the historian to explore the very private world of emotional realities central to women's lives and to the middle-class family in nineteenth century America'.[32] In this private world men were either absent, rarely present or entirely superfluous.

Central to Smith-Rosenberg's analysis was a rejection of the idea that the private sphere was the nexus of women's oppression. Instead she argued that the distinctive feminine culture of the domestic realm benefited women in a number of ways. Most significantly she suggested that world of love and ritual elaborated in these private papers provided women with a secure and empathetic environment and created a milieu in which they could develop an inner security and self-esteem. Implied but not stated in this article is the sense that it was just this distinctive women's culture that allowed for the development of feminist consciousness. While Smith-Rosenberg insisted that the article was not about women's culture but women's sexuality, she nonetheless asserted in later debate that '[W]e cannot understand the public acts of a few women without understanding the private world that produced them. Women's interaction with each other formed an intrinsic component of feminism.'[33] Smith-Rosenberg posited a complex connection between women's experience of their separateness from men and feminism. While she insisted that certain aspects of the interaction between women in the nineteenth century did encourage conformity and resistance to change, she maintained that it was impossible to understand the development of feminism outside this female world.[34]

Many historians of women came to use E. P. Thompson's framework to analyse the development of a specifically feminine culture, connecting this culture with the rise of feminist consciousness. Nancy F. Cott, Mary P. Ryan, Blanche Wiesen Cook, Estelle Freedman, Katherine Kish Sklar and Nancy Sahli argued in their work that the 'cult[ure] of true womanhood' framing women's experience in the past had created a sense of 'gender identification' similar to class-consciousness.[35] This gender identification or 'sisterhood' derived from a sense that women had their own traditions, value systems, ideas and institutional forms. It led eventually to women forming a 'vibrant opposition' to male traditions, value systems, ideas and institutional forms.[36]

The Class Challenge

Historians of women made explicit what was implicit in the work of Thompson and his followers: that there existed in the past distinctly different cultures for men and women. While Thompson claimed to write about the working class, what he wrote about was its masculinist culture.[37] While feminist historians criticised Thompson for such gender-blindness, the focus on women's culture within women's history was critiqued for its absence of class analysis. Following the publication of 'The Female World of Love and Ritual', the 'true woman/separate spheres/woman's culture triad became the most widely used framework for interpreting the experience of American women in the past'.[38] While Smith-Rosenberg regarded her work as speculative and 'carefully noted the parameters of time, region and class', those historians who followed her were less inclined to such specificity.[39] A pattern emerged in American women's history that saw historians trace 'the bonds of womanhood' beyond the domestic enclaves of the Victorian bourgeoisie and into the realms of the working classes. This model of sisterhood was used not only to explain the rise of a feminist consciousness amongst the women of the bourgeoisie, but came to explain all expressions of feminist consciousness during the period.

The idea that the private sphere nurtured a sense of sisterhood that ultimately evolved into first-wave feminism became a major theme of women's history in the late 1970s. This was particularly true of American women's history, although in other countries the emphasis on women's culture was less pronounced. In part this was due to distinctly different national historiographical traditions. In Britain, for instance, the emphasis on class within women's history meant that 'the notion of universal sisterhood' was only rarely broached.[40] Moreover, many historians of women in Britain offered an alternate and somewhat oppositional reading of the private sphere, that saw it operate 'as a pressure cooker generating pent-up frustration which eventually exploded as mass feminist politics'.[41] This difference of emphasis between British and American women's history was in keeping with differences between British and American feminism.

The British movement never immersed itself in practices such as consciousness raising and thus never developed the exclusively feminist networks that characterised the American scene. Ideas of sisterhood and women's culture were less emphatic within British feminism. In France, too, women's historians were highly sceptical of the efficacy of using the idea of a separatist women's culture to explore women's history. Fear of essentialising women's historical role informed their concern. As Michelle Perrot cautioned: '[W]e must also beware of describing a feminine culture that would be no more than the rigid designation of a complementary space and, in the end, another formulation of immutable nature.'[42]

Eventually the emphasis on women's culture within American women's history became the focus of intense debate there, too. Historians critical of women's cultural history argued that such an approach denied the possibility of feminist interpretations of the past. These critics wanted a return to viewing the private sphere as the nexus of women's oppression, arguing that it was the private/public dichotomy that structured women's historical activity and shaped their oppression. More significantly, they asserted that the emphasis on women's private realm meant that historians never really looked beyond the domestic sphere. There was no possibility of analysing how women's culture arose in history and how it has been transformed. Emphasis on women's culture was seen to obscure the very real conflict between men and women, making women's oppression seem less relevant. It did not allow for an analysis of the ways in which women-centred culture might constrain women, or create values antithetical to feminism.

In 1980 *Feminist Studies* published a 'Symposium on Politics and Culture in Women's History', featuring leading historians of women: Ellen DuBois, Temma Kaplan, Gerda Lerner and Carroll Smith-Rosenberg.[43] The forum was sparked by DuBois, who expressed concerns that the current historical interest in women's culture precluded an analysis of the political history of feminism. She argued that the focus on women's culture denied the possibility of feminist interpretations of the past, romanticising and isolating female friendship. She maintained that it forestalled inquiry into the system that structured women's historical activity and shaped their oppression.[44] Her position was that the emphasis on women's culture was dialectically opposed to feminism and feminist history. In her opinion feminist history should focus on a broader, more comprehensive analytical history of women's oppression, reaching beyond questions of political and economic inequality to the total social relations of the sexes. DuBois maintained that women's historians needed to ask how the masses of women experienced their lives, what grievances they had, what traditions of protest and resistance they left behind. She believed the answers to such questions not only enriched women's history, but would enhance the relevance of feminism to it. Such a critique reflected the growing divergence within feminism itself, as socialist and Marxist feminists criticised radical feminism's lack of interest in class politics.

The basis of her criticism was a sense that women's culture could not be understood separately from the men's culture. This lack of integration meant that conflict between women's culture and men's culture was underplayed in such historical analysis and as a consequence women's oppression had little relevance.[45] The focus on separate spheres did not allow for an analysis of the ways in which women-centred culture might constrain women, or create values antithetical to feminism. DuBois claimed that the emphasis on women's culture in women's history was a reaction against the stereotype of the nineteenth-century woman as passive, dependent, content and dedicated to home and family. She likened this reaction to black historiography as it had emerged in the late 1960s, which challenged similar images of the slave. While she agreed that the investigation of women's culture provided new ways of seeing women, as 'creating themselves, not just being created', she maintained that women's culture itself 'did not constitute an open and radical break with the dominant sexual ideology any more than slave culture openly challenged slavery'.[46]

Smith-Rosenberg took issue with many of the points DuBois had raised in relation to the history of women and women's culture, particularly her insistence that women's culture was extrinsic to feminism. Smith-Rosenberg insisted that it was impossible to understand the public acts of a few women without analysing the culture that produced them. While she acknowledged that certain aspects of the interaction between women in the nineteenth century did encourage conformity and resistance to change, she suggested that first-wave feminism was intricately bound by women's experience of their separateness from men and their primary identification with women. Only by studying women's interactions with each other, she maintained, would it be possible to untangle the intricate relationship between the female world and the economic and institutional power structures of the 'external [male]world'.[47]

At the core of this debate were conflicting ideas about the importance of class to an analysis of women's history. The use of culture as a category of analysis within labour history had been necessarily bound by class. Within women's history, gender rather than class emerged as the factor, which shaped solidarity and consciousness. But as DuBois and others pointed out, differences between women created by class and race potentially fractured any sense of gender solidarity. Moreover, it was possible to argue that those aspects of women's culture which allowed middle-class women a sense of gender solidarity constrained and confined working-class women. Other historians came to question the validity of the very notion of separate spheres. As Nancy Hewitt has argued, it was quite possible that neither the working class nor the bourgeoisie actually patterned their lives according to such prescriptions.[48] While in certain instances it was possible to evidence the solidarity of bourgeois women at odds with bourgeois men, there was much evidence of bourgeois women and men functioning in solidarity when their own class interests were threatened.

Critics of women's cultural history were most concerned about was the ways in which women's culture had been conflated with women's politics. DuBois and others argued that the emphasis on women's culture had meant that women's history largely avoided the question of women's resistance to male power. While she grudgingly acknowledged that this rich female subculture might suggest 'a largely inchoate feminist consciousness among nineteenth-century women', she believed that it was necessary to move beyond this, to study women's overt resistance to male authority. Later historians argued that the focus on sisterhood within American women's history had seriously distorted an historical understanding of working-class women and women of colour. By making the experience of bourgeois women hegemonic, historians of women often ignored the evidence of solidarity that melded men and women together in defense of class or racial interests. For working-class women and women of colour, the idea that the separation of the spheres formed an ideological barrier between men's and women's worlds greatly obscured the political realities of their lives.

Women's Culture and Cultural Feminism

In a sense DuBois was articulating in historical terms a debate that had developed within women's liberation between radical feminists, who wished to maintain an active political critique of male power, and cultural feminists, who sought to escape male power by creating separatist women's communities. By the mid-1970s radical feminism was floundering as divisions of class, race and sexual preference split the movement. These tensions were exacerbated by an atmosphere of increasing conservatism generated by the economic recession and the collapse of other radical movements. Much of the optimism generated by feminist initiatives for dealing with male dominance was wearing thin. Many women were disgruntled by the failure of the feminist movement to revolutionise relations between the sexes. Until this point radical feminists had been deeply committed to challenging the cultural meanings attached to male and female sexuality, seeking the liberation of women and men from the damaging effects of sexual stereotyping. Embattled by many hard-fought struggles, certain women felt that the confrontational style of radical feminism had not sufficiently challenged the entrenched sexual dominance of men. Rather than seeking liberation for both women and men, certain feminists came to argue that what was needed was liberation from men.

At the root of these tensions within the women's movement was the implosion of the sexual revolution. The rise of women's liberation had been concomitant with the sexual revolution. The advent of the pill in the early 1960s forever changed heterosexual relations and a new era of sexual permissiveness was born. Underpinned by libertarian notions of the naturally disruptive effects of the sexualisation of culture and enhanced by the new drug subcultures, the sexual revolution began a transformation of all aspects of sexuality, bringing the rise of gay liberation, the end of censorship and dramatic changes in public and private morality. Many believed that the women's liberation movement completed this transformation of (hetero)sexual relations. A desire to change the nature of sexual relations was the driving force behind radical feminism. Feminists such as Kate Millet, Shulamith Firestone, Anne Koedt and Germaine Greer had characterised feminism as the final step towards men and women gaining freedom of sexual expression. With radical feminism, they argued, came the end of phallocentric sexual relations. Radical feminists argued that women's sexuality had been mutilated by years of patriarchy and urged women to embrace their sexuality as a means of ensuring liberation.

Underscoring their optimism was a damning criticism of the failure of the sexual revolution to liberate women. Without feminism the sexual revolution had merely liberated men by reinforcing the primacy of phallocentric heterosexual relations. By the mid-1970s two distinct critiques of the relationship between feminism and the sexual revolution had developed. Certain feminists argued that even with feminism the sexual revolution had only liberated men. Many of these feminists developed a position on sex that was not merely critical of the phallocentric nature of sexuality, but of all forms of heterosexuality. They argued that heterosexual sex was paradigmatic of women's oppression, while simultaneously representing the most potent threat to women's liberation. Other feminists insisted that the emphasis on sexual liberation had skewed an understanding of the true sources of women's oppression. They saw the inequality women experienced within sexual relations as reflective of the more general oppression and degradation women suffered. Freedom from sexual oppression, they believed, was one minor aspect of women's liberation.

Both these critiques saw a diminishing emphasis on the liberating effects of sexuality within feminist theory that reflected the evolution of radical feminism into cultural feminism.[49] Cultural feminism deviated from radical feminism in certain crucial areas. Cultural feminism demanded the creation of a female counterculture, where 'male' values were exorcised and 'female' values nurtured. Whereas radical feminism had been the battle front of sexual politics, many women turned to cultural feminism in retreat from sexual politics. Underpinning the idea of a 'female counterculture' were essentialist notions of gender difference. Whereas radical feminists had tried to de-emphasise gender difference, cultural feminists embraced a theory of gender difference rooted in biology. A belief in women's unique biological difference from men framed their discussions.[50]

The issue of separatism was critical to the development of cultural feminism. Separatism had at first been envisaged by radical feminists as a temporary strategy, a means to separate feminist politics from the politics of other radical movements. As the personal became the political radical feminists argued that separatism could function as a political strategy within personal life. Initially this separation from men was viewed as 'a leave of absence' for women to revitalise their commitment to other women. Far from threatening the institution of heterosexuality, radical feminists believed that separatism would improve women's coexistence with men in the future. Such idealism was short-lived. By the mid-1970s feminist separatism had come to mean complete separation from the world of men. In part this reflected the impact of lesbian feminism within the movement, but the impulse towards separatism was not entirely framed by the issue of sexual preference. While cultural feminists characterised their position as a retreat from the sexual politics of radical feminism, they simultaneously created a new form of sexual politics. Although separatism assumed a women-loving-women community, this was not characterised as a sexual choice framed by desire, but rather a political choice framed by the rejection of a male cultural system. Cultural feminism's essentialist notions of sexual difference de-eroticised their discussion of women's sexuality. Love between women rather than sexual desire was the basis of cultural feminism's sexual revolution. Most forms of sexuality were seen as being essentially masculinist and phallocentric, and even lesbianism came to be regarded as a patriarchal construct.

Cultural feminists sought to re-create the de-eroticised world of female 'love and ritual' celebrated by historians who followed Smith-Rosenberg. In her essay Smith-Rosenberg had suggested that in the past relationships between women tended to be more intense and emotionally charged. She termed these relationships 'romantic friendships' and maintained that they were often deeply passionate. Such relationships were socially acceptable and compatible with heterosexual marriage. She argued that it was only with the advent of sexology that these relationships were pathologised. Historians following Smith-Rosenberg have argued that 'romantic friendships' provided nurturing support systems that allowed women to develop feminist consciousness and political networks bound by these friendships.[51]

More significantly, certain historians came to argue that such friendships allowed women to create a 'separate female sphere'.[52] While historians following DuBois had been quite critical of the separate-sphere model generated within women's cultural history, the ascendancy of cultural feminism gave a new legitimacy to the notion of separatism. Drawing on feminist anthropology and sociology, historians such as Estelle Freedman argued that during certain historical periods 'the creation of a female public sphere [was] the only viable political strategy for women'.[53] This historical discussion of separatism was deeply informed by cultural feminism's impulse towards separatism. Blanche Wiesen Cook and Estelle Freedman saw in their historical analysis of separatist strategies among first-wave feminists distinct lessons for second-wave feminists. As Cook wrote:

> [T]he power of communities of independent women, and of the love between individual women, expressed not only sensually but in a range of ways, is part of the history that has been taken from us by heterosexist culture. To recognise this history is to recognise our personal forces of energy and courage and the power to change.[54]

Such analysis showed that separate female communities could generate and sustain women's participation in social reform and political activism. But the true lesson the past offered to feminists of the present was about the decline of first-wave feminism. Cultural historians of women argued that the gradual decline of female separatism in social and political life precluded the emergence of a strong feminist political movement following the granting of suffrage. Attempts by 'new women' to assimilate into male-dominated institutions saw the erosion of women's culture and the subsequent decline in public feminism.[55]

Cultural feminism only represented one response to the implosion of the sexual revolution. Other feminists upheld their newly found sexual freedom, rejecting the separatist politics of cultural feminism and embracing a more libertarian stance. These 'pro-sex' feminists defended vigorously the potential of freedom of sexual expression offered by radical feminism. Although the sexual politics of radical feminism is now often confused with cultural feminism, radical feminism insisted upon women's sexual autonomy, maintaining that women's freedom of sexual expression was a 'fundamental project' of feminism.[56]

By the late 1970s cultural feminist critique of the sexual revolution had developed into a full-scale attack on pornography and other sexual practices bound by an erotics of dominance and submission, such as sadomasochism and butch/femme role-playing. Although pornography had long been a concern of radical feminism, it was never considered the linchpin of women's oppression.[57] Cultural feminism characterised pornography as the propaganda of male dominance. Such an analysis was derived from the essentialist notions that framed cultural feminism's understanding of sexual difference. Female sexuality was characterised as mute, intimate and reciprocal, while male sexuality was seen as lustful, aggressive and potentially lethal. Cultural feminism assumed that for men sexuality and violence were inextricably linked and that the cultural expression of this connection was pornography.[58] Underpinning this attack on pornography was cultural feminism's deep-seated suspicion that heterosexuality itself forever bound women into an erotics of dominance and submission.

This attack on heterosexuality necessarily created schisms within the women's movement. The impact of the social purity movement upon first-wave feminism provided a critical axis for the development of debates within feminism and women's history. Just as cultural feminists looked to the experience of first-wave feminists to justify and legitimate their position on separatism, pro-sex feminists looked to the past to defend their position on sexual liberation. Cultural and pro-sex feminists tried to explain their position in relation to what they saw as the failure of first-wave feminists to truly liberate women. For cultural feminists this failure arose because the gradual decline of female separatism in social and political life impeded the emergence of a strong feminist political movement during the inter-war period. Pro-sex feminists blamed the decline in feminist militancy to more disparate causes, although the central focus of their critique was the failure of first-wave feminism to embrace sexual radicalism.

Debates about sexuality within feminism necessarily had an enormous impact on the ways in which lesbianism and other forms of alternate sexuality were dealt with in women's history. The sexual experience of women in the past became a critical focal point for late twentieth-century feminists engaged in struggles over separatism, role-playing and identity.

CHAPTER 10

Surpassing the History of Men: Women's History and Lesbian History

> All women's lives are precious, but histories are complicated things. While all lesbian history is women's history, not all women's history is lesbian history. These identities may be intertwined at times, but they are separate, distinct legacies and at other times they may be in conflict.
>
> Joan Nestle, *A Restricted Country*, 1986

Lesbian history has not evolved simply as a sub-genre of women's history, but out of a series of debates within feminism, women's history, the history of sexuality, and within the gay and lesbian community. This chapter will examine the development of lesbian history primarily in relation to feminism and women's historiography. The debates around lesbianism within women's liberation have generated considerable controversy, which was in turn reflected in the historical writings on the subject. The sexual experience of women in the past became a critical discussion point for late twentieth-century feminists engaged in debates about sexuality.

This chapter will explore how these 'sex wars' impacted upon the writing of women's history. It will ask: What was the relationship between feminist debates in the present and the analysis of women's sexuality in the past? What effect did feminism's 'sex wars' have on the conception of lesbianism and on lesbian history? Is it possible to separate lesbian history from women's history?

Sex Wars

On 1 May 1970 some forty women calling themselves the 'Lavender Menace' pre-empted the opening of the second Congress to Unite

Women in New York City, protesting against the heterosexism and homophobia of the women's liberation movement. Taking the stage for over two hours, the protesters spoke of their experiences as lesbians within a heterosexist culture, attempting to raise the movement's consciousness.[1] The protest had been aimed primarily at liberal feminists, particularly the hierarchy of NOW. The term 'Lavender Menace' had been used by Betty Friedan, founder of NOW, who strenuously opposed the presence of lesbians in that organisation.[2] Reacting to the homophobia of the mainstream press, the NOW hierarchy distanced itself from any association with lesbianism. The Daughters of Bilitis, the United States' most prominent lesbian lobby group, had not been mentioned on a NOW press release listing institutional sponsors at the first Congress to Unite Women in 1969. Shortly after this Rita Mae Brown was relieved of her duties as the editor of NOW's New York newsletter. Brown, who became the most famous lesbian of the 1970s, was so angered by her treatment she published a statement detailing the homophobia in the organisation and accusing the leadership of consciously oppressing women on the question of sexual preference.

Although the protest may have begun as a response to the institutionalised homophobia of liberal feminism, it was also a reaction against the intrinsic heterosexism of radical feminism. Until this time, most radical feminists had developed feminist theory around the reform of heterosexual relations. The demands made by the protesters were published as a 'radicalesbian' manifesto entitled 'Woman-Identified-Woman' in *Notes from the Third Year* (1971). Its publication signalled the emergence of a political lesbianism distinct from gay liberation and mainstream feminism, which was condemned as counter-revolutionary. Up until this point most radical feminist theory had called upon women to renegotiate and transform (hetero)sexual relations: 'Woman-Identified Women' sought to revolutionise sexual relations by rejecting heterosexuality entirely. The manifesto created debate within radical feminism on separatism that persisted throughout the decade. While certain radical feminists had tentatively raised the issue of separatism as a 'temporary solution' for women, lesbian feminists asserted that separatism was an imperative political strategy to end male domination. As Jill Johnston, author of the radical text *Lesbian Nation* argued, lesbianism transcended the problem of male dominance by its refusal to engage in the (hetero)sexual institutions that formed women's oppression.[3] Moreover, lesbianism came to symbolise a powerful affirmation of sisterhood and a rejection of patriarchy. As Rita Mae Brown complained, to give a man support and love before giving it to a sister was to uphold a power system that was violently anti-woman.[4]

Such 'lesbian chauvinism'[5] appealed to many women who had already adopted radical feminism. Although at odds with gay liberation for its essentially phallocentric interests, lesbian feminists adopted 'the angry aggressive positioning of the Gay Liberation Front' in their stance against heterosexism within the women's movement.[6] Lesbian feminism did much to explode definitions of lesbianism that had preceded it by 'making it almost a categorical imperative for all women truly interested in the welfare and progress of other women'.[7] Political lesbianism saw radical feminism redefine its critique of men's patriarchal power over women, to focus particularly upon the question of heterosexual sex. Heterosexual sex came to be seen as paradigmatic of women's oppression, while simultaneously representing the most potent threat to women's liberation. Like cultural feminists, political lesbians maintained that women who had sexual relations with men were 'sleeping with the enemy' and were to be despised as collaborators.[8] Whereas radical feminism had focused on protecting women from the worst excesses of phallocentric sex, particularly rape and spousal abuse, political lesbianism called upon women to abandon the institution of heterosexuality altogether and forever eschew the company of men.

Political lesbianism clearly underpinned radical feminism's shift towards cultural feminism. However, with cultural feminism came another dimension to the discussion of separatism. For political lesbians separatism meant not only separation from the world of men, but also separation from heterosexual women. Within the context of cultural feminism both separatism and lesbianism took on new meanings. Cultural feminists embraced an ideal of separation from the world of men, but they did not wholeheartedly endorse political lesbianism as the obvious solution. Instead they attempted to create a new form of sexual politics that assumed a women-loving-women community. This was a political choice rather than a sexual preference. Cultural feminists de-eroticised lesbianism by arguing that lesbianism as a sexual preference was the product of patriarchy.

Women's History and the Lesbian Continuum

In this way cultural feminists marginalised lesbian sexuality, while simultaneously assuming that all women were part of a 'lesbian continuum'.[9] The concept of a lesbian continuum was first articulated by the poet Adrienne Rich, although she drew upon ideas that had emerged from historical discussions of women's separatist culture. Using Carroll Smith-Rosenberg's work as an historical basis as well as numerous literary examples, Rich developed an idea of lesbianism that moved beyond its definition as a sexual practice and suggested that the term be used to embrace all forms of female friendship. Like Smith-Rosenberg, Rich suggested that it was necessary to view women's sexuality in non-dichotomous ways, as neither heterosexuality or homosexuality were adequate categories to explain most women's sexual lives. The 'lesbian continuum' she proposed was defined by 'woman identified experience' that embraced all 'forms of primary intensity between and among women' and was characterised in opposition to the divisions between women generated by 'compulsory heterosexuality'.[10] This broadening of the concept of lesbianism was done to challenge what Rich saw as the patriarchal definitions of lesbianism, which focused only upon the sexual. Rich was concerned to create the possibility of a female erotic free of phallocentricity. The idea of a lesbian continuum was in keeping with the writings of other cultural feminists such as Mary Daly, who sought to de-eroticise the nature of relationships between women.[11]

Cultural feminism's de-eroticisation of lesbianism proved highly divisive. While lesbian feminists welcomed women who rejected the institution of heterosexuality, they were nonetheless suspicious of any feminist position that marginalised lesbian sexuality. Cultural feminism's insistence upon the idea of a 'lesbian continuum' created division because it denied the specificity and difference of lesbian experience.[12] It was sexual preference that defined lesbianism within patriarchal discourses and it was this choice that formed their oppression. The rhetoric of a lesbian continuum obscured lesbian experience, 'by blurring the distinctions between lesbian relationships and non-lesbian female friendships' and 'lesbian identity and female-centred identity', effectively eliminating lesbianism as a meaningful category.[13]

The separatism envisaged by cultural feminists included 'removing all vestiges of male-identified behaviour from the lesbian psyche'.[14] This further placed cultural feminists at odds with political lesbians, who were seeking to devise non-heterosexist and non-patriarchal modes of sexuality, such as non-monogamous sex or non-penetrative sex, that expressed 'collectiveness and connectedness' with other women.[15] Most at issue was butch/femme role-playing, which cultural feminists regarded as a form of false consciousness and as a demeaning imitation of heterosexuality. The question of butch/femme role-playing remained a contentious issue within lesbian feminism and shaped the debate around identity, resistance, agency and sexual practice within lesbian history for the next decade.

The Elusive Question of Female Friendship

Ironically the first moves towards the writing of lesbian history did not emerge from shifting historical perspectives on homosexuality, but rather from the reconceptualisation of heterosexuality first posed by Carroll Smith-Rosenberg. As has been shown, her essay 'The Female World of Love and Ritual' created considerable discussion around the question of a separatist women's culture in the nineteenth century and generated much controversy within the field of women's history. Smith-Rosenberg, however, saw her research as raising questions about the nature of women's sexuality in the past, particularly trying to understand the emotionally intense and erotically charged women's 'friendships' she had uncovered and society's benign approval of such relationships. As she demonstrated, these 'romantic friendships' were often the most long-lived and emotionally rewarding relationships women experienced, in spite of marriage and child-rearing. This observation raised various questions about the fluidity of female (and male) sexuality in the nineteenth century, suggesting that women may have been freer to indulge in a spectrum of love choices in the past. Smith-Rosenberg argued that it was necessary for historians to move beyond the dichotomised understandings of sexuality that had emerged in the twentieth century in the wake of Sigmund Freud. This universe of 'deviance and normality, genitality and Platonic love', she maintained, was alien to the emotions and attitudes of nineteenth-century women.[16] She suggested that historians needed to devise new ways of interpreting these 'romantic friendships' to avoid the hetero/homosexual dichotomy and allow greater understanding of the fluidity of sexuality in the past.

Although often attributed to Carroll Smith-Rosenberg, the idea of 'romantic friendship' was first put forward by Elizabeth Mavor in 1973, in her book *The Ladies of Llangollen*. Like much recuperative history written in the early 1970s, *The Ladies of Llangollen* recounted the story of two aristocratic Irishwomen, Lady Eleanor Butler and Sarah Ponsonby, whose extraordinary lives had previously been lost to history. What made the lives of Butler and Ponsonby extraordinary was the fact that they had eloped from their families and established a household together in the tiny Welsh village of Llangollen, where they spent the rest of their lives together. The women's elopement had created a minor *cause célèbre* in 1788. Speculation about the nature of their relationship began around the period of their elopement and has continued into the present day. Both women held that they deeply loved each other and regarded their bond as sacred as any marriage. Mavor, too, considered that the 'ladies' were 'married'; however, she made no mention of sexual compatibility, a defining feature of modern marriages. Instead she asserted that their friendship was 'so subtle and rare' as to make 'the obvious Freudian interpretation' seem 'a bluntish instrument'.[17] Mavor never considered the possibility that the ladies were lesbians and was at pains to point out that their relationship was 'homoerotic' rather than homosexual, a 'romantic friendship' rather than a sexual relationship. 'Romantic friendships', she suggested, were a particularly womanly institution, 'better suited to the diffuse feminine nature'.[18]

Mavor's analysis of romantic friendships was curiously bound by early twentieth-century sexology. While she does not deny that these women experienced 'passion' she doubted that it was 'biologically defined'.[19] The idea that women in the past experienced a paradise of 'romantic friendship' before the rise of sexology became a defining feature of much early lesbian history. As historians uncovered more examples of such 'rare' friendships in the past, the idea of the lesbian continuum was used to interpret these relationships. Historians interested in the elusive world of female friendship in the past combined the culturally separate world of women described by Smith-Rosenberg with Rich's notion of 'woman-identified experience', to popularise the idea that love between women was not only extremely common before the twentieth century, but that such relationships were widely accepted within society.

Such an analysis led historians to argue that far from being confined to a deviant and marginalised minority, loving relationships between women in the past were the norm. This was the premise of the first historical survey of same-sex relations between women since the Renaissance, *Surpassing the Love of Men*, produced by Lillian Faderman in 1981. Faderman suggested in the introduction to that text: 'it was virtually impossible to study the correspondence of any nineteenth-century woman, not only of America but also of England, France and Germany, and not uncover a passionate commitment to another woman at some time in her life'.[20] Faderman's history of same-sex relationships between women grew out of a study of the life of Emily Dickinson and her sister-in-law Sue Gilbert. In her research on Dickinson Faderman discovered evidence to suggest that it was Sue Gilbert who was the love of Dickinson's life, not any of the men with whom she had been romantically linked by twentieth-century biographers. What most interested Faderman in the Dickinson–Gilbert relationship was the fact that neither woman felt any compunction to hide her feelings, nor did they evidence any feelings of guilt or anxiety about their love. Encouraged by Smith-Rosenberg's analysis, Faderman looked for further evidence of romantic friendships between women. Not only did she discover a mass of evidence of such relationships in the correspondence of women since the Renaissance, but also 'innumerable fictional examples'.[21]

Unlike Carroll Smith-Rosenberg, who argued that the existence of such relationships in the past should not be viewed in dichotomous terms as either heterosexual or homosexual, Faderman suggested that these relationships were 'similar' to lesbian relationships, except they generally precluded 'genital' sexuality.[22] For Faderman this did not discount the potential for seeing such relationships as part of a lesbian continuum, as she argued that even in avowed lesbian relationships 'sexual contact may only be part of the relationship to a greater or lesser degree'.[23] Such a 'feminocentric'[24] analysis was in keeping with cultural feminism's insistence that it was patriarchal institutions such as marriage that inflicted compulsory heterosexuality upon women, distorting and damaging relations between women.

This moved the notion of 'romantic friendships' beyond what had been proposed by Smith-Rosenberg, who saw them largely as coexistent with other heterosexual relationships and into the distinct realm of lesbian history. Faderman's work provided a definite foundation for lesbian history, overturning heterosexist accounts of female friendships and offering insights that depart from the paradigms established within gay history.[25] Like Mavor, Faderman argued that such relationships between women existed in all innocence until the rise of sexology in the late nineteenth century. Sexology 'morbidified' the love between women, rendering all female friendships potentially sexual and thus pathological, while simultaneously inflicting 'compulsory heterosexuality' upon women.

Faderman continued this line of analysis in her next book, *The Scotch Verdict* (1983), which detailed the famous case of two Edinburgh schoolmistresses, Marianne Wood and Jane Pirie, accused of lesbianism in 1811.[26] The accusations brought against the women by Jane Cumming, a young student at their school and the illegitimate granddaughter of the socially prominent and politically powerful Dame Helen Cumming Gordon. Cumming had told her grandmother that Woods and Pirie were lovers and had provided rather graphic details to back up her statement. The scandal that ensued when these accusations became public forced the closure of the school and ruined the reputation of Wood and Pirie. In a valiant effort to rescue their reputations, the schoolmistresses sued Dame Cumming Gordon for libel, eventually winning £1,000 in damages after ten years of litigation. The basis of the judgement in their favour was that it was inconceivable for two ladies to be having sex with each other. This was Faderman's conclusion also, as she believed that sexologists 'invented lesbianism' by investing romantic friendships with sexuality and developing a sexualised mannish stereotype to describe the women involved in such relationships.[27] It was not, however, the opinion of everyone who read the text. Faderman's own lover Ollie was as convinced, as Faderman was sceptical, that these women were lovers and that Jane Cumming had witnessed their lovemaking.

As later critics of Faderman's analysis point out, the very case itself presented ample evidence that middle-class girls and women were aware, if not well-informed about the possibilities of sexual love between women.[28] For Faderman and other historians who followed her analysis the issue of 'lesbian sex' remained problematic. On the one hand the idea of 'romantic friendship' denied the possibility of sexual love between women in the past, yet there was considerable evidence to suggest that such relationships in the past were sexual. The question of whether women involved in romantic friendships 'did it', that is, engaged in sexual relations, remained a site of 'definitional uncertainty' for historians writing on women's relationships in the past.[29]

Lesbian Sex and Sexology

Coupled with the difficulty of definition was the whole question of lesbian invisibility in the past. Women who have achieved historical subjectivity have usually done this through their relationships with men. Women appear in history as the wives, daughters, sisters and mothers of great men. The first excursions of women into historical writing clearly exploited these relationships so women might develop a distinct historical subjectivity. Women who eschew the company of men, who only have relationships with women, have not had the same access to the historical record.

The invisibility of lesbians in history was compounded by the fact that such relationships were frequently the cause of embarrassment and scandal. Women were rarely prosecuted for lesbianism and so there is little mention of sexual acts between women in police or court records.[30] While sodomy and other homosexual practices were commonly referred to in police or medical records, references to lesbian relations in the sources are veiled or coded. Because lesbian sexuality was rarely recognised in law, it was possible to pretend that it did not exist.[31] This in itself has proven particularly problematic for historians of lesbianism, as the resort to medical and psychiatric records, as well as court documents and other sources derived from the criminal justice system, has proven critical to the writing of gay history.

The most important archival material used by gay historians has been that left by sexologists. The idea first expressed by Michel Foucault in the *History of Sexuality* (1979), that sexology 'invented' homosexuality in the late nineteenth century, has been enormously important to gay historians and theoreticians. Foucault did not mean that men did not engage in sex with other men prior to the nineteenth century, rather he was suggesting that homosexuality previously only existed as a set of practices such as sodomy. Men who engaged in such practices did not necessarily define themselves in relation to these practices. Like Smith-Rosenberg, Foucault assumed that sexuality was more fluid in the past and that homosexuality and heterosexuality were constructs of modernity. Where Smith-Rosenberg blamed Freud for the creation of dichotomous sexual identities, Foucault maintained that this transition occurred earlier, with the declining power of the church and the rise of science and medicine in the late eighteenth century. The shift from defining homosexual practices as sin to the emergence of notions of deviance and pathology allowed for the construction of a homosexual identity. As Foucault had written: 'The homosexual became a personage, a past, a case history, a childhood in addition to being a type of life .... Nothing that went into his total composition was unaffected by his sexuality.[32] For Foucault and historians who followed him, discourses such as sexology and psychiatry were seen as critical to the creation of homosexual identity.

While Foucauldians did not naively suggest that sexology and psychiatry were free of prejudice or prescription, they maintained that such discourses would eventually allow homosexual men a role in defining homosexual identity, as well as spreading awareness of homosexuality more generally. A number of prominent sexologists were homosexuals and in their work promoted tolerance of homosexuality. Sexology provided the first 'scientific' definition of lesbianism in 1864 when Karl Ulrichs published a pamphlet that posited the existence of a third sex. Ulrichs, himself a homosexual, believed that such inversion was innate and therefore should be viewed sympathetically, as an accident of heredity. Both sexologists and Foucauldians were primarily concerned with the history of homosexual men.

Foucault's work formed a major paradigm in gay history, with much analysis of the homosexual experience in the past being shaped around his suggestion that the homosexual was an invention of modernity. Some historians, such as Jeffrey Weeks, have closely followed Foucault's analysis, demonstrating in greater detail than Foucault himself, the ways in which sexology established homosexual identity and how this led to the homosexual subcultures in the late nineteenth and early twentieth centuries. These subcultures, Weeks has suggested, were critical prepolitical communities from which homophile movements and gay liberation emerged.[33] Other historians, such as Alan Bray and Randolph Trumbach, have taken issue with Foucault, suggesting that homosexual identities predated the scientific classification of the homosexual in the nineteenth century.[34] Both, however, acknowledge Foucault's importance in establishing the connection between identity and culture within gay history.

Lesbian historians have regarded the impact of sexology on lesbianism somewhat differently. It was the very idea that same-sex relationships between women could be scientifically classified in this way that created dissent among lesbian historians. Historians of lesbianism were quick to point out that sexology before the Second World War was an exclusively masculinist and phallocentric discourse. Lillian Faderman and Sheila Jeffreys complained that it was ahistorical to assume that sexology functioned in the same way for gay men as for lesbians. To do this necessarily marginalised the lesbian experience within gay history by making the homosexual experience in the past a universal model. More significantly, Faderman and Jeffreys suggested that the impact of sexology on lesbians enacted a process of 'morbidification', that thrust previously closeted relationships into the public arena and sexualised all relationships between women.[35]

For gay historians this process was characterised as essentially liberating, for it allowed for the development of a unique gay identity in the modern period, as sexology led to the increased visibility of homosexual relationships, generating gay subcultures and eventually coherent political goals. For gay men, gay sexual practice was a fundamental issue of gay liberation. The relationship between lesbians and lesbian sexual practice was more fraught. Historians of lesbianism saw the increased visibility of lesbianism as problematic. Whereas before the rise of sexology women's relationships with other women received little if any public scrutiny or condemnation, it was argued that the sexualisation of lesbianism had a negative effect, as sexologists classified lesbianism as pathological or perverse. Faderman and Jeffreys maintained that this was not the accidental effect of sexology, but rather reflected its intrinsic phallocentricity and misogyny. Sheila Jeffreys, particularly, cast sexologists such as Havelock Ellis as repressive villains intent on pathologising female sexuality in all its myriad forms.[36] Sexology, in Jeffreys's analysis, became synonymous with anti-feminism, as practitioners such as Ellis were accused of smashing feminist networks by pathologising female friendship and emphasising the dangers of celibacy.

This approach to the role of sexology within lesbian history and politics was quickly challenged. In 1982 Sonja Ruehl published a reassessment of Ellis's contribution, particularly focusing on his influence on Radclyffe Hall, author of the lesbian classic *The Well of Loneliness* (1928). Drawing on Foucault, Ruehl argued that Ellis's theories of inversion allowed Hall to create an positive identity for herself and, through the text and its trials, initiated 'a reverse discourse' that helped lead to the creation of a lesbian subculture and identity.[37] Figures such as Ellis and his contemporaries Edward Carpenter and Karl Pearson were slowly reclaimed by lesbian historians, who represented their influence in more benign terms. By examining the writings of women in their circle, historians such as Liz Stanley and Lucy Bland have adopted a more positive position on the role of sexology, arguing that the classification of lesbians as 'inverts' or 'Uranians' allowed women who loved other women a degree of self-definition previously impossible.[38]

Sex Radical, Butch/Femme

Critiques of Faderman and Jeffreys within lesbian history reflected the interest in women as sex radicals emerging more generally within women's history. Historians of women had been drawn into the 'sex wars' of the late 1970s and early 1980s around the campaigns against pornography and their nineteenth-century equivalent, the 'social purity' movement. These debates called into question the representation of first-wave feminism within women's history and its failure to thrive following suffrage. Cultural and pro-sex feminists saw the period after the granting of suffrage as the nadir of first-wave feminism. For historians influenced by cultural feminism this was due to the fact that feminists who became 'new women' were more interested in free love and assimilation into male-dominated institutions, than the maintenance of a distinctly feminine culture.[39] For historians influenced by the pro-sex argument the decline of first-wave feminism occurred because most feminists failed to embrace the sexual radicalism of the 'new woman'. Sex radicals such as Emma Goldman, Margaret Sanger and Crystal

Eastman were held up as pioneering spirits, who began the exploration of the sexual world late twentieth-century feminists now occupied.[40]

Ironically both pro-sex and cultural feminists blamed early sex radicals for their maintenance of an essentialist heterosexual definition of sexuality. This was seen as the key to the failure of these sex pioneers to sustain the momentum of feminism in the post-suffrage era.[41] While sex radicals encouraged sex education, sex research, abortion and contraception, social puritans often promoted opposition to prostitution, homosexuality and other forms of erotic variation. Pro-sex feminists contended that it was in the best interests of feminism to promote sexual radicalism, as social purity often led to the repression of female sexuality, the denial of women's reproductive rights and the policing of women's sexuality. Cultural feminists argued that sexual libertarianism led to the sexual exploitation of women and children.

Such debates played themselves out within women's history more generally. Historians of women who focused on women's agency in history revised the representation of women traditionally regarded as history's victims. Whereas first-wave and cultural feminists had seen the experience of the prostitute as paradigmatic of women's oppression, feminist historians imbued with such debates tended to describe prostitutes as sexual outlaws, women who disdained their traditional roles and defied male authority to create their own space in the public sphere.[42] They argued that social purity feminists, who sought to 'protect' prostitutes and other such marginalised women, acted in ways that were repressive and stigmatising. Such discussion returned to the attempts by cultural feminists to impose restrictions on contemporary women's freedom of sexual expression. Women's historians sympathetic to pro-sex feminism consistently drew parallels between the campaigns of nineteenth-century social purity feminists and anti-pornography feminists in the twentieth century. Both campaigns were seen as leading inevitably to the restriction of female sexuality, the reassertion of the double standard of sexual morality and the failure to sustain the liberation of women.[43]

At stake here was the place of sexual liberation within the discourses of feminism. Both heterosexual women and lesbians contested what they saw as the 'new puritanism' creeping into the women's movement. While most feminists agreed that the sexual revolution had clearly benefited men, some were now committed to creating another sexual revolution informed by feminism. Such a revolution would challenge both heterosexist and separatist assumptions about sexuality. Lesbian feminists such as Amber Hollibaugh and Cherríe Moraga argued that women needed to go back to consciousness-raising sessions and to build feminist theory around lesbian sex and sexuality. Feminism, according to Hollibaugh, needed to be sexualised if it were not to become a force for conservatism.[44]

Pro-sex feminism challenged the hegemonic ideals of women's cultural history, suggesting that the ideology of separate spheres characterised women as essentially moral, spiritual creatures who needed protection from the carnal urges of men. This worked to constrain and repress the agency of working-class women. In this analysis first-wave feminism did not represent solidarity between working-class and bourgeois women, rather, as Ellen DuBois, Linda Gordon and Judith Walkowitz have argued, the protectionist mechanisms set in place by middle-class women controlled the sexuality of working-class women, imposing a social code that stressed female dependency.[45] Far from challenging such an analysis, histories of first-wave feminism produced by cultural feminists such as Jeffreys and Margaret Jackson merely took issue with the question of intention.[46] The separate and asexual sphere idealised in certain first-wave feminist discourse was characterised in such histories as the means of politicising sexuality, protecting women from brutalisation at the hands of men and generating true feminist consciousness.[47]

Such discussion drew lesbian historians back to the issue of class, because the emphasis on 'romantic friendship' had created the sense within lesbian history that such relationships were the privilege of the upper classes.[48] Taking class into account necessarily generated a different view of lesbian history, particularly around the issue of butch/femme. Within the lesbian feminist politics of the 1970s butch/femme had been a hotly contested issue. Radical and cultural feminists joined with certain lesbian feminists to condemn the practice of butch/femme relations as a crude imitation of heterosexual relationships. For many women who had been involved in butch/femme communities before the rise of women's liberation, such criticism was a denial of their heritage. In the wake of these sex wars certain lesbian historians asserted that to characterise butch/femme as a morbid imitation of 'straight' sexual relationships was to misunderstand how this culture functioned as a site of survival and resistance under homophobic conditions.[49]

The work of historians such as Elizabeth Lapovsky Kennedy and Madelaine D. Davis revised the place of butch/femme within the history of lesbianism and lesbian feminism. Unlike earlier efforts to construct a lesbian past, the Buffalo Oral History Project established by Kennedy and Davis in the 1980s was community-based and drew on oral sources taken from women who had been involved in the Buffalo lesbian community since the 1940s. Oral history was seen as an important vehicle for the recovery of the lesbian past as it allowed lesbians to speak for themselves and was not filtered through the lenses of psychiatry or the courts. Being able to ask their subjects about identity, bar culture, politics and discrimination, as well as sexual practice, allowed Kennedy and Davis to draw a more nuanced and complex history of lesbianism. It also allowed their subjects a degree of agency in the re-creation of their own history.

Whereas earlier discussions of lesbian experience in the 1940s and 1950s had depicted bar subculture 'as passive and therefore tangential to developing lesbian consciousness and politics', Kennedy and Davis's study suggested that butch/femme functioned as a form of resistance for lesbians living in an oppressive environment.[50] Rather than viewing role playing as a 'demeaning imitation of the heterosexual world', they saw this subculture as an important site for the pre-political development of the homophile movement, gay liberation and lesbian feminism.[51] While historians focusing on 'romantic friendships' between women in the past could characterise gay and lesbian experience as separate spheres, Kennedy and Davis's analysis drew obvious parallels with the discussion of gay subcultures.

Kennedy and Davis's analysis reflected the importance of community to the maintenance of lesbian history in the past and in the present. Throughout this period various lesbian communities took a role in shaping their own history. Lesbian 'herstory' archives were established throughout the world and community-based projects flourished.[52] Through their emphasis on oral sources and personal writings such projects could depict the self-conscious development of lesbian communities, while simultaneously reinforcing the importance of sexual practice and sexual identity to the maintenance of these communities.

Doing 'It'?

The development of community-based projects marked the development of a self-conscious lesbian history distinct from histories that stressed the lesbian continuum. This was clearly at odds with histories of 'romantic friendships', which had tended to view women's relationships in isolation. Until this time the dominant approach to lesbian history had 'been premised on the absence of self-consciously lesbian communities'.[53] From this point certain historians came to argue that the idea of a lesbian continuum denied the specificity of the lesbian experience by seeing lesbianism in all forms of female friendship. At the heart of this debate remained the issue of sexual practice. The question of whether women who loved women in the past 'did it', that is, engaged in genital sexuality, became to a certain extent an unfathomable problem within lesbian history. As Martha Vicinus complained, lesbian history came to be 'characterised by a "not knowing" what could be its defining core'.[54]

The rediscovery of the diaries of Anne Lister in 1988 profoundly challenged the rhetoric of 'romantic friendship' within lesbian history, by providing the first detailed evidence of lesbian sexuality in the past. Unlike other historical evidence of lesbian sexuality, this text was not mediated through male voices, nor was it veiled or coy.

The diaries began in 1806 and, although written in code, depicted Lister's extensive network of female friends, her sexual relations with these women and her 'marriage' to Anne Walker, a wealthy neighbouring heiress. The diaries challenged the 'assumptions about the supposed sexual "innocence" of women' in the past.[55] It was no longer possible to maintain that sexual acts between women before the twentieth century had been the product of the masculine imagination. Moreover, it was possible to show that lesbianism was a sexualised practice long before the emergence of sexology.

While Lister may have been a unique figure, the appearance of her diaries called into question many of the assumptions that had previously structured lesbian history. For some the diaries were viewed as 'the Rosetta stone' of lesbian experience, demanding the reassessment of all previous lesbian history. The field of literary studies was particularly welcoming of the discovery, and a number of texts such as Emma Donoghue's *Passions between Women* and Lisa Moore's *Dangerous Intimacies* drew on the evidence of sex between women in the past to revise the idea of 'romantic friendships' in British literature.[56]

For others this discovery merely limited the possibilities of lesbian history. At issue again was the question of the place of sexuality within the definition of lesbianism. Even before the publication of the diaries Sheila Jeffreys had warned that defining lesbianism by 'genital contact' would not breach 'the heterosexual foundations of male supremacy'.[57] Less polemically and in the context of gay sexuality, Eve Kosofsky Sedgwick suggested that defining homosexuality in terms of sexual practice had a 'minoritizing' effect.[58] By this she meant that such a definition was essentialist and did not take into account the great variety of same-sex relationships.

Far from solving the problem of definitional uncertainty within lesbian history, the Lister diaries complicated the picture, suggesting that previously held archetypes such as 'romantic friends' or 'butch/femmes' could not possibly represent the variety of same-sex relationships between women.[59] Their appearance, however, confirmed the idea that female sexuality was more fluid in the past and that binaries such as heterosexuality and homosexuality were insufficient to describe the historical range of sexual practices and identities available to women (and men).

Making Things Perfectly Queer?

Such ideas blended well with the new theoretical understandings of sexuality emerging from the politics of queer in the late 1980s. Queer as a political practice and a theoretical discourse questioned the way in which definitions of heterosexuality and homosexuality had been constructed as oppositions, suggesting that in such formulations homosexuality was represented as 'a miming of heterosexual relationships – as if the latter were the legitimate original and homosexuality an imitation'.[60] Queer theorists were concerned to explode such restrictive sexual categories, suggesting, like Smith-Rosenberg, that sexuality, or rather sexualities, were fluid. More significantly, queer refused to accept the hegemony of heterosexuality, asserting the impossibility of fixed sexual identities. By decentring heterosexuality, queer refused to accept the outsider status often attributed to lesbians and gay men. Decentring heterosexuality allowed the possibility that queer sexualities were the dominant mode of sexuality, questioning all the paradigms that had previously shaped the history of homosexuality and heterosexuality.

Queer embraced a multitude of sexual possibilities and politics. It stood '*across genders, across sexualities, across genres, across perversions*'.[61] As Martha Vicinus has observed: 'Queer theory freed [us] from previously reductive notions of sexual identity, as well as the tedious essentialist versus social construction debate that agitated homosexuals in the late 1980s.'[62] Such freedom allowed historians to question how definitions of heterosexuality and homosexuality have been formed historically, necessitating new ways of thinking about same-sex practice in the past.

While queer theory rendered problematic the idea of fixed sexual identities potentially freeing lesbian history from the 'did they do it?' question, it would be wrong to suggest that it solved the 'conceptual impasse' that has haunted lesbian history. In some ways queer merely reinforced divisions amongst lesbians along similar lines to earlier sex wars.[63] Its emergence has, however, thrown into question all previous ways of thinking about sexuality. Queer's insistence on celebrating diversity, its refusal of 'outsider status' and its rejection of the universalising and heterosexist tendencies of feminist theory have posed significant challenges to the ways in which women's history could be conceived in its wake. Dealing with diversity or 'difference' would become a major theme of feminist politics and women's history in the 1990s.

Conclusion: Dealing with Difference

> The herstory of black women is interwoven with that of white women but this does not mean that they are the same story. Nor do we need white feminists to write our herstory for us, we can and are doing that for ourselves. However when they write their herstory and call it the story of women but ignore our lives and deny their relation to us, that is the moment in which they are acting within the relations of racism and writing *his*tory.
> Hazel V. Carby, 'White Women Listen!', 1986

The fragmentation of the women's movement over issues such as agency and resistance, consent and non-consent, separatism and sexual radicalism was only a small part of a broadening critique of the universalising tendencies of radical feminism. From its inception radical feminism had self-consciously promoted the ideal of sisterhood in an attempt to build up a sense of solidarity amongst women, focusing on their commonalities of experience and their shared oppression. Discussion of 'difference' formed part of the rhetoric of radical feminism. However, in this context difference signified gender difference, or the social meanings attributed to biological difference by patriarchal discourses. Although radical feminists were aware that class, race, age and sexual preference created differences among women, such differences were frequently overlooked. As radical feminism evolved into cultural feminism issues of class, race and age difference came to be regarded as divisive. Cultural feminism reverted to an earlier feminist stance that sought to create an alternate discourse centred on 'female uniqueness'.[1] In its essentialisation of female experience, cultural feminism found little space to consider 'difference' other than differences created by sex.

Even before the end of the 1970s many women began to question the unstated premise of homogeneity among the 'sisterhood'. Radical feminism, and its offspring cultural feminism, were criticised for their failure to take into account the differences between women. The issues of racism and homophobia further fragmented the women's movement, with acceptance of difference becoming a major theme of feminism in the 1980s and 1990s. Difference feminism broke with the universalising and essentialising tendencies of cultural feminism which was criticised as elitist, heterosexist, racist and Eurocentric. Feminists informed by the politics of difference challenged the idea of a 'unique female experience', claiming that the experience of white middle-class women had become hegemonic, suppressing the experiences of women who did not belong to this dominant group.

It is not the purpose of this conclusion to describe the historiography of women of colour. Such a task would involve an essentialist undertaking that would homogenise the historical experience of women from many and diverse cultural backgrounds. Rather this conclusion will explore the various ways in which the debates about difference impacted upon the field of women's history more generally. The very possibility of women's history had been premised upon radical feminism's insistence that women formed an 'unhistoried' minority, absent from history because of their sex. The creation of women's history was dependent upon an ideal of universal sisterhood in the past. Women of colour challenged the very possibility of creating a 'herstory', by suggesting that the experiences of women in the past could not be homogenised in such a way, that those factors that divided women in the present also divided women in the past.[2] They argued that women's historians had represented the experiences of white middle-class women in the past as the experience of all women. Historians informed by debates about difference suggested that what now passed as 'women's history' was not the history of all women, but like men's history, the history of an elite, with little reference to the experience of marginalised and minority women. When women's history did relate the experience of women of colour, working-class women, indigenous women, colonised women, it was always from the perspective of the white middle-class woman.

All the Women Were White?

Debates about difference questioned the historical narrative radical feminists had created about the evolution of women's liberation. Women's historians were forced to acknowledge that this story had only been told from the perspective of white middle-class women. One of the first challenges debates about difference posed to women's history was a need to revise the ways in which they had envisioned the formation of feminist consciousness in the present and in the past. Until women of colour challenged the women's movement to think about issues of race and racism, few historians of women considered how racial and class oppression created different forms of feminist consciousness. More significantly, debates about difference forced feminists and historians of women to recognise how feminism and racism sometimes functioned together in the past. This allowed the suggestion that racism would continue to exist, unless white women acknowledged that the feminism of women of colour was different from their own.

As women of colour described their own experiences of coming to feminism, they criticised the ways in which the experience of certain groups of elite women had become *the* history of women's liberation.[3] The forces that had shaped the development of white middle-class women's feminist consciousness often functioned very differently in relation to women of colour. Around certain issues such as abortion and contraception the experience of women of colour was so different from white women that it precluded any suggestion of sisterhood. Women of colour offered a very different analysis of the rise of feminist consciousness among women following the Second World War. The historical sites that were so formative for white middle-class feminists, such as the publication of Betty Freidan's *The Feminine Mystique*, the formation of NOW and the exodus of women from radical politics, were not only experienced differently by non-white, non-elite women, but were often experienced in ways that heightened their feelings of racial and class oppression. Moreover, such an analysis ignored years of feminist activism undertaken by women of colour in the civil rights movement, in independence and decolonisation movements and more generally in anti-racist politics.

Although all women were subjected to similar messages encouraging them to return to the constraints of domesticity during the 1950s, only white middle-class women had the economic freedom to do so. Women of colour, from economic necessity, remained in the workforce unbound by the return of quasi-Victorian domestic ideology that so troubled middle-class white women during this period. In the United States many African-American women found work as maids propping up the domestic ideal created by white consumer culture.[4] In Europe women from the West Indies, Turkey, India and Pakistan were allowed to immigrate in order to replace white women in the industries they had taken up during the war.[5] This disparity of experience created much resentment among women of colour. While white women complained of domestic constraint, lack of fulfilment and the overbearing demands of the new femininity, women of colour complained of long hours, poor pay and racist assumptions that forever condemned them to menial work.

Women of colour positioned themselves rather differently in relation to the new femininity of the 1950s. While white women saw this as the key to their oppression, women of colour often actively pursued these prescriptions for femininity. Unlike white women, who became discontented with the role of home-maker, many women of colour sought the right not to work during this period. They wanted only to be housewives. The right not to work served as a symbol of their improved economic status and their continued survival in a racist society. When these feelings of domestic entrapment were theorised into a politics of women's liberation with Betty Friedan's *The Feminine Mystique*, many women of colour were incredulous. As Paula Giddings has written, 'Friedan's observation that "I never knew a woman, when I was growing up, who used her mind, and played her own part in the world and also loved, and had children" seemed to come from another planet.'[6] The solutions posed by Friedan were aimed specifically at middle-class, college-educated white women. The exhortation for women to go back to work depended on white women attaining domestic help from working-class women of colour. White women's liberation was to be achieved on the shoulders of their black 'sisters'. That Friedan did not even consider the experience of non-white women in her text, that she rendered invisible the femininity of her domestic help, convinced many women of colour that her feminism merely revealed the extent to which white women had 'been socialised to accept and perpetuate racist ideology'.[7]

The disparity of experience between white women and women of colour was further exacerbated by the way in which radical feminists positioned themselves in relation to other forms of radical politics. Many white middle-class feminists claimed to have come to feminism through a rejection of radical politics. In so doing they were not merely rejecting what they perceived to be the sexist and patriarchal culture of radical politics, they were also asserting that sexual oppression formed the most fundamental form of oppression in society. Such an understanding created a culture of implied racism within radical feminism. The ideal of universal sisterhood had obscured the differences between women and essentialised their experiences of oppression. The experience of white middle-class women, the dominant group within the movement, became hegemonic. It was their experience that shaped feminist consciousness.

Women of colour were quick to point out that their experience of such movements was often fundamentally different from the experience of white women. The difference of experience between African-American women and white women in the US civil rights movement presents perhaps the most telling example of this disparity. While initially the experience of working in the civil rights movement allowed white women to develop political skills and to break out of confining roles, many complained of sexual discrimination and harassment. They believed that all women were relegated to menial tasks within the movement and were rarely allowed to take part in decision- and policy-making, because this had been the experience of white women. These complaints led white women within the movement to liken sexual supremacy to racial supremacy. Eventually such analysis formed the basis of radical feminism, which posited sexual oppression as the key to all other forms of oppression.

The experience of white women within the movement was necessarily different, if not oppositional, to women of colour. African-American women were baffled by the complaints of their white co-workers and resented them likening their experience of sexual discrimination to racial discrimination. African-American women had held positions of authority within the movement and were often responsible for the success of reform initiatives. In the civil rights movement's most critical moments they were in the vanguard. African-American women thought themselves capable of doing anything men could do, including facing physical dangers. Their experiences made them assume that white women were only relegated to menial tasks because they were incapable of more strenuous involvement.[8]

Women of colour resented the ways in which white women made their experience of the movement *the* feminist position, while totally neglecting the experience of women of colour. What was for African-American women an incredibly empowering experience came to be represented in radical feminism as a site of women's oppression and a catalyst for reform. Although women of colour eventually formed alliances with white feminists, their engagement with women's liberation sprang from a long tradition of women's activism in the struggle against racism. Their history of feminism was fundamentally at odds with the narrative of exclusion from and rejection of radical politics generated within radical feminism.

The scepticism of women of colour was merely heightened when they worked to form alliances with women's liberation groups. Unlike the civil rights movement and other radical black movements, women's liberation was primarily concerned with revolutionary sexual politics. Whereas women of colour active in the struggle against racism had been violently attacked in confrontations with the government and the police, few white women saw the necessity of such violence in the sex war they were fighting. Few women involved in women's liberation maintained an interest in black politics and many considered racist oppression a secondary concern to sexual oppression. This often led to intense confrontations between white women and women of colour. At a NOW rally in California 1970, African-American women involved in the rally were holding up posters of the exiled activist Angela Davis and demanding her safety. One of the leaders of NOW approached these women and stated: 'Angela Davis has nothing to do with women's liberation.' Frances Beal, leader of the Third World Women's Alliance, retorted: 'It has nothing to do with the kind of liberation you're talking about but it has everything to do with the kind of liberation we're talking about.'[9] Similar encounters were to be repeated wherever women of colour sought to forge connections within the women's movement.

This lack of understanding between white women and women of colour was only intensified by the refusal of white feminists to acknowledge the implied racism of their position. As bell hooks has argued, white feminists assumed that racism took the form of overt expressions of hatred, and did not recognise that the ways in which the experiences of women of colour were represented (or not represented) within women's liberation was also implicitly racist.[10] White women failed to understand that women of colour might perceive them as the enemy.[11] The experience of slavery and colonisation left many women of colour in no doubt that white women benefited from their racial identity and they continued to form a partnership with white men when their racial or class interests were threatened, as they had been in the past. This made women of colour highly sceptical of the sisterhood offered them by women's liberationists.

Women of colour also resented the appropriation of the language of racial oppression by white middle-class women. Radical feminists used language and images borrowed from the civil rights movement, black power and other struggles against racial oppression to highlight the oppression of women. Techniques such as 'consciousness raising' were appropriated by radical feminism from Maoism and black power, only to be used in ways that made hegemonic the experience of white women. The insularity of women's liberation and its failure to acknowledge the importance of other radical political positions made women of colour highly suspicious, and they felt betrayed by their experiences of the movement. This experience led many women of colour to believe that the women's movement 'was consciously and deliberately structured ... to serve primarily the interests of middle- and upper-class college-educated women seeking equality with middle- and upper-class white men'.[12]

Dealing with Difference?

In the rhetoric of women's liberation the term 'woman' had been used exclusively to signify white women, while the term 'black' was used exclusively to refer to men of colour. Feminists of colour were highly critical of this universalising tendency, arguing that it allowed white feminists to 'proclaim white men world oppressors while making it appear linguistically that no alliance existed between white women and white men on the basis of shared racial imperialism'.[13] This created the illusion that all women were united in the shared oppression formed by white patriarchy, deflecting attention away from the elitism and racism of the women's movement.

Until debates about difference fractured the movement, the writing of women's history both reflected and replicated this tendency. History was the history of 'white elite males', black historiography dealt with the history of black males and women's history dealt with the 'universal sisterhood' of women. By universalising the experience of women, women's historians made hegemonic the experience of white middle-class women, while rendering invisible the experience of women of colour. Just as women's liberation focused almost exclusively on the sexual oppression of women, women's history initially failed to examine how race and class mitigated the historical experiences of women.

The issues that had emerged within women's history during the 1970s, questions of visibility and invisibility, agency and resistance, were all rendered more complex and ambiguous when the historical experiences of women of colour were brought into consideration. Debates about difference forced historians of women not only to focus on issues of race and class, but also to understand that the historical experience of women could not be fully explored, unless sexual oppression was contextualised with reference to race and class. Women's historians could not merely add the history of women of colour to create a broader, more inclusive history of women. Rather, considering how race and class shaped the experience of women in the past created major shifts in the ways in which women's history was written. Ultimately this undercut the very possibility of 'women's history' as women of colour argued that:

> the 'herstory' that white women use to trace the roots of women's oppression ... is an imperial history rooted in the prejudices of colonial and neo-colonial periods, a 'herstory' which suffers the same form of historical amnesia of white male historians, by ignoring the fundamental ways in which white women have benefited from the oppression of Black people.[14]

The impact of such criticism fundamentally challenged many of the paradigms established by historians to create women's history. When white women came to first challenge history their focus had been on their lack of representation within traditional historical narrative. Women's historical experience, they argued, had been consciously neglected, obscured and suppressed. The principal aim of the new historians of women was to 'restore women to history and history to women'.[15] Issues of visibility and invisibility within history were rendered more complicated by the inclusion of women of colour into these historical debates. Historians informed by theories of difference argued that it was essential to recognise that white women and women of colour have been differently represented in history. Historians informed by radical feminism were concerned to highlight the invisibility of [white] women in history. Black feminist historians argued that it was important to not only recognise the absence of women of colour from historical narrative, but also to deconstruct the ways in which history had made women of colour visible.[16] Such ideas not only challenged historians of women, but also set up new parameters within black and post-colonial historiography. Just as white women historians were criticised for writing a history of women that paid little heed to racial difference, men of colour were criticised for adopting alternative historical narratives that paid scant attention to sexual difference.

Historians such as Hazel V. Carby and Darlene Clark Hine argued that the idea that women were historically 'invisible' was premised only upon the experience of white middle-class women.[17] Women of colour were represented somewhat differently within history. Ultimately this difference in historical representation existed because the nexus between racism and sexism shaped the gendered construction of white and black womanhood in oppositional terms. While 'womanhood' excluded white women from history, the systematic denial of 'womanhood' to women of colour made them overly visible within history. This visibility did not ensure that women of colour were seen as independent historical subjects, rather they worked symbolically within history, to signify the 'Other' and in opposition to the 'chaste, domesticated and morally pure' middle-class white woman.[18]

Women of colour have most often been represented in history as racist stereotypes. 'Hypersexuality' was a defining feature of such stereotypes and was attributed to women of colour in the context of slavery and colonisation. This uniformity can be attributed to overarching racist assumptions about all non-white women, but also because such stereotypes were formed in opposition to an ideal of white womanhood. This ideal was manipulated to defend slavery and colonisation as 'civilising missions' that would eventually lead to the elevation of all women. The difference between this ideal of womanhood and the experiences of women burdened by colonisation and slavery was used to justify their continued subordination. Such representations obscured the sexual exploitation of women of colour that slavery and colonisation necessarily produced. Rape was the underside of the sanctioned mode of colonial rule and an economic imperative of slavery.

As post-colonial historians have demonstrated, colonisation and its attendant practices such as slavery were intensely gendered.

Discourses of imperialism used the gendered ideology of separate spheres to establish racial boundaries, defining men and women subject to colonisation as 'incapable of self-government', 'primitive', 'akin to nature', 'childlike' and hence, feminine. Moreover, they argued, it was critical to the practice of colonisation and its historical understanding that divisions were established between those women who colonised and those who were colonised. The myth that colonisation was a 'civilising mission' was largely dependent upon a prescriptive and restrictive ideal of European womanhood. Western Europe was represented the high point of civilisation because women did not have to work, because they were sexually pure and because they were subject to male authority. The supposed elevation of the status of women in colonised countries was seen as major goal of colonisation. This myth functioned on a number of levels, controlling women's sexuality at home and in the colonies, while simultaneously justifying the sexual exploitation of colonised women.

Poststructuralist Postscript

As post-colonial and poststructuralist critiques have emerged the very viability of Western historiography to produce alternate narratives has been called into question. While historians informed by post-colonialism have come to argue that the writing of history has merely acted as an extension of the colonial endeavour and that history as discourse was often a powerful instrument in the control of colonised people.[19] The idea that colonisation functioned as 'the motor of historical progress', bringing the gifts of freedom and democracy to those societies it touched, was shown to be a product of historiography's Eurocentricity.[20] Such ideas, coupled with debates around difference, have enabled historians to show that very different histories of women exist with 'respect to the particular inheritance ... of slavery, enforced migration, plantation and indentured labour, colonialism, imperial conquest and genocide'.[21]

Poststructural accounts of the past have called into question the very possibility of writing history, while simultaneously fragmenting the concept of 'woman' so that it no longer can be considered a unified subject.[22] Such critiques have necessarily called into question the possibility of writing 'the history of women'. Emerging alongside debates about difference, such critiques have shown the category 'woman' to be fragmented by the 'various systematic networks of class, race, (hetero)sexuality and nation'.[23] While on the one hand this has led certain historians to claim that it is impossible to write women's history, on the other hand this fragmentation has led to a more nuanced approach to the analysis of women in the past. Debates about difference have forced women's historians to acknowledge the link between racism and feminism in the present and in the past. Historians of women have come to see that is impossible to understand the experience of women in the past without acknowledging how race, class and sexuality have shaped their lives.[24]

Poststructuralist accounts of history have also forced the recognition that the prescriptions of gender have shaped the way in which men and women have written history in the past. This gendering of history has allowed for a positive reassessment of earlier traditions of women's historical writings. Beliefs about sexual difference have shaped the development of history as a modern discipline and have always functioned in ways that excluded women from history as both subjects and practitioners in the past. These insights have forced a reassessment of both women's historical writing in the past and the 'new' women's history that emerged out of women's liberation. Women's historical production can no longer be dismissed as 'quaint' or 'worthy', because it is unlike masculinist historical writing, rather it must be viewed as part of a diverse but distinct tradition that has seen women since the Renaissance manipulate the prescriptions of gender and genre to carve out a history of their own.

Notes

Introduction

1. From ancient Rome there is fragmentary evidence of a history of the Julio-Claudian family written by the Empress Agrippina (15–59 CE), wife of the Emperor Claudius and mother of the Emperor Nero, which is mentioned by Tacitus and other ancient writers. See Estelle C. Jelinek, *The Tradition of Women's Autobiography from Antiquity to the Present* (Boston: Twayne Publishers, 1986) p. 13. From China we know of the efforts of Pan Chao (*c.* 45–114 CE), Daughter of Pan Piao and sister of Pan Ku, court historians to the Emperor Chang. With her father and brother, Pan Chao contributed to the official history of the Hang Dynasty. See Nancy Lee Swann, *Pan Chao: Foremost Woman Scholar of China* (New York: Century, 1932).
2. Christina Crosby, *The Ends of History: Victorians and 'the Woman Question'* (New York: Routledge, 1991) p. 2.
3. See Gerda Lerner, 'New Approaches to the Study of Women in American History', *Journal of Social History*, 4, 4 (1969): 333–56; Linda Gordon, Persis Hunt, Elizabeth Pleck, Rochelle Goldberg Ruthchild and Marcia Scott, 'Historical Phallacies: Sexism in American Historical Writing' and Ann D. Gordon, Mari Jo Buhle and Nancy Schrom Dye, 'The Problem of Women's History', in Berenice A. Carroll (ed.), *Liberating Women's History: Theoretical and Critical Essays* (Urbana: University of Chicago Press, 1976), pp. 55–74, 75–92.
4. Despite the explosion of interest in women's history during the 1970s, only two articles were published that focused on women's historiography in previous centuries. See Kathryn Kish Sklar, 'American Female Historians in Context 1770–1930', *Feminist Studies*, 3, 1 (1975–76): 169–83 and Natalie Zemon Davis, 'Gender and Genre: Women as Historical Writers 1400–1820', *University of Ottawa Quarterly*, 50, 1 (1980), reprinted in Patricia H. Labalme (ed.), *Beyond their Sex: Learned Women of the European Past* (New York: New York University Press, 1983), pp. 153–82.

5. Jane Lewis, 'Women, Lost and Found: The Impact of Feminism on History', in Dale Spender (ed.), *Men's Studies Modified: The Impact of Feminism on the Academic Disciplines* (Oxford: Pergamon Press, 1981), pp. 55–72.
6. Judith Allen, 'Evidence and Silence: Feminism and the Limits of History', in Carole Pateman and Elizabeth Gross (eds), *Feminist Challenges: Social and Political Theory* (Sydney: Allen & Unwin, 1986), p. 173.
7. Joan W. Scott, *Gender and the Politics of History* (New York: Columbia University Press, 1988), p. 3.
8. Linda Gordon, 'What is Women's History?', in Juliet Gardiner (ed.), *What is History Today?* (London: Macmillan, 1988), p. 93.
9. Allen, 'Evidence and Silence', p. 187.
10. For various critiques of masculinist historical methodology see the collection *Liberating Women's History* edited by Berenice A. Carroll (Urbana: University of Chicago Press, 1976); and Natalie Zemon Davis, ' "Women's History" in Transition: The European Case', *Feminist Studies*, 3, 3/4 (1976): 83–103; Joan Kelly-Gadol, 'Did Women Have a Renaissance?', in Renate Bridenthal and Claudia Koonz (eds), *Becoming Visible: Women in European History* (Boston: Houghton Mifflin, 1977), pp. 139–65; Michelle Perrot (ed.), *Writing Women's History* (Oxford: Blackwell, 1984).
11. Allen, 'Evidence and Silence', p. 187.
12. Scott, *Gender and the Politics of History*, p. 2.
13. *Ibid.*, p. 183.
14. *Ibid.*, p. 7.
15. *Ibid.*, p. 7.
16. *Ibid.*, p. 26.
17. Crosby, *Ends of History*, p. 2.
18. Bonnie G. Smith, 'The Contribution of Women to Modern Historiography in Great Britain, France and the United States 1750–1940', *American Historical Review*, 89 (1985): 307.
19. Davis, ' "Women's History" in Transition', p. 83.
20. See for instance Jane Lewis, 'Women, Lost and Found: The Impact of Feminism on History' and Marilyn J. Boxer and Jean H. Quataret, 'Restoring Women to History', in *Connecting Spheres: Women in the Western World 1500 to the Present* (New York: Oxford University Press, 1987), pp. 3–17; Olwen Hufton, 'What is Women's History?', in Juliet Gardiner (ed.), *What is History Today?* (London: Macmillan,

1980), pp. 82–5; Elizabeth H. Pleck, 'Women's History: Gender as a Category of Historical Analysis', in James B. Gardiner and George Rollie Adams (eds), *Ordinary People and Everyday Life: Perspectives on the New Social History* (Nashville: American Association for State and Local History, 1990), pp. 51–65.
21. See introduction to *The Gender of History* (Cambridge, MA: Harvard University Press, 1998), pp. 1–13.
22. Smith, 'Contribution of Women to Modern Historiography', p. 711.
23. Between 1985 and 1998 Smith published numerous articles on this theme. In 1998 she published her groundbreaking text *The Gender of History*, in which she reprised these earlier essays.
24. Joan Thirsk, 'Foreword', in Mary Prior (ed.), *Women in English Society 1500–1800* (London: Methuen, 1985), pp. 1–21; 'The History Women', in Mary O'Dowd and Sabine Wichert (ed.), *Chattel, Servant or Citizen: Women's Status in Church, State and Society* (Belfast: Institute of Irish Studies, 1995), pp. 1–11; and 'Woman Local and Family Historians', in David Hey (ed.), *Oxford Companion to Local and Family Historians* (Oxford: Oxford University Press, 1996), pp. 498–504; Billie Melman, 'Gender, History and Memory: The Invention of Women's Past in the Nineteenth and Early Twentieth Century', *History and Memory*, 5, 1 (1993): 5–41; Rohan Amanda Maitzen, *Gender, Genre and Victorian Historical Writing* (New York: Garland, 1998) Rosemary Mitchell, ' "The Busy Daughters of Clio": Women Writers of History from 1820–1880', *Women's History Review* 7, 1 (1998): 107–34; Miriam Elizabeth Burstein, ' "From Good Looks to Good Thoughts": Popular Women's History and the Invention of Modernity, ca. 1830–1870', *Modern Philology*, 97, 1 (1999): 46–75.
25. Greg Kucich, 'Romanticism and Feminist Historiography', *Wordsworth Circle,* 24, 3 (1993): 133–40; Jane Rendall, 'Writing History for British Women: Elizabeth Hamilton and the Memoirs of Agrippina', in Clarissa Campbell Orr (ed.), *Wollstonecraft's Daughters: Womanhood in England and France 1780–1920* (Manchester: Manchester University Press, 1996), pp. 79–93.
26. Daniel R. Woolf, 'A Feminine Past? Gender, Genre and Historical Knowledge in England 1500–1800', *American Historical Review*, 102, 3 (1997): 645–79.
27. Gerda Lerner, *The Creation of Feminist Consciousness: From the Middle Ages to Eighteen-Seventy* (New York: Oxford University Press: 1993), pp. 249–73.

Chapter 1

1. Barbara Caine, *Victorian Feminists* (Oxford: Oxford University Press, 1992), p. 39.
2. Euan Cameron, 'The Power of the Word: Renaissance and Reformation', in *Early Modern Europe: An Oxford History* (Oxford: Oxford University Press, 1999), p. 72.
3. Barbara F. McManus, *Classics and Feminism: Gendering the Classics* (New York : Twayne, 1997) p. 2.
4. Walter J. Ong, 'Latin Language Study as a Renaissance Puberty Rite', *Studies in Philology*, 57, 2 (1959): 105.
5. Anthony Grafton and Lisa Jardine, *From Humanism to the Humanities: Education and the Liberal Arts in Fifteenth- and Sixteenth-century Europe* (London: Duckworth, 1986), p. 4.
6. *Ibid.*, p. 5.
7. *Ibid.*, p. 6.
8. Joseph Levine, *Humanism and History: Origins of Modern English Historiography* (Ithaca: Cornell University Press, 1987), p. 74.
9. T.S. Eliot, 'What is a Classic?', in *On Poetry and Poets* (London: Faber, 1957), p. 67.
10. Donald R. Kelley, *Faces of History from Herodotus to Herder* (New Haven: Yale University Press, 1998), p. 134.
11. E. B. Fryde, *Humanism and Renaissance Historiography* (London: Hambledon Press, 1983), p. 4.
12. Donald R. Kelley, *Versions of History from Antiquity to the Enlightenment* (New Haven: Yale University Press, 1991), p. 218.
13. Peter Burke, *The Renaissance Sense of the Past: Documents of Modern History* (London: Edward Arnold, 1969), pp. 50–76.
14. *Ibid.*, p. 219.
15. Phyllis Rackin, *Stages of History: Shakespeare's English Chronicles* (New York: Cornell University Press, 1990), p. 8.
16. *Ibid.*, p. 9.
17. Donald R. Kelley, 'Humanism and History', in Albert Rabil Jr (ed.), *Renaissance Humanism: Foundations, Forms and Legacy*, Vol. 3, *Humanism and the Disciplines* (Philadelphia: University of Pennsylvania Press, 1988), p. 241.
18. Richard Schlatter (ed.), *Hobbes's Thucydides* (New Brunswick: Rutgers University Press, 1975), p. 6.

19. Peter Burke, 'A Survey of the Popularity of Ancient Historians 1450–1700', *History and Theory* 5 (1966): 136.
20. *Ibid.*, 138.
21. *Ibid.*, 141.
22. Kelley, *Versions of History*, p. 219.
23. Eric Cochrane, *Historians and Historiography in the Italian Renaissance* (Chicago: University of Chicago Press, 1981), p. 3.
24. Arnaldo Momigliano, 'The Introduction of the Teaching of History as an Academic Subject and its Implications', *Minerva* 21, 1 (1983): 2–3.
25. A. Dwight Culler, *The Victorian Mirror of History* (New Haven: Yale University Press, 1981), p. 4.
26. Cited in Rackin, *Stages of History*, p. 2.
27. *Ibid.*, p. 4.
28. I owe this insight to Ian Plant. Thank you.
29. Arthur Marwick, *The Nature of History* (London: Macmillan, 1970), p. 26.
30. Kelley, *Faces of History*, p. 147.
31. T. J. Luce, *The Greek Historians* (London: Routledge, 1997), p. 125.
32. J. B. Bury, *The Ancient Greek Historians* (New York: Dover, 1958), p. 197.
33. Luce, *Greek Historians*, p. 127.
34. Arthur Eckstein, *Moral Vision in the Histories of Polybius* (Berkeley: University of California Press, 1995), p. 118.
35. Burke, 'Survey of the Popularity of Ancient Historians', pp. 145–51.
36. David Harvey, 'Women in Thucydides', *Arethusa* 18, 1 (1985): 70. Other historians suggest there are fifty references to women.
37. Book 2, 45.2. J. S. Rusten, *Thucydides: The Peloponnesian War, Book II* (Cambridge: Cambridge University Press, 1989), p. 175.
38. As late as 1893 the German classicist Ulrich von Wilamowitz-Moellendorff would celebrate the elision of women from the Thucydidean tradition of historiography. Referring to Aspasia, he would write:

> I am not so foolish as to bear ill-will to a dead female, but one should leave her where she is – dead and a female. People who do not want to sniff out any history without women's perfume and do not consider their heroes to be complete unless they coo and bleat from time to time may read Hamerling instead of Thucydides. But it is no small sign of the dignity of Attic history that only one woman is found in it, although she commands it all-the maiden of the Acropolis [The Goddess Athena].

39. Frank M. Turner, *The Greek Heritage in Victorian Britain* (New Haven: Yale University Press, 1981), p. 187.
40. ' "[T]he chief glory of a woman is not to be talked of," said Pericles, himself a much talked of man'. Virginia Woolf, *A Room of One's Own* (London: Hogarth, 1929), p. 76.
41. T. E. Page et al. (eds), *Plutarch's Moralia* (London: Heinemann, 1931), p. 475.
42. Crosby, *Ends of History*, p. 1.
43. Glenda McLeod, *Virtue and Venom: Catalogs of Women from Antiquity to the Renaissance* (Ann Arbor: University of Michigan Press, 1991), p. 1.
44. *Ibid.*, p. 15.
45. *Ibid.*, p. 16.
46. Froma I. Zeitlin, 'Foreword', in Nicole Loraux, *Children of Athena: Athenian Ideas about Citizenship and the Division between the Sexes* (Princeton: Princeton University Press, 1993), p. xii.
47. McLeod, *Virtue and Venom*, p. 27.
48. On Agrippina see Anthony A. Barrett, *Agrippina: Mother of Nero* (London: Batsford, 1995). For Messalina see Sandra R. Joshel, 'Female Desire and the Discourse of Empire: Tacitus's Messalina', in Barbara Laslett et al. (eds), *History and Theory: Feminist Research, Debates and Contestations* (Chicago: University of Chicago Press, 1997), pp. 383–415.
49. On the authority of Tacitus see, for instance, Burke, 'Survey of the Popularity of Ancient Historians', and Donald R. Kelley, 'Tacitus Noster: The Germania in the Renaissance and Reformation', in T. J. Luce and A. J. Woodman (eds), *Tacitus and the Tacitean Tradition* (Princeton: Princeton University Press, 1993), pp. 152–67.
50. Ernest Breisach, *Historiography: Ancient, Medieval and Modern* (Chicago: University of Chicago Press, 1983), p. 64.
51. R.G. Collingwood, *The Idea of History* (Oxford: Clarendon Press, 1993), p. 37.
52. The story of the Sabine women is also found in Ennius, *Sabine Women*, Cicero's *De Republica*, Plutarch's *Romulus*, Ovid's *Fasti* and Dionysius of Halicarnassus' *Antiquitates Romanæ*.
53. Titus Livius, *The History of Rome* (London: T. Cadell, 1822), Book 1, XIII, p. 25.
54. N. Davidson, 'Theology, Nature and the Law: Sexual Sin and Sexual Crime in Italy from the Fourteenth to the Seventeenth Century',

in T. Dean and K. J. P. Lowe (eds), *Crime, Society and the Law in Renaissance Italy* (Cambridge: Cambridge University Press, 1994), pp. 83–4.
55. Patricia Klindienst Joplin, 'Ritual Work on Human Flesh: Livy's Lucretia and the Rape of the Body Politic', *Helios* 17 (1990): 55.
56. *Ibid.*, p. 55.
57. Sandra R. Joshel, 'The Body Female and the Body Politic: Livy's Lucretia and Verginia', in Amy Richlin (ed.), *Pornography and Representation in Greece and Rome* (New York: Oxford University Press, 1992), p. 115.
58. Froma I. Zeitlin, 'Foreword', in Nicole Loraux, *The Children of Athena: Athenian Ideas about Citizenship and the Division of the Sexes* (Princeton: Princeton University Press, 1993), p. xii.
59. Erica Mathieson, 'Women in the Ecclesiastical History of Eusebius: A Comparison with Women in the New Testament', MA thesis, Macquarie University (1996), p. 42.
60. *Ibid.*, p. 43.
61. Marina Warner, *Alone of all her Sex: The Myth and the Cult of the Virgin Mary* (New York: Alfred Knopf, 1976), p. xxi.
62. Ronald Syme, perhaps the most highly regarded Tacitus specialist of the twentieth century, wrote of his portrayal of Agrippina that 'Tacitus's portrayal is terrible and truthful. Julia Agrippina, the mother of Nero, is wholly authentic.' Syme's only reference to Tacitus's authentic portrait of Julia Agrippina is, however, Tacitus. See Ronald Syme, *Tacitus* (London: Oxford University Press, 1958), pp. 334–5.
63. Kelley, 'Tacitus Noster', pp. 152–67.
64. *Ibid.*, p. 154.
65. Howard D. Weinbrot, 'Politics, Taste and National Identity: Some Uses of Tacitism in Eighteenth-Century Britain', in T. J. Luce and A. J. Woodman (eds), *Tacitus and the Tacitean Tradition* (Princeton: Princeton University Press, 1993), p. 178.
66. Joshel, 'Female Desire and the Discourse of Empire', p. 401.
67. *Ibid.*
68. Francesca Santoro L'Hoir, 'Tacitus and Women's Usurption of Power', *Classical World*, 88 (1994): 5.
69. See, for instance, his treatment of Zenobia, wife of the fugitive King Radamistus, Antisitius Pollita, Sextia and Paxaea.
70. See especially his treatment of Messalina, Agrippina the Younger and Poppaea.

71. Cited in Nicole Loraux, *The Experiences of Tiresias: The Feminine and the Greek Man* (Princeton: Princeton University Press, 1995), p. 236.
72. Thomas E. J. Wiedmann, 'Thucydides, Women and the Limits of Rational Analysis', *Greece & Rome*, 30, 2 (1983): 162.
73. Loraux, *Experiences of Tiresias*, pp. 231–40.
74. Rusten, *Thucydides: The Peloponnesian War*, p. 127.
75. Thomas Harrison, 'Herodotus and the Ancient Greek Idea of Rape', in Susan Deacy and Karen F. Pierce (eds), *Rape in Antiquity* (London: Duckworth, 1997), p. 199.
76. Eckstein, *Moral Vision in the Histories of Polybius*, p. 119.
77. *Ibid.*, p. 154.
78. *Ibid.*, p. 156.
79. Marnie Hughes-Warrington, *Fifty Key Thinkers in History* (London: Routledge, 2000), pp. 156–64.
80. John Gould, *Herodotus* (London, Weidenfeld & Nicolson, 1989), p. 129.
81. Carolyn Dewald, 'Women and Culture in Herodotus' *Histories*', *Women's Studies* (1975): 92.
82. *Ibid.*, p. 93.
83. John L. Myres, *Herodotus: Father of History* (Oxford: Clarendon Press, 1953) p. 16.
84. Kelley, *Faces of History*, p. 20.
85. For a revisionist perspective on Herodotus see Harrison, 'Herodotus and the Ancient Greek Idea of Rape'.

Chapter 2

1. Mary Astell, *The Christian Religion as Profess'd by a Daughter of the Church of England* (1705), in Bridget Hill (ed.), *The First English Feminist* (Aldershot: Gower, 1986), p. 201.
2. Kelley, *Versions of History*, p. 311.
3. Donald R. Kelley, 'History as a Calling: The Case of La Popelinière', in A. Mohlo and J. A. Tedeschi (eds), *Renaissance Studies in Honour of Hans Baron* (Florence: G. C. Sansoni, SPA, 1971), p. 775.
4. *Ibid.*
5. Rackin, *Stages of History*, p. 13.
6. *Ibid.*, p. 10.
7. Sarah Colvin, '*Die Zung ist dieses Schwet*: Classical Tongues and Gendered Curricula in German Schooling to 1908', in Yun Lee Too and

Niall Livingstone (eds), *Power and Pedagogy: Rhetorics of Classical Learning* (Cambridge: Cambridge University Press, 1998), p. 84.
8. Sara Mendelson and Patricia Crawford, *Women in Early Modern England* (Oxford: Clarendon Press, 1998), p. 369.
9. Jodi Mikalachki, *The Legacy of Boadicea: Gender and Nation in Early Modern England* (New York: Routledge, 1998), p. 11.
10. *Ibid.*, p. 12.
11. See, for instance, the representation of these queens in Holinshed's *Chronicles*.
12. Lyndal Roper, *The Holy Household: Women and Morals in Reformation Augsburg* (Oxford: Clarendon Press, 1985), p. 1.
13. *Ibid.*, pp. 1–2.
14. Richard Braverman, *Plots and Counterplots: Sexual Politics in English Literature 1660–1730* (Cambridge: Cambridge University Press, 1993), p. 18.
15. Carole Pateman, *The Sexual Contract* (London: Polity, 1989), pp. 78–82, 102.
16. Constance Jordan, 'Feminism and the Humanists: The Case of Sir Thomas Elyot's Defence of Good Women', in Maureen W. Ferguson, Maureen Quilligan and Nancy J. Vickers (eds), *Rewriting the Renaissance: The Discourse of Sexual Difference in Early Modern Europe* (Chicago: University of Chicago Press, 1986), p. 243.
17. Sheila ffolliott, 'Exemplarity and Gender: Three Lives of Queen Catherine de' Medici', in Thomas F. Mayer and D. R. Woolf (eds), *The Rhetorics of Life Writing in Early Modern Europe: Forms of Biography from Casandra Fedele to Louis XIV* (Ann Arbor: University of Michigan Press, 1995), p. 321.
18. McLeod, *Virtue and Venom*, p. 60.
19. Giovanni Boccaccio, *Concerning Famous Women* (New Brunswick: Rutgers University Press, 1963), p. x.
20. Constance Jordan, 'Boccaccio's Infamous Women: Gender and Civic Virtue in the *De Claris mulieribus*', in Carole Levin and Jeanie Watson (eds), *Ambiguous Realities: Women in the Middle Ages and Renaissance* (Detroit: Wayne State University Press, 1987), p. 25.
21. Boccaccio, *Concerning Famous Women*, p. xxxiv.
22. Jordan, 'Boccaccio's Infamous Women', p. 25.
23. Boccaccio, *Concerning Famous Women*, p. xxxvii.
24. Pamela Joseph Benson, *The Invention of the Renaissance Woman* (Philadelphia: Pennsylvania State University Press, 1992), p. 16.

25. Jordan, 'Boccaccio's Infamous Women', p. 27.
26. *Ibid.*
27. Ian Maclean, *The Renaissance Notion of Woman: A Study in the Fortunes of Scholasticism and Medical Science in European Intellectual Life* (Cambridge: Cambridge University Press, 1980).
28. Benson, *Invention of the Renaissance Woman*, pp. 9–11.
29. Stephen Kolsky, 'Bending the Rules: Marriage in the Biographies of Famous Women', in Trevor Dean and K. J. P Lowe (eds), *Marriage in Italy 1300–1650* (Cambridge: Cambridge University Press, 1998), p. 229.
30. Brita Rang, ' "Learned Wave": Women of Letters and Science from the Renaissance to the Enlightenment', in Tjitske Akkerman and Siep Stuurman (eds), *Perspectives on Feminist Political Thought in European History from the Middle Ages to the Present* (London: Routledge, 1998), pp. 51–2.
31. Jordan, 'Feminism and the Humanists', p. 244.
32. Patrick Collinson, *The Birthpangs of Protestant England: Religious and Cultural Change in the Sixteenth and Seventeenth Centuries* (New York: St Martin's Press, 1988), p. 60.
33. Roper, 'Luther: Sex, Marriage and Motherhood', *History Today*, 33 (1983): 38.
34. Roper, *Holy Household*, pp. 1–5.
35. Braverman, *Plots and Counterplots*, p. 14.
36. Margarita Stocker, *Judith Sexual Warrior: Women and Power in Western Culture* (New Haven: Yale University Press, 1988), p. 70.
37. Constance Jordan, 'Woman's Rule in Sixteenth Century British Political Thought', *Renaissance Quarterly*, 40, 3 (1987): 42–3.
38. Stocker, *Judith Sexual Warrior*, p. 73.
39. Jordan, 'Woman's Rule', p. 428.
40. Amanda Shepherd, *Gender and Authority in Sixteenth Century England* (Keele: Keele University Press, 1994), p. 37.
41. Jordan, 'Feminism and the Humanists', p. 246.
42. Shepherd, *Gender and Authority*, pp. 149–50.
43. Thomas Heywood, *Gunaikeion or, nine bookes of various history concerninge women* (London: T. H. Gent, 1624) and *The Exemplary Lives and Memorable Acts of Nine of The Most Worthy Women of the World* (London: Richard Royston, 1640).
44. Celeste Turner Wright, 'The Elizabethan Female Worthies', *Studies in Philology*, 43 (1946): 641–2.

45. Shepherd, *Gender and Authority*, p. 161.
46. Penny Roberts, 'Martyrologies and Martyrs in the French Reformation: Heretics to Subversives in Troyes', in Diana Wood (ed.), *Martyrs and Martyrology* (Oxford: Blackwell, 1993), p. 227.
47. Shepherd, *Gender and Authority,* p. 14.
48. Elaine V. Beilin, 'Anne Askew's Self-Portrait in the Examinations', in Margaret Patterson Hannay (ed.), *Silent but for the Word: Tudor Women as Patrons, Translators and Writers of Religious Work* (Kent: Kent State University Press, 1985), p. 80.
49. Carole Levin, 'Women in the Book Of Martyrs as Models of Behaviour in Tudor England', *International Journal of Women's Studies,* 4, 2 (1981): 196.
50. David Loades, 'John Foxe and the Editors', in David Loades (ed.), *John Foxe and the English Reformation* (London: Scolar Press, 1997), p. 17.
51. Breisach, *Historiography*, p. 191.
52. Richard Olsen, *The Emergence of the Social Sciences 1642–1792* (New York: Twayne, 1992), p. 10.
53. P. J. Marshall and Glyndwr Williams, *The Great Map of Mankind: British Perceptions of the World in the Age of Enlightenment* (London: Dent, 1982), p. 7.
54. G. P. Gooch, *History and the Historians in the Nineteenth Century* (London: Longman, 1967), p. 5.
55. Breisach, *Historiography*, p. 191.
56. Kelley, *Faces of History*, p. 196.
57. Levine, *Humanism and History*, p. 148.
58. Robert Mayer, *History and the Early English Novel: Matters of Fact from Bacon to Defoe* (Cambridge: Cambridge University Press, 1997), p. 27.
59. Genevieve Lloyd, *The Man of Reason* (London: Methuen, 1984), p. 10.
60. Londa Schiebinger, *The Mind has No Sex? Women in the Origins of Modern Science* (Cambridge, MA: Harvard University Press, 1989), p. 137.
61. Lloyd, *Man of Reason*, p. 11.
62. Woolf, 'Feminine Past?', p. 659.
63. Michael Bentley, 'Approaches to Modernity: Western Historiography since the Enlightenment', in Michael Bentley (ed.), *Companion to Historiography* (Routledge: London, 1997), p. 396.
64. G. J. Whitrow, *Time in History: Views of Time from Prehistory to the Present Day* (Oxford: Oxford University Press, 1986), p. 129.

65. Joyce Appleby, Lynn Hunt and Margaret Jacob, *Telling the Truth about History* (New York: W. W. Norton, 1994), p. 17.
66. *Ibid.*, pp. 15–16.
67. Rosemary Jann, *The Art and Science of Victorian History* (Columbus: Ohio State University Press, 1985), p. xvii.
68. Thomas Goddard and Max Harold Fisch, *The New Science of Giambattista Vico* (1744) (Ithaca: Cornell University Press, 1968), p. 14.
69. Ronald L. Meek, *Social Science and the Ignoble Savage* (Cambridge: Cambridge University Press, 1976), pp. 5–37.
70. Jann, *Art and Science of Victorian History*, p. xvii.
71. David Carrithers, 'The Enlightenment Science of Society', in Christopher Fox, Roy Porter and Robert Wokler (eds), *Inventing Human Science: Eighteenth Century Domains* (Berkeley: University of California Press, 1995), p. 235.
72. Culler, *Victorian Mirror of History*, p. 22.
73. Bentley, 'Approaches to Modernity', p. 401.
74. Jane Rendall, *The Origins of the Scottish Enlightenment* (London: Macmillan, 1978), p. 123.
75. Jann, *Art and Science of History*, p.xii.
76. François Furet, 'From Savage Man to Historical Man: The American Experience in Eighteenth Century French Culture', in *In the Workshop of History* (Chicago: University of Chicago Press, 1984), p. 153.
77. Sylvana Tomaselli, 'The Enlightenment Debate on Women', *History Workshop Journal*, 28 (1985): 114.
78. Antoine-Nicolas de Condorcet, *Sketch for a Historical Picture of the Progress of the Human Mind* (1793) (London: Weidenfeld & Nicolson, 1955), p. 27.
79. Henry Home, Lord Kames, *Sketches of the History of Man*, Vol. 1 (Edinburgh: William Creech, 1813), p. 404.
80. Condorcet, *Sketch for a Historical Picture*, p. 27.
81. Robert Wokler, 'Anthropology and Conjectural History in the Enlightenment', in Christopher Fox, Roy Porter and Robert Wokler (eds), *Inventing Human Science: Eighteenth Century Domains* (Berkeley: University of California Press, 1995), p. 39.
82. G. J. Barker-Benfield, *The Culture of Sensibility: Sex and Society in Eighteenth Century Britain* (Chicago: University of Chicago Press, 1992), p. 2.
83. Rosemary Zagarri, 'Morals, Manners and the Republican Mother', *American Quarterly*, 44 (1992): 194.

84. *Ibid.*, p. 195.
 85. Tomaselli, 'Enlightenment Debate on Women', p. 106.
 86. William Alexander, *The History of Women from Earliest Antiquity, to the Present Time, giving some account of almost every interesting particular concerning that sex among all nations, ancient and modern* (London: W. Strahan, 1792), p. 10.
 87. *Ibid.*, pp. 10–11.
 88. *Ibid.*, p. 11.
 89. Woolf, 'Feminine Past ?', pp. 658–78.
 90. Peter Burke, 'Ranke The Reactionary', in Georg G. Iggers and James M. Powell (eds), *Leopold von Ranke and the Shaping of the Historical Discipline* (Syracuse: Syracuse University Press, 1990), p. 43.
 91. Bentley, 'Approaches to Modernity', p. 405.
 92. *Ibid.*, p. 400.
 93. *Ibid.*
 94. See Culler, *Victorian Mirror of History* and Jann, *Art and Science of Victorian History.*
 95. Culler, *Victorian Mirror of History*, p. 5.
 96. *Ibid.*
 97. Burke, *Renaissance Sense of the Past*, p. 143.
 98. Avrom Fleishman, *The English Historical Novel* (Baltimore: Johns Hopkins University Press, 1972), p. 18.
 99. Cited in Norman Vance, *The Victorians and Ancient Rome* (Oxford: Blackwell, 1997), p. 68.
100. Kelley, 'Tacitus Noster', p. 154.
101. Linda Dowling, *Hellenism and Homosexuality in Victorian Oxford* (Ithaca: Cornell University Press), p. 18.
102. Turner, *Greek Heritage in Victorian Britain,* p. 4.
103. Richard Jenkyns, *The Victorians and Ancient Greece* (Cambridge, MA: Harvard University Press, 1980), p. 15.
104. Turner, *Greek Heritage in Victorian Britain*, pp. 187–263.
105. Dowling, *Hellenism and Homosexuality*, p. 16.
106. Joan B. Landes, *Women and the Public Sphere in the Age of the French Revolution* (Ithaca: Cornell University Press, 1988), pp. 66–89.
107. Geneviève Fraisse, *Reason's Muse: Sexual Difference and the Birth of Democracy* (Chicago: University of Chicago Press, 1994), pp. 14–20.
108. Joshel, 'Female Desire and the Discourse of Empire', p. 384.
109. Edmund Burke, *Reflections on the French Revolution* (London: J. M. Dent & Sons, 1916), p. 73.

110. Linda M.G. Zerilli, *Signifying Woman: Culture and Chaos in Rousseau, Burke and Mill* (Ithaca: Cornell University Press, 1994), pp. 60–95.
111. Crosby, *Ends of History*, p. 2.
112. Caine, *Victorian Feminists*, p. 39.
113. Josine Blok, 'Sexual Asymmetry: A Historiographical Essay', in Josine Blok and Peter Mason (eds), *Sexual Asymmetry: Studies in Ancient Society* (Amsterdam: J. C. Gieben, 1987), pp. 1–57 and Marilyn A. Katz, 'Ideology and "the Status of Women" in Ancient Greece', in Ann-Louise Shapiro (ed.), *Feminists Revision History* (New Brunswick: Rutgers University Press, 1994), pp. 120–45.
114. Katz, 'Ideology and "the Status of Women" in Ancient Greece', pp. 120–45.
115. Cited in *ibid.*, p. 124.
116. Thomas Carlyle, *The French Revolution* Vol. 1 (London: Macmillan, 1906), pp. 248–9.
117. L.M. Findlay, '"Maternity Must Forth": The Poetics and Politics of Gender in Carlyle's *French Revolution*', *Dalhousie Review*, 66 (1986): 134.
118. Jules Michelet, *Les Femmes de la Révolution* (Paris: Calmann-Lévy, 1898), p. 213.
119. Melman, 'Gender, History and Memory', p. 11.
120. Reba N. Soffer, *Discipline and Power: The University History and the Making of an English Elite 1870–1930* (Stanford: Stanford University Press, 1994), p. 33.
121. *Ibid.*, p. 7.
122. Leonard Krieger, *Ranke: The Meaning of History* (Chicago: University of Chicago Press, 1977), pp. 3–4.
123. Doris S. Goldstein, 'History at Oxford and Cambridge: Professionalisation and the Influence of Ranke', in Georg G. Iggers and James M. Powell (eds), *Leopold von Ranke and the Shaping of the Historical Discipline* (Syracuse: Syracuse University Press, 1990), p. 142.
124. Smith, *Gender of History*, pp. 103–29.
125. *Ibid.*
126. *Ibid.*, p. 111.
127. *Ibid.*
128. According to Philippa Levine, the English community of historical scholars in the nineteenth century was almost entirely male. See *The Amateur and the Professional: Antiquarians, Historians and*

Archaeologists in Victorian England 1838–1886 (Cambridge: Cambridge University Press, 1986), pp. 1–6. For discussion of the American experience see Joan Wallach Scott, 'American Women Historians 1884–1984', in *Gender and the Politics of History*, pp. 178–97 and Jacqueline Goggin, 'Challenging Sexual Discrimination in the Historical Profession: Women Historians and the American Historical Association 1890–1940', *American Historical Review*, 97/3 (1992): 769–802.

Chapter 3

1. Kelly-Gadol, 'Did Women Have a Renaissance?', pp. 139–65.
2. Maclean, *Renaissance Notion of Woman*, p. 64.
3. Margaret L. King, 'Book-lined Cells: Women and Humanism in the Early Italian Renaissance', in Patricia H. Labalme (ed.), *Beyond Their Sex* (New York: New York University Press, 1980), p. 75.
4. R. A. Day, 'Muses in the Mud: The *Female Wits* Anthropologically Considered', *Women's Studies*, 7 (1980): 68.
5. Cited in Woolf, 'Feminine Past?', p. 656.
6. Jenny R. Redfern, ' "Christine de Pisan and the *Treasure of the City of Ladies*": A Medieval Rhetorician and her Rhetoric', in Andrea A. Lunsford (ed.), *Reclaiming Rhetorica: Women in the Rhetorical Tradition* (Pittsburgh: University of Pittsburgh, 1995), p. 75.
7. Joan Kelly-Gadol, 'Early Feminist Theory and the *Querelle des Femmes, 1400–1789*', *Signs*, 8, 11 (1982): 4.
8. Alice Kemp-Welch, *Of Six Medieval Women* (London: Macmillan, 1913), p. 46.
9. Christine de Pisan, *The Book of the City of Ladies*, trans. Earl Jeffrey Richards (New York: Persea Books, 1982), p. xxviii.
10. Marina Warner, 'Foreword', in *ibid.*, p. xv.
11. McLeod, *Virtue and Venom*, p. 116.
12. Davis, 'Gender and Genre', p. 154.
13. *Ibid.*, p. 257.
14. Weaver, 'Convent Muses', pp. 134–7.
15. Davis, 'Gender and Genre', p. 161.
16. Charlotte Woodford, 'Women as Historians: The Case of Early Modern German Convents', *German Life and Letters*, 52, 3 (1999): 271–4.

17. Suzanne W. Hull, *Chaste, Silent and Obedient* (San Marino: Huntington Library, 1982), p. 85.
18. Lerner, *Creation of Feminist Consciousness*, p. 251.
19. Isobel Grundy, 'Women's History, Writings by English Nuns', in Isobel Grundy and Susan Wiseman (eds), *Women, Writing, History 1640–1740* (London: Batsford, 1992), p. 126.
20. Mendelson and Crawford, *Women in Early Modern England*, p. 388.
21. As Susan Broomhall has pointed out, because we know so little about who read texts produced by women in the early modern period, the terms 'public' and 'voice' are somewhat problematic. Following Broomhall, I would suggest that the fact of women writing meant that women 'perceived themselves to be making a public display of their opinions and were participating in political debate'. Susan Broomhall, ' "In My Opinion": Charlotte de Minut and Female Political Discussion in Print in Sixteenth Century France', *Sixteenth Century Journal*, 31, 1 (2000): 26.
22. Davis, 'Gender and Genre', p. 161.
23. Cynthia Skenazi, 'Marie Dentière et la Prédication des Femmes', *Renaissance and Reformation*, 21, 1 (1997): 5–18 and Irena Backus, 'Marie Dentière: Un cas de Féminisme Théologique à l'Epoque de la Réforme?', *Bulletin de la Société d'histoire du Protestantisme Français*, 137, 2 (1991): 177–95.
24. Woodford, 'Women as Historians', p. 273.
25. Davis, 'Gender and Genre', p. 161.
26. Randall Martin, *Women Writers in Renaissance England* (London: Longman, 1997), pp. 337–8.
27. Elaine V. Beilin, *Redeeming Eve: Women Writers of the English Renaissance* (New Haven: Princeton University Press, 1987), p. 103.
28. Janet Todd, *The Sign of Angellica: Women, Writing and Fiction 1660–1800* (London: Virago, 1989), p. 43.
29. Mary Beth Rose, 'Gender, Genre and History', in Mary Beth Rose (ed.), *Women in the Middle Ages and the Renaissance: Literary and Historical Perspectives* (Syracuse: University of Syracuse Press, 1986), p. 245.
30. Davis, 'Gender and Genre', p. 163.
31. Catherine Randall, 'Shouting Down Abraham: How Sixteenth Century Huguenot Women Found Their Voice', *Renaissance Quarterly*, 50 (1997): 433.
32. *Ibid.*, pp. 432–3.

33. Margaret Cavendish, *Life of the Thrice Noble, High and Puissant Prince William Cavendish* (London: J.M. Dent & Sons, 1915), p. 11.
34. John Loftis (ed.), *Memoirs of Anne, Lady Halkett and Anne, Lady Fanshawe* (Oxford, Clarendon: 1979), p. 111.
35. Cavendish, *Life of Prince William Cavendish*, p. 11.
36. N.H. Keeble, ' "Obedient Subjects": The Loyal Self in Some Later Seventeenth Century Royalist Women's Memoirs', in Gerald MacLean (ed.), *Culture and Society in the Stuart Restoration* (Cambridge: Cambridge University Press, 1995), p. 205.
37. Lucy Hutchinson, *Memoirs of the Life of Colonel Hutchinson* (London: Longman, 1806).
38. Stevie Davies, *Unbridled Spirits: Women of the English Revolution 1640–1660* (London, Women's Press: 1998), p. 206.
39. N.H. Keeble, ' "The Colonel's Shadow": Lucy Hutchinson, Women's Writing and the Civil War', in Thomas Healy and Jonathan Sawday (eds), *Literature and the English Civil War* (Cambridge: Cambridge University Press, 1990), p. 235.
40. Davies, *Unbridled Spirits*, p. 248.
41. *Ibid.*, p. 257.
42. Rose, 'Gender, Genre, and History', pp. 245–78.
43. Keeble, 'Obedient Subjects', p. 216.
44. See, for instance, the example of Samuel Pepys cited in Sara Heller Mendelson, 'Stuart Women's Diaries and Occasional Memoirs' in Mary Prior (ed.), *Women in English Society 1500–1800* (London: Methuen, 1985), p. 184.
45. Faith Beasley, *Revising Memory: Women's Fiction and Memoirs in Seventeenth-Century France* (New Brunswick: Rutgers University Press, 1990), p. 47.
46. *Ibid.*, p. 46.
47. A number of memoirs exist of middle-class French women involved in the political and religious upheavals of the late seventeenth century. However, they do not really offer anything more than personal anecdotes. See Carolyn Lougee Chappell, ' "The Pains I Took to Save My/His Family": Escape Accounts by a Huguenot Mother and Daughter after the Revocation of the Edict of Nantes', *French Historical Studies*, 22, 1 (1999): 1–39.
48. Devoney Looser, *British Women Writers and the Writing of History 1670–1820* (Baltimore: Johns Hopkins University Press, 2000), p. 45.

49. As Looser points out, while Hutchinson tries to suppress the romantic quality of the text, there remain certain aspects of her tale that resemble romance writing. *Ibid.*
50. *Ibid.*, p. 61.
51. Madeleine de Scudéry, *Artamenes, or the Grand Cyrus: an excellent new romance* (London: Humphrey Mosely, 1653).
52. Anne Marie Louise Henriette d'Orléans, for example, wrote her *Memoirs* while in political exile for her part in the Fronde.
53. Catherine Gallagher, 'Political Crimes and Fictional Alibis: The Case of Delarivier Manley', *Eighteenth Century Studies*, 23, 4 (1990): 502–21.
54. Mary Wortley Montagu reportedly burned her 'History of my own Life', although her 'Account of the Court of King George I' appears to be a fragment of this text. Looser, *British Women and the Writing of History*, p. 65.
55. *Ibid.*, p. 71.
56. *Ibid.*, p. 65.
57. Beasley, *Revising Memory*, p. 245.
58. Keeble, 'The Colonel's Shadow', p. 236.
59. Marilyn L. Williamson, *Raising their Voices: British Women Writers 1650–1750* (Detroit: Wayne State University Press, 1990), p. 55. See also Mary Ann McGuire, 'Margaret Cavendish, Duchess of Newcastle, On the Nature and Status of Women', *International Journal of Women's Studies*, 1, 1 (1978): 193–206.
60. Margaret Cavendish, *A True Relation of My Birth, Breeding and Life* in Elspeth Graham et al. (eds), *Her Own Life: Autobiographical Writings by Seventeenth Century English Women* (London: Routledge, 1989), p. 89.
61. *Ibid.*, p. 99.
62. Joan Thirsk, 'Women, Local and Family Historians', in David Hey (ed.), *The Oxford Companion to Family and Local History* (Oxford: Oxford University Press, 1996), p. 498.
63. Woolf, 'Feminine Past?', p. 654.
64. Richard T. Spence, *Lady Anne Clifford: Duchess of Pembroke, Dorset and Montgomery 1590–1676* (Thrupp: Sutton, 1997), p. 160.
65. Katharine Hodgkin, 'The Diary of Lady Anne Clifford: A Study of Class and Gender in the Seventeenth Century', *History Workshop Journal*, 19 (1985): 155.
66. Levine, *Amateur and the Professional*, pp. 1–6.
67. Thirsk, 'Women, Local and Family Historians', p. 499.

68. Nina Baym, *American Women Writers and the Work of History 1790–1860* (New Brunswick: Rutgers University Press, 1995), p. 93.
69. Jennifer Scanlon and Shaaron Cosner, *American Women Historians: A Biographical Dictionary* (Westport, CT: Greenwood, 1996), p. 148.
70. Sklar, 'American Female Historians', p. 173.
71. *Ibid.*, 171–6.
72. Barker-Benfield, *Culture of Sensibility*, p. 2.
73. Macaulay has often been considered the first woman to write political history in Great Britain. Recently this status has been challenged as historians have come to some consensus that Elizabeth Cary, Lady Fawkland (1585–1639), was the author of *The History of the Life, Reign and Death of Edward II* (1627). See Martin, *Women Writers in Renaissance England*, pp. 160–3.
74. Bridget Hill, *Republican Virago: The Life and Times of Catherine Macaulay* (Oxford: Clarendon Press, 1997), p. 26.
75. John Kenyon, *The History Men* (London: Weidenfeld & Nicolson, 1993), p. 55.
76. Hill, *Republican Virago*, p. 24.
77. Sklar, 'American Female Historians', 173.
78. Scalon and Cosner, *American Women Historians*, p. 236.
79. Maud Macdonald Hutchinson, 'Mercy Warren 1728–1814', *William and Mary Quarterly*, 10 (1953): 397–8.
80. Theresa Freda Nicolay, *Gender Roles, Literary Authority and Three American Women Writers* (New York: Peter Lang, 1995), p. 34.
81. *Ibid.*
82. Lester H. Cohen, 'Explaining the Revolution: Ideology and Ethics in Mercy Otis Warren's Historical Theory', *William & Mary Quarterly*, 37 (1980): 202.
83. Susan Phinney Conrad, *Perish the Thought: Intellectual Women in Romantic America 1830–60* (New York: Oxford University Press, 1976), p. 95.
84. *Ibid.*
85. Smith, *Gender of History*, pp. 39–41.
86. Catherine Macaulay, *Letters on Education, with Observations on Religious and Metaphysical Subject* (New York: Garland Publishing, 1974), p. 212.
87. Hill, *Republican Virago*, pp. 130–1.
88. *Ibid.*, p. 132.
89. *Ibid.*

90. Macaulay, *Letters on Education*, p. 212.
91. Alice Browne, *The Eighteenth Century Feminist Mind* (Detroit: Wayne State University Press, 1987), p. 5.
92. Bridget Hill, 'The Links between Mary Wollstonecraft and Catherine Macaulay: New Evidence', *Women's History Review*, 4, 2 (1995): 177–93.
93. Barbara Caine, *English Feminism 1780–1980* (Oxford: Oxford University Press, 1997), p. 25.
94. Mary Wollstonecraft, *The Vindication of the Rights of Woman (1792)* (London: Penguin, 1985), p. 206.
95. *Ibid.*, p. 317.
96. Caine, *English Feminism 1780–1980*, p. 28.
97. Wollstonecraft, *Vindication*, p. 313.
98. *Ibid.*, p. 295.
99. *Ibid.*, p. 119.

Chapter 4

1. Anne K. Mellor, *Romanticism and Gender* (New York: Routledge, 1993).
2. Landes, *Women and the Public Sphere*, p. 22.
3. *Ibid.*
4. Carolyn C. Lougee, *Les Paradis des Femmes: Women, Salons and Social Stratification in Seventeenth-Century France* (Princeton: Princeton University Press, 1976), p. 5.
5. *Ibid.*, p. 6.
6. Dena Goodman, 'Enlightenment Salons: The Convergence of Female and Philosophic Ambitions', *Eighteenth Century Studies*, 2, 2/3 (1989): 331–2.
7. *Ibid.*
8. Landes, *Woman and the Public Sphere*, p. 23.
9. Smith, 'Contribution of Women to Modern Historiography', p. 711.
10. *Ibid.*, 711.
11. During her lifetime Marguerite de Lussan's histories included *Anecdotes de la cour de Philippe Auguste* (1733); *Anecdotes de la cour de François I* (1748); *Annales galantes de la cour de Henri II* (1749); and *La Révolution du Royaume de Naples dans les annèes 1647–1648* (1757). Marie Geneviève Charlotte d'Arlus published *Vie de Marie de*

Médicis (1774); *Vie du Cardinal d'Ossat* (1771) and *Histoire de François II, roi de France* (1783). See Davis, 'Gender and Genre', p. 179.
12. Pauline de Lézardière published the four-volume *Théorie des loix politiques de la monarchie françoise in 1792*. See Davis, 'Gender and Genre', p. 179.
13. Smith, *Gender of History*, p. 259.
14. According to Carla Hesse, the French journalist, Jacques Mallet du Pan created this new word *historienne* to describe Louise de Keralio (Roberts). See Carla Hesse, 'Revolutionary Histories: The Literary Politics of Louise de Kéralio', in Barbara B. Diefendorf and Carla Hesse (eds), *Culture and Identity in Early Modern Europe 1500–1800* (Ann Arbor: University of Michigan Press, 1993), p. 237.
15. Beasley, *Revising History,* pp. 53–4. See also Marguerite Buffet (d. 1680), *L'Eloge des illustres savantes, tantes anciennes que modernes* (n.p., 1662).
16. Joan DeJean, 'Classical Reeducation: Decanonizing the Feminine', *Yale French Studies*, 75 (1988): 29–30.
17. Hesse, 'Revolutionary Histories', p. 241.
18. *Ibid.*, p. 245.
19. *Ibid.*, pp. 246–7.
20. Lynn Hunt, *The Family Romance of the French Revolution* (Berkeley: University of California Press, 1992), pp. 98–9, 120, 122, 142.
21. *Ibid.*, p. 93.
22. *Ibid.*, p. 130.
23. Sarah Maza, 'The Diamond Necklace Affair Revisited (1785–1786): The Case of the Missing Queen' in Lynn Hunt (ed.), *Eroticism and the Body Politic* (Baltimore: Johns Hopkins University Press, 1991), p. 82.
24. Hesse, 'Revolutionary Histories', p. 244.
25. Cited in Hunt, *Family Romance of the French Revolution*, p. 110.
26. *Ibid.*, p. 253.
27. *Ibid.*
28. Cited in Leigh Whaley, 'Revolutionary Networking 1789–1791', *Consortium on Revolutionary Europe* (1996), p. 46.
29. Carla Hesse, 'Revolutionary Histories', p. 245.
30. Hunt, *Family Romance of the French Revolution*, p. 121.
31. Cited in Darline Levy, Harriet Applewhite and Mary Johnson (eds), *Women in Revolutionary Paris 1789–1795* (Urbana: University of Illinois Press, 1979), pp. 167–8.

32. Madelyn Gutwirth, *The Twilight of the Goddesses: Women and Representation in the French Revolutionary Era* (New Brunswick: Rutgers University Press, 1992), p. 310.
33. *Ibid.*
34. Marilyn Butler, *Burke, Paine, Godwin and the Revolution Controversy* (Cambridge: Cambridge University Press, 1984), p. 80. *Lettres de cachet* were used by kings/fathers/husbands to order those subject to their authority under house arrest.
35. Janet Todd, *Mary Wollstonecraft: A Revolutionary Life* (London: Weidenfeld & Nicolson, 2000), pp. 212–13.
36. *Ibid.*, pp. 212–14.
37. Gary Kelly, *Women, Writing and Revolution 1790–1827* (Oxford: Clarendon Press, 1993), pp. 3–29.
38. *Ibid.*, pp. 30–79.
39. *Ibid.*, p. 39.
40. Richard C. Sha, 'Expanding the Limits of Feminine Writing: The Prose Sketches of Sydney Owenson (Lady Morgan) and Helen Maria Williams', in Paula R. Feldman and Theresa M. Kelley (eds), *Romantic Women Writers: Voices and Countervoices* (Hanover: University Press of New England, 1995), p. 197.
41. Ruth Perry, *Women, Letters and the Novel* (New York: AMS Press, 1980), p. 17.
42. Catherine Sawbridge Macaulay, *The History of England from the Revolution to the Present Time in a Series of Letters to a Friend* (Bath: R. Crutwell, 1778).
43. Looser, *British Women Writers and the Writing of History*, pp. 141–51.
44. *Ibid.* and Margaret Kirkham, *Jane Austen, Feminism and Fiction* (Sussex: Harvester, 1983), p. 12.
45. Helen Maria Williams, *Letters Written in France 1790* (Oxford, Woodstock Books, 1989), p. iv and Gary Kelly, 'Women Novelists and the French Revolution Debate: Novelising the Revolution/Revolutionising the Novel', *Eighteenth Century Fiction*, 6, 4 (1994): 378.
46. Mellor, *Romanticism and Gender*, p. 73.
47. *Ibid.*
48. Matthew Bray, 'Helen Maria Williams and Edmund Burke: Radical Critique and Complicity', *Eighteenth Century Life*, 16 (1992): 1–24.
49. *Ibid.*, p. 1.
50. *Ibid.*, pp. 5–20.

51. Williams, *Letters Written in France 1790*, p. 38.
52. Kelly, *Women, Writing and Revolution*, p. 36.
53. Steven Blakemore, 'Revolution and the French Disease: Laetitia Matilda Hawkin's Letters to Helen Maria Williams', *Studies in English Literature*, 36 (1996): 676. James Boswell was reported to have removed the word 'amiable' from his description of Williams in his biography of Johnson following the execution of Louis XVI in 1792.
54. Cited in *ibid.*, p. 671.
55. *Ibid.*, p. 674.
56. *Ibid.*, p. 675.
57. Mellor, *Romanticism and Gender*, p. 40.
58. Alan Ruston, 'Two Unitarians in France during the Revolution', *Transactions of the Unitarian Historical Society*, 17, 1 (1979): 20.
59. *Ibid.*
60. Anne K. Mellor, 'English Women Writers and the French Revolution', in Sara E. Maza and Leslie W. Rabine (eds), *Rebel Daughters: Women and the French Revolution* (New York: Oxford University Press, 1992), p. 263.
61. *Ibid.*
62. Gary Kelly, *Revolutionary Feminism: The Mind and Career of Mary Wollstonecraft* (London: Macmillan, 1992), p. 141.
63. *Ibid.*, p. 149.
64. Todd, *Mary Wollstonecraft*, p. 236.
65. Barbara Caine, 'Victorian Feminism and the Ghost of Mary Wollstonecraft', *Women's Writing*, 4, 2 (1997): 266.
66. Harriet Devine Jump, ' "The Cool Eye of Observation": Mary Wollstonecraft and the French Revolution', in Kelvin Everest (ed.), *Revolution in Writing: British Literary Responses to the French Revolution* (Milton Keynes: Open University Press, 1991), pp. 104–5.
67. Kelly, *Revolutionary Feminism*, p. 153.
68. *Ibid.*
69. Kelly, *Revolutionary Feminism*, p. 152.
70. Mary Wollstonecraft, *A Moral and Historical View of the Origin and Progress of the French Revolution* (New York: Scholars' Facsimiles & Reprints, 1975), p. 6.
71. Jump, 'The Cool Eye of Observation', p. 105.
72. For further discussion of Wollstonecraft's debt to philosophical history see Jane Rendall, ' "The Grand Causes Which Combine to

Carry Mankind Forward": Wollstonecraft, History and Revolution', *Women's Writing*, 4, 2 (1997): 155–72.
73. Mary Wollstonecraft, *The Vindication of the Rights of Man* (1790) (Cambridge: Cambridge University Press, 1995), p. 30.
74. Hill, 'Links between Mary Wollstonecraft and Catherine Macaulay', p. 185.
75. Ashley Tauchert, 'Maternity, Castration and Mary Wollstonecraft's *Historical and Moral View of the French Revolution*', *Women's Writing*, 4, 2 (1997): 175. Tauchert also argues that Wollstonecraft developed a genderless narrative voice in *Historical and Moral View* as a response to her pregnancy.
76. *Ibid.*, p. 175.
77. Todd, *Mary Wollstonecraft*, p. 220.
78. Jump, 'The Cool Eye of Observation', pp. 101–3 and Rendall, 'The Grand Causes', p. 161.
79. Rendall, 'Grand Causes', pp. 103, 161.
80. Cited in Jon Klancher, 'Godwin and the Genre Reformers: On Necessity and Contingency in Romantic Narrative Theory', in Tilottama Rajan and Julia M. Wright (eds), *Romanticism, History and the Possibilities of Genre* (Cambridge: Cambridge University Press, 1998), pp. 21–22.
81. *Ibid.*, p. 21.
82. Tilottama Rajan and Julia M. Wright (eds), 'Introduction', in *Romanticism, History and the Possibilities of Genre* (Cambridge: Cambridge University Press, 1998), pp. 10–11.
83. Vivien Jones, 'Women Writing Revolution: Narratives of History and Sexuality in Wollstonecraft and Williams', in Stephen Copley and John Whale (eds), *Beyond Romanticism: New Approaches to Texts and Contexts 1780–1832* (London: Routledge, 1992), p. 179.
84. Pam Hirsch, 'Mary Wollstonecraft: A Problematic Legacy' in Clarissa Campbell Orr (ed.), *Wollstonecraft's Daughters* (Manchester: University of Manchester Press, 1996), p. 51.
85. Todd, *Sign of Angellica*, p. 215.
86. Charlotte Smith, *Desmond*, ed. Antje Blank and Janet Todd (London: Pickering & Chatto, 1997), p. xx.
87. Cited in Marilyn Butler, *Jane Austen and the War of Ideas* (Oxford: Clarendon, 1975), p. 15.
88. Kelly, 'Women Novelists and the French Revolution Debate', pp. 369–88.

89. *Ibid.*, p. 382.
90. Avril Goldberger, 'Introduction', in Germaine de Staël, *Corinne, or Italy* (New Brunswick: Rutgers University Press, 1987), p. xx.
91. Eve Sourian, 'Germaine de Staël and the Position of Women in France, England and Germany', in Avriel H. Goldberger (ed.), *Woman as Mediatrix: Essays on Nineteenth Century European Women Writers* (New York: Greenwood Press, 1987), p. 32.
92. Paula Blanchard, '*Corinne* and the "Yankee Corinna": Madame de Staël and Margaret Fuller', in Avriel H. Goldberger (ed.), *Woman as Mediatrix: Essays on Nineteenth Century European Women Writers* (New York: Greenwood Press, 1987), pp. 39–46.
93. Madelyn Gutwirth, *Madame de Staël, Novelist: The Emergence of the Artist as Woman* (Urbana: University of Illinois Press, 1978), p. 204.
94. Beasley, *Revising Memory*, pp. 31–41.
95. *Ibid.*, p. 5.
96. Doris Y. Kadish, 'Narrating the French Revolution: The Example of *Corinne*', in Madelyn Gutwirth, Averiel Goldberger and Karyna Szmurlo (eds), *Germaine de Staël: Crossing the Borders* (New Brunswick: Rutgers University Press, 1991), p. 113.
97. *Ibid.*, p. 115.
98. *Ibid.*
99. Kelly, *Revolutionary Feminism*, p. 154.
100. Gutwirth, *Madame de Staël, Novelist*, p. 154.
101. Kelly, *Women, Writing and Revolution*, p. 229.
102. Charlotte Hogsett, 'Generative Factors in the Considerations on the French Revolution,' in Madelyn Gutwirth, Averiel Goldberger and Karyna Szmurlo (eds), *Germaine de Staël: Crossing the Borders* (New Brunswick: Rutgers University Press, 1991), p. 40.
103. John Clairborne Isbell, *The Birth of European Romanticism: Truth and Propaganda in de Staël's De l'Allemagne* (Cambridge: Cambridge University Press, 1994), p. 12.
104. *Ibid.*, p. 5.
105. *Blackwood's Magazine*, 4 December 1818, p. 278.
106. Isbell, *Birth of European Romanticism*, p. 3.
107. Although de Staël was married to a Swedish aristocrat she engaged in affairs with a number of prominent revolutionary figures, including the Comte de Carbonne and Benjamin Constant. Bonnie G. Smith has argued that de Staël's unconventional erotic life has negatively

affected critical analysis of her work into the late twentieth century. See *Gender of History*, p. 16.
108. Roberta J. Forsberg, *Madame de Staël and the English* (New York: Astra Books, 1967), p. 120.
109. Emma Gertrude Jaeck, *Madame de Staël and the Spread of German Literature* (New York: Oxford University Press, 1915), p. 141.
110. Kurt Mueller-Vollmer, 'Staël's *Germany* and the Beginnings of an American National Literature', in Madelyn Gutwirth, Averiel Goldberger and Karyna Szmurlo (eds), *Germaine de Staël: Crossing the Borders* (New Brunswick: Rutgers University Press, 1991), p. 147.
111. *Ibid.*, p. 152.
112. Blanchard, '*Corinne* and the "Yankee Corinna" ', p. 39.
113. Phylllis Stock-Morton, 'Daniel Stern, Historian', *History of European Ideas*, 8, 4/5 (1987): 491.
114. Phylllis Stock-Morton, *The Life of Marie d'Agoult, Alias Daniel Stern* (Baltimore: Johns Hopkins University Press, 2000), p. 127.
115. *Zur Geschichte der deutschen demokratischen Legion aus Paris* (Grunberg, 1849). Phylllis Stock-Morton reports that after a period of mutual suspicion Emma and Marie became friends. *Ibid.*, pp. 96–7. A number of German women wrote histories of the revolutions of 1848. See Lia Secci, 'German Women Writers and the Revolution of 1848', in John C. Fout (ed.), *German Women in the Nineteenth Century: A Social History* (New York: Holmes & Meier, 1984), pp. 151–71.
116. Secci, 'German Women Writers', and Beth Archer Brombert, *Cristina: Portraits of a Princess* (London: Hamish Hamilton, 1978), and Whitney Walton, 'Writing the 1848 Revolution: Politics, Gender and Feminism in the Works of French Women of Letters', *French Historical Studies*, 18, 4 (1994): 1001–24.
117. Whitney Walton, *Eve's Proud Descendants: Four Women Writers and Republican Politics in Nineteenth-Century France* (Stanford: Stanford University Press, 2000), p. 128.
118. Stock-Morton, *Life of Marie d'Agoult*, p. 130 and Walton, *Eve's Proud Descendants*, p. 177.
119. Walton, *Eve's Proud Descendants*, p. 177.
120. *Ibid.*, p. 93.
121. Claire Marrone, 'Cristina Trivulzio Belgiojoso's Western Feminism: The Poetics of a Nineteenth-Century Nomad', *Italian Quarterly*, 34 (1997): 22.

122. Cited in Perry Miller, *Margaret Fuller: American Romantic: A Selection from Her Writings and Correspondence* (New York: Doubleday, 1963), p. xxi.
123. Blanchard, '*Corinne* and the "Yankee Corinna"', p. 39.
124. Larry J. Reynolds and Susan Belasco (eds), *These Sad but Glorious Days: Dispatches from Europe* (New Haven: Yale University Press, 1991), p. 8.
125. Madelyn Gutwirth, *Madame de Staël*, p. 222.
126. Harriet Martineau, *The History of England during the Thirty Years Peace* (London: Charles Knight, 1849).

Chapter 5

1. Rohan Maitzen, '"This Feminine Preserve": Historical Biographies by Victorian Women', *Victorian Studies*, 38, 3 (1995): 371–2.
2. Cited in *Ibid.*, p. 372.
3. Natalie Zemon Davis, '"Women's History" in Transition: The European Case', *Feminist Studies*, 3, 3/4 (1975): 83–103.
4. Donna Dickenson, *Margaret Fuller: A Woman's Life* (New York: St Martin's Press, 1993), p. xvi.
5. Crosby, *Ends of History* and Melman, 'Gender, History and Memory'.
6. Melman, 'Gender, History and Memory', p. 11.
7. Joseph W. Reed, *English Biography in the Early Nineteenth Century 1810–1838* (New Haven: Yale University Press, 1966), p. 15.
8. Alison Booth, 'The Lessons of the Medusa: Anna Jameson and Collective Biographies of Women', *Victorian Studies*, 42, 2 (1999): 260.
9. Beasley, *Revising Memory*, p. 53.
10. Anthony Fletcher, *Gender, Sex and Subordination in England 1500–1800* (New Haven: Yale University Press, 1995), pp. 384.
11. *Ibid.*, pp. 384–8.
12. Mitzi Myers, 'Ruin or Reform: A Revolution in Female Manners', *Studies in Eighteenth Century Culture*, 11 (1982): 200.
13. Elizabeth Kowaleski-Wallace, *Their Fathers' Daughters: Hannah More, Maria Edgeworth, and Patriarchal Complicity* (New York: Oxford University Press, 1991), p. 11.
14. Nancy Armstrong, *Fiction: A Political History of the Novel* (New York: Oxford University Press, 1987), p. 60.

15. Barbara Miller Solomon, *In The Company of Educated Women: A History of Women and Higher Education in America* (New Haven: Yale University Press, 1985), p. 16.
16. Hannah More, *Coelebs in Search of a Wife* (Bristol: Thoemmes Press, 1995), p. 71.
17. Hannah More, *Essays on Various Subjects designed for Young Ladies* (London: J. Wilkie: n.d.), p. iii.
18. Veronica Webb Leahy, 'Women Who Have Dared but Deterred Other Women: Hannah More and Beverly LaHaye', in Ann C. Hall (ed.), *Delights, Desires and Dilemmas: Essays on Women in the Media* (Westport, CT: Praeger, 1998), pp. 137–52.
19. *Ibid.*, p. i.
20. Woolf, 'Feminine Past?', p. 669.
21. Hannah More, *Hints towards forming the character of a young princess* (London: T. Cadell & Davies, 1805), p. 191.
22. *Ibid.*, p. 193.
23. Alison Plowden, *Caroline & Charlotte, The Regent's Wife and Daughter 1795–1821* (London: Sidgwick & Plowden, 1989), p. 104.
24. *Ibid.*, p. 104.
25. Katherine M. Rogers, 'The Contribution of Mary Hays', *Prose Studies*, 10, 2 (1987): 132.
26. Mary Hays, *Letters and Essays, Moral and Miscellaneous* (London: T. Knott, 1793), p. iii.
27. Barbara Caine, *English Feminism 1780–1980*, p. 47.
28. Kelly, *Women, Writing and Revolution*, p. 109.
29. *Ibid.*, p. 110.
30. Elizabeth Hamilton, *Memoirs of Agrippina, Wife of Germanicus* (London: G. & J. Robinson, 1804), pp. 18–19.
31. Jane Rendall, 'Writing History for British Women: Elizabeth Hamilton and the Memoirs of Agrippina', in Clarissa Campbell Orr (ed.), *Wollstonecraft's Daughters: Womanhood in England and France 1780–1920* (Manchester: Manchester University Press, 1996), p. 84.
32. *Ibid.*, p. iv.
33. *Ibid.*, p. v.
34. Kelly, *Women, Writing and Revolution*, pp. 237–47.
35. Mary Hays, *Female Biography, or memoirs of illustrious and Celebrated Women of All Ages and Countries*, Vol. 1 (R. Phillips: London, 1803), p. 4.

36. It is commonly noted that the publication of Lytton Strachey's canonical *Eminent Victorians* revolutionised the genre of biography, as he moved out of the realm of hagiography by showing his subjects to be flawed, lusty and susceptible to flattery. I would however argue that this 'new biography' began with Hays in 1802.
37. Jerry C. Beasley, 'Politics and Moral Idealism: The Achievement of Some Early Women Novelists', in Mary Anne Schofield and Cecilia Macheski (eds), *Fetter'd or Free?: British Women Novelists 1670–1815* (Athens, OH: Ohio University Press, 1986), p. 217.
38. Nancy Armstrong, *Desire and Domestic Fiction: A Political History of the Novel* (New York: Oxford University Press, 1987), p. 4.
39. *Ibid.*, p. 5.
40. George L. Mosse, *Nationalism and Sexuality: Respectability and Abnormal Sexuality in Modern Europe* (New York: Howard Fertig, 1985), p. 8.
41. Robert A. Colby, ' "Rational Amusement": Fiction vs. Useful Knowledge in the Nineteenth Century', in James R. Kincaid and Albert J. Kuhn (eds), *Victorian Literature and Society* (Ohio: Ohio State University Press, 1984), p. 51.
42. Miriam Elizabeth Burstein, 'The Reduced Pretensions of the Historic Muse', p. 220.
43. Mrs John Sandford, *Lives of English Female Worthies* (London: Longman, 1833), p. x.
44. Martha Vicinus, 'Models for Public Life: Biographies of "Noble Women" for Girls' in Claudia Nelson and Lynne Vallone (eds), *The Girl's Own: Cultural Histories of the Anglo-American Girl 1830–1915* (Athens, GA: University of Georgia Press, 1994), p. 55.
45. *Ibid.*
46. Lucy Aitkin, 'Memoir of Miss Benger', in Elizabeth Ogilvy Benger, *Anne Boleyn: Queen of Henry VIII* (London: Longman, 1827), p. ix.
47. Deirdre David, *Intellectual Women and Victorian Patriarchy* (London: Macmillan, 1987), pp. vii–viii.
48. Hannah Adams, *A Memoir of Hannah Adams* (Boston: Gray & Bowen, 1832), pp. 34–35.
49. Miriam Elizabeth Burstein, ' "The Reduced Pretensions of the Historic Muse": Agnes Strickland and the Commerce of Women's History', *Journal of Narrative Technique*, 28 (1998): 220.
50. *Ibid.*, 229.

51. Levine, *Amateur and the Professional*, pp. 24–7.
52. Rosemary Mitchell, *Picturing the Past: English History in Text and Image 1830–1870* (Oxford: Clarendon Press, 2000), p. 150.
53. M. A. Stodart, *Female writers' thoughts on their proper sphere, and on their powers of usefulness* (London: Thames Ditton, 1842), p. 128.
54. *Ibid.*, pp. 128–9.
55. Maitzen, 'This Feminine Preserve', p. 374.
56. Anonymous, *Select Female Biography, or Eminent British Ladies* (London: John & Arthur Arch, 1821), p. vii.
57. Adams, *Memoir*, p. iv.
58. Burstein, 'From Good Looks to Good Thoughts', p. 50.
59. Hamilton, *Memoirs of Agrippina*, p. xiii.
60. Una Pope Hennessy, *Agnes Strickland: Biographer of the Queens of England* (London: Chatto & Windus, 1940), p. 67.
61. Cited in Mary Delorme, '"Facts, Not opinions": Agnes Strickland', *History Today*, 38 (1988): 47.
62. Mitchell, 'Busy Daughters of Clio', p. 115.
63. Alison Booth, 'Illustrious Company: Victoria among other Women in Anglo-American Role Model Anthologies', in Margaret Homans and Adrienne Munich (eds), *Remaking Queen Victoria* (Cambridge: Cambridge University Press, 1997), pp. 72–7.
64. Mitchell, 'Busy Daughters of Clio', pp. 123–4.
65. In Britain one of the first 'patriotic' or nationalist collections was published in the revolutionary year of 1848. See Elizabeth Starling's *Noble Deeds of Woman* (London: Bohn, 1848). An American supplement appeared several years later. See Jesse Clement's *Noble Deeds of American Women* (Buffalo: Derby, 1851).
66. Jeanne Moskal, 'Gender, Nationality, and Textual Authority in Lady Morgan's Travel Books', in Paula R. Feldman and Theresa M. Kelley (eds), *Romantic Women Writers: Voices and Countervoices* (Hanover: University of New England Press, 1995), p. 178.
67. Katie Trumpener, *Bardic Nationalism: The Romantic Novel and the British Empire* (Princeton: Princeton University Press, 1997), p. 131.
68. Ina Ferris, 'Narrating Cultural Encounter: Lady Morgan and the Irish National Tale', *Nineteenth Century Literature*, 51, 3 (1996): 287–303.
69. Cited in Sha, 'Expanding the Limits of Feminine Writing', p. 200.
70. Smith, 'Contribution of Women to Modern Historiography', p. 722.
71. Baym, *American Women Writers and the Work of History*, p. 214.

72. See, for instance, Conrad, *Perish the Thought*, pp. 93–133; and Scott E. Caspar, 'An Uneasy Marriage of Sentiment and Scholarship: Elizabeth F. Ellet and the Domestic Origins of American History', *Journal of Women's History*, 4 (1992): 10–35; Nina Baym, 'Onward Christian Women: Sarah J. Hale's History of the World', *New England Quarterly*, 63, 2 (1990): 249–70; Nicole Tonkovich, *Domesticity with a Difference: The Nonfiction of Catherine Beecher, Sarah J. Hale, Fanny Fern and Margaret Fuller* (Jackson: University of Mississippi Press, 1997).
73. Elizabeth Ellet, *Women of the American Revolution*, Vol. 1 (New York: Charles Scribner, 1852), p. 23.
74. Caspar, 'Uneasy Marriage of Sentiment and Scholarship', pp. 17–18.
75. Fraisse, *Reason's Muse*, p. 48.

Chapter 6

1. Mary R. Beard, *On Understanding Women* (London: Longman, 1931), p. 31.
2. Numerous articles on this subject were published in Carroll (ed.), *Liberating Women's History*. See those by Gerda Lerner, Sheila Ryan Johansson, Ann D. Gordon, Mari Jo Buhle, Nancy Schrom Dye and Berenice A. Carroll.
3. For discussion of the limitations of Beard's analysis see Carol Ellen DuBois, 'Making Women's History: Activist Historians of Women's Rights 1880–1940', *Radical History Review*, 49 (1991): 61–84 and Bonnie G. Smith, 'Seeing Mary Beard', *Feminist Studies*, 10, 3 (1984): 399–416.
4. Donna Dickenson, 'Introduction', in Margaret Fuller, *Woman in the Nineteenth Century and Other Writings* (Oxford: Oxford University Press: 1994), p. viii.
5. *Ibid.*, p. 27.
6. Maitzen, 'This Feminine Preserve', p. 374.
7. Fuller, *Woman in the Nineteenth Century*, p. 27.
8. *Ibid.*, p. ix.
9. Eleanor Flexnor, *A Century of Struggle: The Women's Rights Movement in the United States* (Cambridge, MA: Belknap Press, 1986), p. 45.
10. Jane Rendall, *The Origins of Modern Feminism: Women in Britain, France and the United States* (London: Macmillan, 1985), p. 227.

11. Two volumes of this text were published in 1881, volumes 3 and 4 between 1886 and 1902 and volumes 5 and 6 in 1922.
12. Dubois, 'Making Women's History', p. 63.
13. 'Declaration of Sentiments', in Judith Papachristou (ed.), *Women Together* (New York: Alfred A. Knopf, 1976), p. 27.
14. William Blackstone, *Commentaries on the Laws of England*, Vol. One (1783) (New York: Garland, 1978), p. 442.
15. Caine, *English Feminism 1780–1980*, pp. 66–70.
16. *Ibid.*, p. 69.
17. Lynne E. Withey, 'Catherine Macaulay and the Use of History: Ancient Rights, Perfectionism and Propaganda', *Journal of British Studies*, 16, 1 (1976): 59–83.
18. Sandra Stanley Holton, 'The Making of Suffrage History', in June Purvis and Sandra Stanley Holton (eds), *Votes for Women* (London: Routledge, 1999), p. 14.
19. Sandra Stanley Holton, 'British Freewomen: National Identity, Constitutionalism and Languages of Race in Early Suffrage Histories', in Eileen Janes Yeo (ed.), *Radical Feminity: Women's Self-Representation in the Public Sphere* (Manchester: Manchester University Press, 1999), p. 150.
20. *Ibid.*, p. 14.
21. Holton 'Making of Suffrage History', p. 19.
22. Florence Griswold Buckstaff, 'Married Women's Property Rights in Anglo-Saxon and Anglo-Norman Law', *Annals of the American Academy* (1886). For discussion of such texts see Susan Mosher Stuard, 'A New Dimension? North American Scholars Contribute their Perspective', in *Women in Medieval History and Historiography* (Philadelphia: University of Pennsylvania Press, 1986), pp. 85–7.
23. Emmeline Pankhurst, *My Own Story* (New York: Hearst International Library, 1914); E. Sylvia Pankhurst, *The Suffragette Movement: An Intimate Account of Persons and Ideas* (London: Longman, 1931); Christabel Pankhurst, *Unshackled: The Story of How We Won the Vote* (London: Hutchinson, 1959).
24. Lerner, *Creation of Feminist Consciousness*, p. 268.
25. See for instance Catherine H. Birney, *The Grimke Sisters: The First American Advocates of Abolition* (Boston: Lee & Shephard, 1885); G.W. and A.L. Johnson, *Josephine Butler: An Autobiographical Memoir* (London, J.W. Arrowsmith, 1909); Elizabeth Raikes, *Dorothea Beale of Cheltenham* (London: Archibald & Constable, 1908); Ray

Strachey, *Frances Willard: Her Life and Work* (London: T.F. Unwin, 1912). Collections such as *Noble Works by Noble Women* (London: S.W. Patridge, 1900) began to routinely include figures such as Millicent Garrett Fawcett alongside women engaged in more acceptably feminine works, such as Angela Burdett-Coutts, Elizabeth Fry and Octavia Hill.
26. Ray Strachey, *The Cause: A Short History of the Women's Movements in Great Britain* (Washington, DC: Kennikat Press, 1928), pp. 418–19.
27. See, for instance, Ray Strachey, *Millicent Garrett Fawcett* (London: John Murray, 1931); Alma Lutz, *Created Equal: A Biography of Elizabeth Cady Stanton* (New York: J. Day, 1940).
28. Kathryn Dodd, 'Cultural Politics and Women's Historical Writing: The Case of Ray Strachey's *The Cause*', *Women's Studies International Forum*, 13, 2 (1990): 127–37.
29. Laura E. Nym Mayhall, 'Creating the "Suffragette Spirit": British Feminism and the Historical Imagination', *Women's History Review*, 4, 3 (1995): 329.
30. As well as the autobiographical works produced by the Pankhursts a number of suffrage memoirs were produced between 1914 and the 1970s. For discussion of these texts see ibid., pp. 319–44.
31. Kathryn Dodd, *A Sylvia Pankhurst Reader* (Manchester: Manchester University Press, 1993), p. 18.
32. Anna Davin, 'Redressing the Balance or Transforming the Art? The British Experience', in S. Jay Kleinberg (ed.), *Retrieving Women's history: Changing Perceptions of the Role of Women in Politics and Society* (Oxford: Berg, 1988), p. 61.
33. Barbara Caine, 'Vida Goldstein and the English Militant Campaign', *Women's History Review*, 2, 3 (1993): 363–76.
34. Diane Kirkby, *Alice Henry: The Power of Pen and Voice* (Melbourne: Cambridge University Press, 1991), p. 70.
35. Maxine Berg, 'The First Women Economic Historians', *Economic History Review*, 45, 2 (1992): 308–12.
36. Scott, *Gender and the Politics of History*, p. 187.
37. Terry Crowley, 'Isabel Skelton: Precursor to Canadian Cultural History', in Beverley Boutilier and Alison Prentice, 'Locating Women in the Work of History', in *Creating Historical Memory: English-Canadian Women and the Work of History* (Vancouver: University of British Columbia Press, 1997). See Isabel Skelton, 'Canadian Woman and Suffrage', *Canadian Magazine*, 41 (1913): 162–5.

38. T.S. Ashton, 'A Memoir', in Frances Collier, *The Family Economy of the Working Classes in the Cotton Industry 1784–1833* (Manchester: Manchester University Press, 1964), pp. v-viii.
39. France and Italy would be notable exceptions.
40. Hilda Kean, 'Searching for the Past in Present Defeat: The Construction of Historical and Political Identity in British Feminism in the 1920s and 1930s', *Women's History Review*, 3, 1 (1994): 59–60.
41. Dubois, ' Making Women's History', pp. 72–6.
42. Lerner, *Creation of Feminist Consciousness*, p. 269.
43. Dubois, 'Making Women's History', p. 61. In spite of their best efforts, suffrage history would become marginalised in political and national histories in the post-war period. Indeed, certain vituperative masculinist tradition had emerged by the 1970s in the wake of second-wave feminism. See especially David Mitchell, *Queen Christabel* (London: MacDonald & Janes, 1972). For discussion of this literature see June Purvis, ' "A Pair of Infernal Queens": A Reassessment of the Dominant Representations of Emmeline and Christabel Pankhurst, First-Wave Feminists in Edwardian Britain', *Women's History Review*, 5, 2 (1996): 259–80.
44. Dodd, 'Cultural Politics and Women's Historical Writing', p. 128.
45. Kean, 'Searching for the Past in Present Defeat', p. 61.
46. On social purity see Josephine Butler, *Personal Reminiscences of a Great Crusade* (London: Marshall, 1896) and Christabel Pankhurst, *The Great Scourge and How to End It* (London: E. Pankhurst, 1913). On marriage see Cicely Hamilton, *Marriage as a Trade* (London: Chapman & Hill, 1909). On education see Elizabeth Blackwell, *Pioneer Work in Opening the Medical Profession to Women* (London: K. Barry, 1895) and Barbara Stephen, *Emily Davies and Girton College* (London, Constable, 1927).
47. Eileen Janes Yeo, *The Contest for Social Science: Relations and Representations of Gender and Class* (London: Rivers Oram Press, 1996), pp. 3–31.
48. *Ibid.*; Helen Silverberg, 'Towards a Gendered Social Science History', in *Gender and American Social Science: The Formative Years* (Princeton: Princeton University Press, 1998), pp. 3–32.
49. See, for instance, Harriet Martineau, 'Female Industry', *Edinburgh Review*, 222, (1859): 293–336; Caroline Dall, *The College, the Market and the Court: Or Women's Relation to Education, Labor and the Law* (Boston: Lee & Shepherd, 1859); Frances Power Cobbe, 'What Shall

we do with our Old Maids?', *Fraser's Magazine*, 66 (1862): 594–610 and 'Wife Torture in England', *Contemporary Review*, 32 (1878): 56–87.
50. Yeo, *Contest for Social Science*, pp. 120–47.
51. Silverberg, 'Towards a Gendered Social Science History', p. 6 and Kathleen E. McCrone, 'The National Association for the Promotion of Social Science and the Advancement of Victorian Women', *Atlantis*, 8, 1 (1982): 47.
52. Cited in Kathryn Kish Sklar, 'Hull House Maps and Papers: Social Science as Women's Work in the 1890s', in Martin Bulmer, Kevin Bales and Kathryn Kish Sklar (eds), *The Social Survey in Historical Perspective* (Cambridge: Cambridge University Press, 1991), pp. 111–12.
53. *Ibid.*, pp. 127–55.
54. Kirkby, *Alice Henry*, p. 69.
55. Denise Riley, *Am I That Name: Feminism and the Category of 'Women' in History* (Minneapolis: University of Minnesota Press, 1988), p. 50.
56. Cited in Conrad, *Perish the Thought*, pp. 166–7.
57. Bonnie G. Smith argues that one of the massive tasks of amateur women historians in the nineteenth century was to generate a history of women's cultural achievements. This emerged not so much as an explicit feminist project but rather as the result of interest in the daily life of women in the past, what clothes they wore, what they read, etc. 'Contribution of Women to Modern Historiography', pp. 718–21.
58. Cited in Thirsk, 'Foreword', p. 4.
59. Georgiana Hill, *Women in English Life from Medieval to Modern Times*, Vol 1. (London: Richard Bentley & Sons, 1896), p. vii.
60. *Ibid.*, p. ix.
61. Mabel A. Atkinson, *The Economic Foundations of the Women's Movement* (London: Fabian Women's Group, 1914), p. 6 and Barbara L. Hutchins, *Women in Modern Industry* (London: G. Bell, 1915).
62. Helen Laura Sumner Woodbury, *The History of Women in Industry in the United States* (1910) (New York: Arno Press, 1974) and Rolla Milton Tyron, *Household Manufactures in the United States 1640–1860* (Chicago: University of Chicago Press, 1917).
63. Stewart A. Weaver, *The Hammonds: A Marriage in History* (Stanford: Stanford University Press, 1997), p. 67.

64. Maxine Berg, 'Women's Work, Mechanisation and the Early Phases of Industrialisation in England', in Patrick Joyce (ed.), *The Historical Meanings of Work* (Cambridge: Cambridge University Press, 1987), pp. 64–9.
65. Alon Kadish, *Historians, Economists and Economic History* (London: Routledge, 1989).
66. E.J. Hobsbawm, 'From Social History to the History of Society', in M. Flinn and T.C. Smout (eds), *Essays in Social History*, Vol. One (Oxford: Clarendon Press, 1974), p. 2.
67. *Ibid.*, p. 49.
68. Berg, 'First Women Economic Historians', pp. 308–27.

Chapter 7

1. Baym, *American Women Writers and the Work of History*, p. 11.
2. Scott, *Gender and the Politics of History*, pp. 181–93.
3. Elizabeth Seymour Eschbach, *The Higher Education of Women in England and America 1865–1920* (New York: Garland, 1993), p. 62.
4. Helen Lefkowitz Horowitz, *Alma Mater: Design and Experience in the Women's Colleges from their Nineteenth-Century Beginnings to the 1930s* (New York: Knopf, 1984), p. 40.
5. *Ibid.*, p. 38.
6. Peter Novick, *That Noble Dream: The 'Objectivity Question' and the American Historical Profession* (Cambridge: Cambridge University Press, 1988), pp. 47–9.
7. *Ibid.*, p. 48.
8. William B. Hesseltine and Louis Kaplan, 'Women Doctors of Philosophy in History', *Journal of Higher Education*, 14 (1943): 254.
9. Goggins, 'Challenging Sexual Discrimination in the Historical Profession', p. 771.
10. Horowitz, *Alma Mater*, p. 179.
11. James C. Albisetti, *Schooling German Girls and Women: Secondary Schooling and Higher Education in Nineteenth-Century Germany* (Princeton: Princeton University Press, 1988), pp. 128–9.
12. McManus, *Classics and Feminism*, p. 2.
13. *Ibid.*, p. 26.
14. Penina Migdal Glazer and Miriam Slater, *Unequal Colleagues: The Entrance of Women into the Professions 1890–1940* (New Brunswick: Rutgers University Press, 1987), pp. 14–15.

15. *Ibid.*, p. 28.
16. *Ibid.*, pp. 35–6.
17. Stuard, 'New Dimension?', p. 82.
18. Herbert B. Adams, *The Study of History in American Colleges and Universities* (Washington, DC: Government Printing Office, 1887), pp. 210–24.
19. Scott, *Gender and the Politics of History*, p. 181.
20. Goggin, 'Challenging Sexual Discrimination in the Historical Profession', p. 771.
21. Eschbach, *Higher Education of Women*, p. xii.
22. Edward Shils and Carmen Blacker (eds), *Cambridge Women: Twelve Portraits* (Cambridge: Cambridge University Press, 1996), p. xii.
23. *Ibid.*, p. 46.
24. *Ibid.*, p. 41.
25. Peter Slee, *Learning and A Liberal Education: The Study of Modern History at the Universities of Oxford, Cambridge and Manchester* (Manchester: Manchester University Press, 1986), pp. 56–7.
26. *Ibid.*, p. 86.
27. Vera Brittain, *Women at Oxford: A Fragment of History* (London: George G. Harrap: 1960), p. 46.
28. Melman, 'Gender, History and Memory', p. 20.
29. Berg, 'First Women Economic Historians', p. 309.
30. Stuard, 'New Dimension?', pp. 83–8.
31. See entries on Eileen Power and Helen Maud Cam in Shils and Blacker, *Cambridge Women*.
32. Maxine Berg, *A Woman in History: Eileen Power 1889–1940* (Cambridge: Cambridge University Press, 1996), p. 63.
33. Mary O'Dowd, 'From Morgan to MacCurtain', in Maryann Gialnella Valiulis and Mary O'Dowd (eds), *Women and Irish History: Essays in Honour of Margaret MacCurtain* (Dublin: Wolfhound Press, 1997), p. 50.
34. *Ibid.*
35. Glazer and Slater, *Unequal Colleagues*, p. 26.
36. Natalie Zemon Davis, 'Women and the World of the Annales', *History Workshop Journal,* 33 (1992): 124.
37. *Ibid.*
38. Jo Burr Margadant, *Madame le Professeur: Women Educators in the Third Republic* (Princeton: Princeton University Press, 1990), pp. 14–15.

39. Karen Offen, 'The Second Sex and the Baccalauréat in Republican France, 1880–1924', *French Historical Studies*, 13, 2 (1983): 252–86.
40. Smith, *Gender of History*, pp. 86–102.
41. Albisetti, *Schooling German Girls and Women*, p. 117.
42. *Ibid.*
43. Smith, *Gender of History*, pp. 103–29.
44. Novick, *That Noble Dream*, p. 23.
45. Smith, *Gender of History*, p. 123.
46. Albisetti, *Schooling German Girls and Women*, p. 200.
47. *Ibid.*, p. 228.
48. Brittain, *Women at Oxford*, p. 136.
49. Maxine Berg, 'Preface', in Eileen Power, *Medieval Women* (Cambridge: Cambridge University Press, 1995), p. xiv.
50. Maryanne Dever, ' "Conventional Women of Ability": M. Barnard Eldershaw and the Question of Women's Cultural Authority', in Maryannne Dever (ed.), *Wallflowers and Witches: Women and Culture in Australia 1910–1945* (St Lucia: University of Queensland Press, 1994), p. 134.
51. Patricia Albjerg Graham, 'Expansion and Exclusion: A History of Women in Higher Education', *Signs*, 3 (1978): 764.
52. Anne Firor Scott, *Unheard Voices: The First Historians of Southern Women* (Charlotteville: University of Virginia, 1993), p. 4.
53. Goggins, 'Challenging Sexual Discrimination in the Historical Profession', p. 771.
54. Scott, *Gender and the Politics of History*, p. 184.
55. Goggins, 'Challenging Sexual Discrimination in the Historical Profession', p. 777.
56. Janet Sondheimer, 'Helen Cam, 1885–1968', in Edward Shils and Carmen Blacker (eds), *Cambridge Women: Twelve Portraits* (Cambridge: Cambridge University Press, 1996), p. 104.
57. Berg, 'First Women Economic Historians', pp. 318–19.
58. Susan Davies, 'Kathleen Fitzpatrick: Sculptor with Words' and Susan Janson, 'Jessie Webb and the Predicament of the Female Historian', in Stuart Macintyre and Julian Thomas, *The Discovery of Australian History* (Melbourne: Melbourne University Press, 1995).
59. Beverley Boutilier and Alison Prentice, 'Locating Women in the Work of History', in Boutilier and Prentice (eds), *Creating Historical Memory: English-Canadian Women and the Work of History* (Vancouver: University of British Columbia Press, 1997), p. 3.

60. Alison Prentice, 'Laying Seige to the History Professoriate', in Beverley Boutilier and Alison Prentice (eds), *Creating Historical Memory: English-Canadian Women and the Work of History* (Vancouver: University of British Columbia Press, 1997), pp. 197–232.
61. I owe this reference to Nikola Mueller, University of Bremen. For further discussion of Hintze see Brigitta Oestreich, 'Hedwig & Otto Hintze: Eine Biographische Skizze', *Geschicte und Geschilschaft*, 11, 4 (1985): 397–419.
62. Davis, 'Women and the World of the Annales', pp. 119–37. Davis provides a number of examples of women in France who produced innovative and important historical work, but who were by and large excluded from the academy.
63. *Ibid.*, p. 122.
64. *Ibid.*, p. 123.
65. *Ibid.*, p. 122.
66. Paul Schöttler, 'Lucie Varga: A Central European Refugee in the Circle of the French "Annales" 1934–1941', *History Workshop Journal*, 33 (1992): 103. This was published as a monograph, *Das Schlagwort vom finsteren Mittelalter*, in 1932.
67. George Huppert, 'Review Essay: Lucie Varga: *Les Autorités Invisibles*', *History & Theory*, 33, 2 (1994): 220–30.
68. Both Barbara A. Hanawalt and Susan Mosher Stuard make this argument in their articles in *Women in Medieval History and Historiography* (Philadelphia: University of Pennsylvania Press, 1987).
69. Françoise Thébaud, 'The Great War and the Triumph of the Sexual Division', in Françoise Thébaud (ed.), *A History of Women in The West: Towards a Cultural Identity* (Cambridge, MA: Belknap Press, 1994), pp. 30–1.
70. Soffer, *Discipline and Power*, p. 50.
71. *Ibid.*
72. Berg, 'Women's Work, Mechanisation and the Early Phases of Industrialisation in England', pp. 66–7.
73. Although most historians focused on the impact of the Industrial Revolution in Europe, these questions were also taken up by American women who looked at its impact in the United States. See Scott, *Unheard Voices*, pp. 1–71.
74. Thirsk, 'Foreword', p. 7.
75. M. Dorothy George, *London Life in the Eighteenth Century* (London: Kegan Paul, 1925). George would also savage the Hammonds' analysis

of the Industrial Revolution. See Stewart Angus Weaver, *The Hammonds: A Marriage in History* (Stanford: Stanford University Press, 1997), pp. 195–7.
76. Miranda Chaytor and Jane Lewis, 'Introduction', in Alice Clark, *The Working Life of Women in the Seventeenth Century* (London: Routledge, 1982), p. xv.
77. Ivy Pinchbeck, *Women Workers and the Industrial Revolution 1750–1850* (London: Frank Cass, 1968), p. v.
78. Deborah Valenze, *The First Industrial Woman* (New York: Oxford University Press, 1995), p. 9.
79. Sara Evans, *Personal Politics: The Roots of Women's Liberation in the Civil Rights Movement and the New Left* (New York: Alfred A. Knopf, 1979), p. 5.
80. Graham, 'Expansion and Exclusion', p. 764.
81. Evans, *Personal Politics*, p. 7.
82. Denise Riley, *War in the Nursery: Theories of Child and Mother* (London: Virago, 1983), pp. 150–96.
83. For information on Flexner, see Leila J. Rupp, 'Eleanor Flexner's *Century of Struggle*: Women's History and the Women's Movement', *National Women's Studies Association Journal*, 4, 2 (1992): 157–169 and Ellen Fitzpatrick, 'Foreword', in Eleanor Flexner, *Century of Struggle* (Cambridge, MA: Belknap Press, 1996), pp. ix–xxvi.
84. Smith, 'Seeing Mary Beard', pp. 399–416.
85. Nancy F. Cott, *A Woman Making History: Mary Ritter Beard through her Letters* (New Haven: Yale University Press, 1991), pp. 53–7.
86. Smith, 'Seeing Mary Beard', p. 407.
87. Cott, *Woman Making History*, p. 47.
88. Ellen C. Dubois, 'Eleanor Flexner and the History of American Feminism', *Gender & History*, 3, 1 (1991): 86.
89. *Ibid.*, p. 87.
90. In *The Feminine Mystique* Friedan called *Century of Struggle* the 'definitive history of the woman's rights movement' and wrote that she was 'much indebted to Miss Flexner for many factual clues I might otherwise have missed in my attempt to get to the truth behind the feminine mystique and its monstrous image of the feminists'. Betty Friedan, *The Feminine Mystique* (New York: Penguin, 1963), p. 333.
91. *Ibid.*, p. 22.

Notes

92. Daniel Horowitz, *Betty Friedan and the Making of the Feminine Mystique: The American Left, The Cold War and American Feminism* (Amherst: University of Manchester Press, 1998), p. 227.

Chapter 8

1. Ann Curthoys, 'Shut up you Bourgeois Bitch: Sexual Identity and Political Action in the Anti-Vietnam War Movement', in Marilyn Lake and Joy Damousi (eds), *Gender and War: Australians at War in the Twentieth Century* (Melbourne: Cambridge University Press, 1995), p. 332.
2. Gisela Kaplan, *Contemporary Western Feminism* (New York: New York University Press, 1992), p. 9.
3. Alice Echols, *Daring to be Bad: Radical Feminism in America 1967–1975* (Minneapolis: University of Minnesota Press, 1989), p. 3.
4. *Ibid.*, p. 84.
5. Kaplan, *Contemporary Western Feminism*, pp. 116–17, 154–5.
6. Arthur Marwick, *The Sixties: Cultural Revolution in Britain, France, Italy and the United States* (Oxford: Oxford University Press, 1998), pp. 592–618.
7. *Ibid.*, p. 586.
8. Jane Lewis, 'Women, Lost and Found: The Impact of Feminism on History', in Dale Spender (ed.), *Men's Studies Modified: The Impact of Feminism on the Academic Disciplines* (London: Pergamon Press, 1981), p. 55.
9. James Green, 'Engaging in People's History: The Massachusetts History Workshop', in Susan Porter, Stephen Brier and Roy Rosenweig (eds), *Presenting the Past: Essays on History and the Public* (Philadelphia: Temple University Press, 1986), p. 347.
10. David Selbourne, 'On the Methods of the History Workshop', *History Workshop Journal*, 9 (1980): 150–61.
11. Georg G. Iggers, *Historiography in the Twentieth Century: From Scientific Objectivity to the Postmodern Challenge* (Hanover: Wesleyan, 1997), p. 94.
12. Davin, 'Redressing the Balance', p. 63.
13. Ava Baron, 'Gender and Labor History: Learning from the Past, Looking to the Future', in *Work Engendered: Toward a New History of American Labor* (Ithaca: Cornell University Press, 1991), pp. 1–46.

14. Scott, *Gender and the Politics of History*, p. 69.
15. Judith P. Zinnser, *History and Feminism: A Glass Half Full?* (New York: Twayne Publishers, 1993), p. 21.
16. Scott, *Gender and the Politics of History*, p. 72.
17. E. P. Thompson, *The Making of the English Working Class* (London: Gollancz, 1963), p. 13.
18. Peter Burke, *Varieties of Cultural History* (London: Polity, 1997), p. 192.
19. Davin, 'Redressing the Balance', pp. 63–4.
20. Lewis, 'Women, Lost and Found', p. 56.
21. See, for instance, Eileen Boris and Nupur Chaudhuri, *Voices of Women Historians: The Personal, the Political, The Professional* (Bloomington: University of Indiana Press, 1999).
22. Zinnser, *History and Feminism*, p. 101.
23. *Ibid.*
24. Delores Barracano Schmidt and Earl Robert Schmidt, 'The Invisible Woman: The Historian as Professional Magician', in Berenice A. Carroll (ed.), *Liberating Women's History: Theoretical and Critical Essays* (Urbana: University of Illinois Press, 1976), p. 423.
25. Zinnser, *History and Feminism*, p. 47.
26. Linda K. Kerber, *Toward an Intellectual History of Women: Essays* (Chapel Hill: University of North Carolina Press, 1997), p. 9.
27. Linda K. Kerber, 'On the Importance of Taking Notes', in Eileen Boris and Nupur Chaudhuri, *Voices of Women Historians: The Personal, the Political, The Professional* (Bloomington: University of Indiana Press, 1999) p. 53.
28. Goggin, 'Challenging Sexual Discrimination in the Historical Profession', pp. 781, 802. For discussion of courses that developed in the United States in the 1970s see Zinnser, *History and Feminism*, pp. 77–84.
29. Deborah Gorham, 'Making History: Women's History in Canadian Universities in the 1970s', in Beverley Boutilier and Alison Prentice (eds), *Creating Historical Memory: English-Canadian Women and the Work of History* (Vancouver: University of British Columbia Press, 1997), pp. 273–7.
30. Michelle Perrot, 'Twenty Years of Women's History in France', in Michelle Perrot (ed.), *Writing Women's History* (Oxford: Blackwell, 1984), p. viii.
31. Jill Roe, 'From Sydney to Boston and Back in Twenty-Five Years, with an Account of Many Strange and Unexpected Happenings

along the Way, or There's No Place like Home', *Australian Historical Studies*, 106 (1996): 37.
32. Rosalind Miles, *The Women's History of the World* (London: Paladin, 1988).
33. Anna Davin, 'Women and History', in Michelene Wandor, *The Body Politic: Women's Liberation in Great Britain 1969–1972* (London: Women's Liberation Workshop, 1972), p. 224.
34. For a detailed discussion of the development of women's history internationally see Karen Offen, Ruth Roach Pierson and Jane Rendall (eds), *Writing Women's History: International Perspectives* (Bloomington: Indiana University Press, 1991).
35. Zinnser, *History and Feminism*, p. 23.
36. Joan Wallach Scott, 'Women's History and the Rewriting of History', in Christine Farnham (ed.), *The Impact of Feminist Research in the Academy* (Bloomington: Indiana University Press: 1987), p. 36.
37. Allen, 'Evidence and Silence', pp. 173–4.
38. Joan Kelly-Gadol, 'The Social Relations of the Sexes: Methodological Implications of Women's History', *Signs*, 4, 1 (1976): 809.
39. Gerda Lerner, *The Majority Finds Its Past: Placing Women in History* (New York: Oxford University Press, 1979), p. 3.
40. See, for instance, Sheila Johansson, ' "Herstory" as History: A New Field or Another Fad', in Berenice A. Carroll (ed.), *Liberating Women's History: Theoretical and Critical Essays* (Urbana: University of Illinois Press, 1973) and Ann Forfreedom (ed.), *Women out of History: A Herstory Anthology* (Los Angeles: Forfreedom, 1973).
41. Glenda Riley, 'Continuity and Change: Interpreting Women in Western History', *Journal of the West*, 22, 3 (1993): 7.
42. David M. Potter, 'American Women in the American Character', in John Hague (ed.), *American Character and Culture: Some Twentieth Century Perspectives* (Deland: Everett Edwards Press, 1964).
43. Between 1970 and 1980 numerous revisionist texts were published about the role of women of the Frontier. See, for instance, Lillian Schlissel (ed.), *Women's Diaries of Westward Journey* (New York: Schocken Books, 1982) and Sandra L. Myres (ed.), *Westward Ho for California! Women's Overland Diaries from the Huntington Library* (San Marino: Huntington Library Press, 1980).
44. Margaret Walsh, 'Women's Place on the American Frontier', *Journal of American Studies*, 29, 2 (1995): 243–8.
45. Allen, 'Evidence and Silence', p. 178.

46. *Ibid.*, p. 174.
47. E.A. Grosz, 'The In(ter)vention of Feminist Knowledges', in Barbara Caine, E.A. Grosz and Marie de Lepervance (eds), *Crossing Boundaries: Feminisms and the Critiques of Knowledges* (Sydney: Allen & Unwin, 1988), p. 94.
48. *Ibid.*, p. 174.
49. Scott, *Gender and the Politics of History*, p. 17.
50. Boxer and Quataret, 'Restoring Women to History', p. 5.
51. Allen, 'Evidence and Silence', p. 176.

Chapter 9

1. Judith Evans, *Feminist Theory Today: An Introduction to Second-Wave Feminism* (London: Sage, 1995), p. 67.
2. Simone de Beauvoir, *The Second Sex* (London: Penguin, 1986), p. 561.
3. See, for instance, Berenice A. Carroll, 'Mary Beard's *Woman as Force in History*: A Critique', in Berenice A. Carroll (ed.), *Liberating Women's History: Theoretical and Critical Essays* (Urbana: University of Illinois Press, 1976), p. 29.
4. Joan Wallach Scott, 'Feminism and History', in *Feminism and History* (Oxford: Oxford University Press, 1996), p. 1.
5. Diane Purkiss, *The Witch in History: Early Modern and Twentieth Century Representations* (London: Routledge, 1996), p. 11.
6. Lerner, *Majority Finds its Past*, p. 37.
7. See also Carroll, 'On Mary Beard's *Woman as Force in History*', p. 31.
8. Iggers, *Historiography in the Twentieth Century*, p. 87.
9. Peter Way, *Common Labour: Workers and the Digging of North American Canals 1780–1860* (Cambridge: Cambridge University Press, 1993), p. 5.
10. Thompson, *Making of the English Working Class*, p. 9.
11. *Ibid.*, pp. 9–10.
12. Perry Anderson, *Arguments Within English Marxism* (London: New Left Books: 1980), p. 30.
13. Robert L. Harris, 'Coming of Age: The Transformation of Afro-American Historiography', *Journal of Negro History*, 67, 2 (1982): 107.
14. See, for instance, *Acculturation: The Study of Culture Contact* (New York: Augustin, 1938); *The American Negro: A Study in Racial Crossing* (Bloomington: University of Indiana Press, 1964) and *Cultural Dynamics* (New York: Knopf, 1964).

15. Patricia Morton, *Disfigured Images: The Historical Assault on Afro-American Women* (New York: Praeger, 1991), p. 99.
16. Way, *Common Labour*, pp. 6–7.
17. See especially Lionel Tiger, *Men in Groups* (London: Nelson, 1969), p. 140. In this text Tiger wrote: 'I do not claim that females have no organisations; obviously they join and are active in a number of social and services clubs, but female organisations affect political activity far less than male ones ... women do not form bonds. Dependent as most women are on the earnings and genes of men, they break ranks very soon.'
18. Kerber, *Toward an Intellectual History of Women*, p. 166.
19. *Ibid.*, p. 162.
20. Barbara Welter, 'The Cult of True Womanhood 1820–1860', *American Quarterly*, 18 (1966): 151–74 and Aileen Kraditor, *Up from the Pedestal: Selected Writings in the History of American Feminism* (Chicago: Quadrangle Books, 1968). See also Gerda Lerner, 'The Lady and the Mill Girl: Changes in the Status of Women in the Age of Jackson', *Midcontinent American Studies Journal*, 10, 1 (1969): 5–15.
21. Beard, *On Understanding Women*, pp. 6–13.
22. For further discussion of 'contribution' history see Gerda Lerner, 'Placing Women in History: A 1975 Perspective', in Berenice A. Carroll (ed.), *Liberating Women's History: Theoretical and Critical Essays* (Urbana: University of Illinois Press, 1976), p. 358 and Lewis, 'Women, Lost and Found', p. 59.
23. Lerner, *Majority Finds its Past*, p. 178.
24. Nancy F. Cott, *The Bonds of Womanhood: Woman's Sphere in New England 1780–1835* (New Haven: Yale University Press, 1977), p. 197.
25. Amanda Vickery, 'Golden Age to Separate Spheres? A Review of the Categories and Chronology of English Women's History', *Historical Journal*, 36, 2 (1993): 383.
26. See Michelle Zimbalist Rosaldo, 'Women, Culture and Society: A Theoretical Overview', in Michelle Zimbalist Rosaldo and Louise Lamphere (eds), *Women, Culture and Society* (Stanford: University of California Press, 1974), pp. 17–42; 'The Use and Abuse of Anthropology: Reflections on Feminism and Cross-Cultural Understanding', *Signs*, 3 (1980): 389–417 and Sherry B. Ortner, 'Is Female to Male As Nature is to Culture?', in Michelle Zimbalist Rosaldo and Louise Lamphere (eds), *Women, Culture and Society* (Stanford: University of California Press, 1974), pp. 67–88.

27. Rosaldo, 'Use and Abuse of Anthropology', p. 396.
28. Jo Freeman, *The Politics of Women's Liberation: A Case Study of an Emerging Social Movement and its Relation to the Policy Process* (New York: David McKay, 1974).
29. Linda Kerber, 'Separate Spheres, Female Worlds and Woman's Place', in Kerber, *Toward an Intellectual History of Women*, p. 166.
30. Carroll Smith-Rosenberg, 'The Female World of Love and Ritual: Relations between Women in Nineteenth Century America', *Signs*, 1 (1975): 3.
31. *Ibid.*
32. *Ibid.*
33. Carroll Smith-Rosenberg, 'Politics and Culture in Women's History: A Symposium', *Feminist Studies*, 6 (1980): 55.
34. *Ibid.*, p. 62.
35. Mary P. Ryan, 'The Power of Women's Networks', in Judith Newton, Mary P. Ryan and Judith R. Walkowitz (eds), *Sex and Class in Women's History* (London: Routledge & Kegan Paul, 1983), pp. 167–86; Blanche Wiesen Cook, 'Female Support Networks and Political Activism: Lillian Wald, Crystal Eastman, Emma Goldman', in Nancy F. Cott and Elizabeth H. Pleck (eds), *A Heritage of Her Own* (New York: Simon & Schuster, 1979), pp. 412–44; Estelle Freedman, 'Separatism as Strategy: Female Institution Building and American Feminism 1870–1930', *Feminist Studies*, 5, 3 (1979): 512–29; Katherine Kish Sklar, 'Hull House in the 1890s: A Community of Women Reformers', *Signs*, 4 (1985): 658–77 and Nancy Sahli, 'Smashing: Women's Relationships Before the Fall', *Chrysalis*, 8 (1979): 17–27.
36. Cott, *Bonds of Womanhood*, p. 194.
37. E.P. Thompson's later works showed more interest in the place of women within working-class culture.
38. Nancy A. Hewitt, 'Beyond the Search for Sisterhood: American Women's history in the 1980s', *Social History*, 10, 3 (1985): 301.
39. *Ibid.*, p. 303.
40. Vickery, 'Golden Age to Separate Spheres?', p. 388.
41. *Ibid.*, p. 388.
42. Perrot, *Writing Women's History*, p. 7.
43. 'Politics and Culture in Women's History: A Symposium', *Feminist Studies*, 6 (1980): 26–64.
44. *Ibid.*, p. 31.
45. *Ibid.*

46. *Ibid.*, p. 30.
47. Smith-Rosenberg, 'Politics and Culture in Women's History', p. 57.
48. Hewitt, 'Beyond the Search for Sisterhood', p. 304.
49. Echols, *Daring to be Bad*, p. 6.
50. Evans, *Feminist Theory Today*, p. 77.
51. See, for instance, Cook, 'Female Support Networks and Political Activism'; Freedman, 'Separatism as Strategy' and Sahli, 'Smashing'.
52. The phrase comes from Freedman, 'Separatism as Strategy', p. 514.
53. Freedman, 'Separatism as Strategy', p. 513.
54. Cook, 'Female Support Networks and Political Activism', p. 60.
55. Freedman, 'Separatism as Strategy', pp. 514–15.
56. Ann Snitow, Christine Stansell and Sharon Thompson (eds), *Desire: The Politics of Sexuality* (London: Virago, 1984), p. 18.
57. Echols, *Daring to be Bad*, p. 289.
58. Alice Echols, 'The New Feminism of Yin and Yang', in Ann Snitow, Christine Stansell and Sharon Thompson (eds), *Desire: The Politics of Sexuality* (London: Virago, 1984), p. 71.

Chapter 10

1. Echols, *Daring to be Bad*, p. 214.
2. *Ibid.*, p. 215.
3. Jill Johnston, *Lesbian Nation: The Feminist Solution* (New York: Simon & Schuster, 1973), p. 149.
4. Rita May Brown, 'Take a Lesbian Out to Lunch', in *Plain Brown Rapper* (Oakland: Diana Press, 1976), pp. 79–96.
5. The term comes from Johnston's *Lesbian Nation*.
6. Johnston, *Lesbian Nation*, p. 149.
7. Lillian Faderman, *Odd Girls and Twilight Lovers: A History of Lesbian Life in Twentieth-Century America* (New York: Columbia University Press, 1991), p. 207.
8. See, for instance, Leeds Revolutionary Feminist Group, 'Political Lesbianism: The Case Against Heterosexuality' (1979) or 'The Clit Statement' (1974). Both these pamphlets were published by radical lesbians critical of heterosexual women in the women's movement, who characterised heterosexuality as the root of all women's oppression.
9. Adrienne Rich, 'Compulsory Heterosexuality and Lesbian Existence', *Signs*, 8, 4 (1980): 631–60.

10. *Ibid.*, p. 632.
11. See, for instance, Mary Daly, *Beyond God the Father: Toward a Philosophy of Women's Liberation* (Boston: Beacon Press, 1973) and *Gyn/Ecology* (Boston: Beacon Press, 1978).
12. Chris Weedon, *Feminism, Theory and the Politics of Difference* (Oxford: Blackwell, 1999), p. 62.
13. *Ibid.*, p. 62.
14. Emma Healey, *Lesbian Sex Wars* (London: Virago, 1996), p. 77.
15. *Ibid.*
16. Smith-Rosenberg, 'The Female World of Love and Ritual', p. 8.
17. *Ibid.*, p. vii.
18. *Ibid.*
19. *Ibid.*
20. Lillian Faderman, *Surpassing the Love of Men: Romantic Friendship and Love between Women from the Renaissance to the Present* (New York: William Morrow, 1981), p. 16.
21. *Ibid.*
22. *Ibid.*, pp. 17–20.
23. *Ibid.*, p. 18.
24. This term comes from Ros Ballaster, ' "The Vices of Old Rome Revived": Representations of Female Same-Sex Desire in Seventeenth and Eighteenth Century England', in Suzanne Riatt (ed.), *Volcanoes and Pearl Divers: Essays in Lesbian Feminist Studies* (London: Onlywomen Press, 1994), p. 16.
25. Sheila Jeffreys, 'Does It Matter If They Did It?', in Lesbian History Group (eds), *Not a Passing Phase: Reclaiming Lesbian History 1840–1985* (London: The Women's Press, 1989), p. 27.
26. Lillian Faderman, *The Scotch Verdict* (New York: Quill, 1983).
27. Liz Stanley, 'Romantic Friendship? Some Issues in Researching Lesbian History and Biography', *Women's History Review*, 1, 2 (1992): 196.
28. Jeffreys, 'Does It Matter If They Did It?', p. 27.
29. Judith Bennett, cited in Martha Vicinus, 'Lesbian History: All Theory and No Facts and All Facts and No Theory?' *Radical History Review*, 60 (1994): 57.
30. There are of course notable exceptions. See Louis Crompton, 'The Myth of Lesbian Impunity: Capitol Laws from 1270–1791' and Brigitte Eriksson, 'A Lesbian Execution in Germany 1721: The Trial Records', in Salvatore J. Licata and Robert P. Petersen (eds), *Historical Perspectives on Homosexuality* (New York: Haworth Press, Stein &

Day, 1980), pp. 3–20, 27–40; Theo van der Meer, 'Tribades on Trial: Female Same-Sex Offenders in Late Eighteenth-Century Amsterdam', in John C. Fout (ed.), *Forbidden History: The State, Society, and the Regulation of Sexuality in Modern Europe* (Chicago: University of Chicago Press, 1992), pp. 189–210; and Ruth Ford, 'The "Man-Woman Murderer": Sex Fraud, Sexual Inversion and the "Unmentionable Article" in 1920s Australia', *Gender & History*, 12, 1 (2000): 158–96.
31. Healey, *Lesbian Sex Wars*, p. 18.
32. Michel Foucault, *The History of Sexuality: An Introduction*, vol. 1 (London: Penguin, 1976), p. 43.
33. Jeffrey Weeks, *Coming Out: Homosexual Politics in Great Britain from the Nineteenth Century to the Present* (London: Quartet Books, 1977) and *Against Nature: Essays on History, Sexuality and Identity* (London: Rivers Oram Press, 1991).
34. Alan Bray, *Homosexuality in Renaissance England* (London: Gay Men's Press, 1982) and Randolph Trumbach, *Sex and the Gender Revolution* (Chicago: University of Chicago Press, 1998).
35. Faderman first articulated this notion in her article 'The Morbidification of Love between Women by Nineteenth-century Sexologists', *Journal of the History of Homosexuality*, 4, 1 (1978): 73–90.
36. Sheila Jeffreys, ' "The Spinster and her Enemies": Sexuality and the Last Wave of Feminism', *Scarlet Woman*, 13, 2 (1981): n.p. and *The Spinster and Her Enemies: Feminism and Sexuality 1880–1930* (London: Pandora Press, 1985).
37. Alison Oram, ' "Friends, Feminists and Sexual Outlaws": Lesbianism and British History', in Gabrielle Griffin and Sonya Andermahr (eds), *Straight Studies Modified: Lesbian Interventions in the Academy* (London: Cassell, 1997), p. 175.
38. See, for instance, Liz Stanley, 'Romantic Friendships? Some Issues in Researching Lesbian History and Biography', *Women's History Review*, 1, 2 (1992): 193–216 and Lucy Bland, *Banishing the Beast: English Feminism and Sexual Morality 1885–1914* (London: Penguin, 1995). See also Sylvia Martin, 'Rethinking Passionate Friendship: The Writings of Mary Fullerton', *Women's History Review*, 2, 3 (1993): 395–406.
39. Freedman, 'Separatism as Strategy', pp. 514–15 and Jefferys, *Spinster and Her Enemies*, p. 26.
40. Linda Gordon and Ellen Carol DuBois, 'Seeking Ecstasy on the Battlefield', in Carole A. Vance (ed.), *Pleasure and Danger: Exploring Female*

Sexuality (Boston: Routledge, 1984), p. 41. Ironically a number of these women were seen as heroines of cultural feminism because of their contribution to a separatist sexual politics. See Cook, 'Female Support Networks and Political Activism'.

41. Gordon and DuBois, 'Seeking Ecstasy on the Battlefield', p. 42.
42. With the exception of Frances Finnegan's *Poverty and Prostitution: A Study of Victorian Prostitutes in York* (Cambridge: Cambridge University Press, 1979), most historical texts on prostitution written in the 1980s followed this pattern. See especially Judith Walkowitz, *Prostitution and Victorian Society: Women, Class and the State* (Cambridge: Cambridge University Press, 1980) and Christine Stansell, *City of Women: Class and Sex in New York 1789–1860* (New York: Knopf, 1986).
43. Gordon and DuBois, 'Seeking Ecstasy on the Battlefield', p. 38.
44. Amber Hollibaugh & Cherríe Moraga, 'What We're Rolling around in Bed with: Sexual Silences in Feminism', in Ann Snitow, Christine Stansell and Sharon Thompson (eds), *Desire: The Politics of Sexuality* (London: Virago, 1984), p. 412.
45. Judith Walkowitz, 'Male Vice and Female Virtue: The Politics of Prostitution in Nineteenth Century Britain', in Ann Snitow, Christine Stansell and Sharon Thompson (eds), *Desire: The Politics of Sexuality* (London: Virago, 1984), p. 50.
46. See Jeffreys, *Spinster and her Enemies*; Margaret Jackson, 'Sex and the Experts', *Scarlet Woman*, 13 (1981) n.p. and 'Sex Research and the Construction of Sexuality: A Tool of Male Supremacy?', *Women's Studies International Forum*, 7, 1 (1983): 43–51.
47. Margaret Hunt, 'The De-Eroticisation of Women's Liberation: Social Purity Movements and the Revolutionary Feminism of Sheila Jeffreys', *Feminist Review*, 34 (1990): 25.
48. Joan Nestle, *Lesbian History Archives News*, 8 (1984): 15.
49. Madeline Davis and Elizabeth Lapovsky Kennedy, 'Oral History and the Study of Sexuality in the Lesbian Community: Buffalo, New York, 1940–1960', in Martin Bauml Duberman, Martha Vicinus and George Chauncey Jr (eds), *Hidden from History: Reclaiming the Gay and Lesbian Past* (New York: New American Books, 1989), p. 427.
50. Elizabeth Lapovsky Kennedy and Madeline Davis, *Boots of Leather, Slippers of Gold: The History of a Lesbian Community* (Buffalo: Routledge, 1993).
51. *Ibid.*, p. 13.

52. Lisa Duggan, 'History's Gay Ghetto: The Contradiction and Growth in Lesbian and Gay History', in Susan Porter Benson, Stephen Brier and Roy Rosenweig (eds), *Presenting the Past: Essays on History and the Public* (Philadelphia: Temple University Press, 1986), pp. 281–302.
53. Laura Gowing, 'History', in Andy Medhurst and Sally Munt (eds), *Lesbian and Gay Studies* (London: 1997), p. 62.
54. Martha Vicinus, 'Lesbian History: All Theory and No Facts or All Facts and No Theory', *Radical History Review*, 60 (1994): 57.
55. Jill Liddington, *Female Fortune: Land Gender and Authority* (London: Rivers Oram Press, 1998), p. xvi.
56. Emma Donoghue, *Passions between Women: British Lesbian Culture 1668–1801* (New York: HarperCollins, 1993) and Lisa L. Moore, *Dangerous Intimacies: Toward a Sapphic History of the British Novel* (Durham: Duke University Press, 1997).
57. Jeffreys, 'Does It Matter If They Did?', p. 28.
58. Eve Kosofsky Sedgwick, *Epistemology of the Closet* (Berkeley: University of California Press, 1990), p. 40.
59. Vicinus, 'Lesbian History', p. 60.
60. *Ibid.*, p. 61.
61. Eve Kosofsky Sedgwick, *Tendencies* (Durham: Duke University Press, 1993), p. xii, her emphasis.
62. Vicinus, 'Lesbian History', p. 61.
63. Anna Marie Jagose, *Queer Theory* (Melbourne: University of Melbourne Press, 1996), pp. 101–26.

Conclusion

1. Linda Gordon, 'On Difference', *Genders*, 10 (1991): 90.
2. Evelyn Brook Higginbotham, 'Beyond the Sounds of Silence: Afro-American Women in History', *Gender and History*, 1, 1 (1989): 53.
3. bell hooks, *Ain't I a Woman: Black Women and Feminism* (Boston: South End Press, 1981), p. 137.
4. Paula Giddings, *When and Where I Enter: The Impact of Black Women on Race and Sex in America* (New York: William Morrow, 1984), p. 298.
5. Hazel V. Carby, 'White Women Listen!', in Centre for Contemporary Cultural Studies (eds), *The Empire Strikes Back: Race and Racism in 70s Britain* (London: Hutchinson, 1982), pp. 218–19.

6. Giddings, *When and Where I Enter*, p. 299.
7. hooks, *Ain't I a Woman*, p. 137.
8. Cited in Echols, *Daring to be Bad*, p. 31. Casey refers to Casey Hayden, who wrote the position paper on (white) women in the civil rights movement.
9. Giddings, *When and Where I Enter*, p. 305.
10. hooks, *Ain't I a Woman*, p. 137.
11. Giddings, *When and Where I Enter*, p. 307.
12. hooks, *Ain't I a Woman*, p. 147.
13. *Ibid.*, p. 140.
14. Valerie Amos and Pratibha Parmar, 'Challenging Imperial Feminism', *Feminist Review*, 17 (1984): 5.
15. Joan Kelly-Gadol, 'The Social Relations of the Sexes', *Signs*, 1, 4 (1976): 809.
16. Carby, 'White Women Listen!', p. 212.
17. *Ibid.*, and Darlene Clark Hine, *Hinesight: Black Women and the Re-Construction of American History* (Bloomington: Indiana University Press, 1994), pp. xxv– xxxv.
18. Chandra Talpade Mohanty, 'Cartographies of Struggle: Third World Women and the Politics of Feminism', in Chandra Talpade Mohanty, Ann Russo and Lourdes Torres (eds), *Third World Women and the Politics of Feminism* (Bloomington: Indiana University Press: 1991), p. 13.
19. See, for instance, Gayatri Chakravorty Spivak, 'Can the Subaltern Speak?', in Cary Nelson and Lawrence Grossberg (eds), *Marxism and the Interpretation of Culture* (London: Macmillan, 1988), and Homi Bhabha, *Nation and Narration* (London: Routledge, 1990).
20. Dipesh Chakrabarty, 'Postcoloniality and the Artifice of History: Who Speaks for "Indian" Pasts?', in H. Aram Veeser (ed.), *The New Historicism Reader* (New York: Routledge, 1994), pp. 342–69.
21. Mohanty, 'Cartographies of Struggle', p. 10.
22. See, for instance, Riley, *Am I That Name?*
23. *Ibid.*, p. 13.
24. Joan Wallach Scott, 'Introduction', in *Feminism and History* (New York: Oxford University Press, 1996), pp. 8–9.

Index

abolitionism
  and feminism, 133, 134, 139
abortion, 172, 175, 222, 231
Adams, Abigail, 84, 125
Adams, Hannah
  Memoirs, 120, 122
Adams, Henry, 157
Adams, Herbert Baxter, 152, 157
Adams, John
  relationship with Catherine Sawbridge Macaulay, 80
  relationship with Mercy Otis Warren, 80
age, 229
Agoult, Marie d'
  Essai sur la liberté, 206
  feminism, 105–6
  rejection of romanticism, 106
  relationship with Franz Liszt, 106
  role in 1848 revolution, 105
  salon, 105
Agrippina, Julia
  archetype of female evil, 25, 43, 91, 247n
  feminine view of history, 90
  Memoirs, 20, 28, 241n
Aikin, Lucy, 120
Alexander, Sally, 183
Alexander, William
  History of Women from the Earliest Antiquity to the Present Time, 50
Allart, Hortense
  criticism of masculinist history, 106
  feminism, 106
  historical writing, 106
  relationship with Chateaubriand, 106
  relationship with Edward Bulwer-Lytton, 106
  salon, 10
Allen, Judith, 185
American Historical Association
  Committee on the Status of Women, 181
  discrimination towards women, 181
  formation, 152, 154
  women's breakfasts, 162
American Historical Review, 152
American Political Science Association, 180
American Social Science Association, 144, 146
anachronism, 17–18, 32, 36, 46
Annales/Annalistes
  influence in postwar period, 177
  treatment of private life, 177
  treatment of women, 177, 182
  treatment of women working on journal, 164
Anne of Austria, 73
Anstey, Vera, 162
Anthony, Susan B.
  History of Woman Suffrage, 135
  influence of Margaret Fuller, 132
  role in suffrage campaigns, 140
anthropology, 48, 182, 197, 206
Anti-Jacobin Review, 100
antiquarianism
  as feminine pursuit, 78, 121
Arbaleste, Charlotte
  biographer, 7, 70
  Life of Philippe du Plessis de Mornay, 70
  memoir, 70
archaeology, 18
archives
  women denied access to, 123
Aristophanes
  Thesmophoriazousa, 30
Aristotle
  medicine, 31
  misogyny, 20,
  philosophy, 31, 46
  representation of women, 38–9
Armstrong, Edward, 156
Arundell, Lady, 125
Askew, Anne, 43–4

Astell, Mary
  The Christian Religion, 63
  women as 'men in petticoats', 35, 63, 85
Atkinson, Mabel, 147
Augustus, 24
Austen, Jane
  feminism, 94
  on history, 1
  Northanger Abbey, 1
  Persuasion, 34
  romantic heroines, 115
autobiography
  spiritual, 68
  as women's history, 73, 122, 138,

Bachofen, Johann Jacob, 126
Bacon, Francis, 45–6, 47
Bale, John, 43
Ballard, George, 7
Bancroft, George, 104–5
Banks, Joseph, 79
Banks, Sarah Sophia, 79
Barnard, Marjorie, 160
Baym, Nina, 126
Beal, Frances, 235
Beard, Mary Ritter
  Centre for Women's Archives, 170
  on feminist history, 131, 191–2
  as transitional figure, 169
  Woman as Force in History, 169–70, 189
  on women's culture, 196
Beauvoir, Simone de
  Memoirs of a Dutiful Daughter, 61
  The Second Sex, 175, 190–1
  women as 'Other' 190
Belgiojoso, Cristina
  Emina, 107
  feminism, 106
  role in Risorgimento, 106–7
  salon, 105
  translation of *New Science*, 107
Benger, Elizabeth Ogilvy, 120
Bentley, Michael, 51
Berkshire Women's History Conferences, 161, 181–2

Biggs, Caroline Ashurst
  editor of *Englishwoman's Review*, 136
  entry on Britain in *History of Woman Suffrage*, 136
biography
  commercial success of, 119
  as domesticated history, 121–3, 128
  as feminist history, 128–9, 138, 273n
  as gendered diminutive of history, 10, 25, 121
  of husbands, 70–3
  as men's history, 111
  as women's history, 9, 63, 109–13, 115–18, 119, 121
  saintly, 68, 122
Bisticci, Vespasiano da, 39
black nationalism, 193
black history, 177, 193–4, 238
black power, 193
Blackburn, Helen
  editor of *Englishwoman's Review*, 136
  Woman's Suffrage, 136
Blackstone, William
  Commentaries, 135
  on coverture, 135, 137
Blackwood's Magazine, 103
Bland, Lucy, 221
Bloch, Marc
  Feudal Society, 13
Bloch, Simone Vidal, 164
Boadicea, 36–7, 139
Boccaccio, Giovanni
  Decameron, 38
  De claris mulieribus, 38–40, 66
  representation of women, 38
  women worthies, 6
Bock, Fabienne, 182
Bonaparte, Napoleon,
  bureaucracy, 57
  the Napoleonic Wars, 55, 96, 101, 110
  treatment of women, 55
Bray, Alan, 219
Bray, Matthew, 95
Bridenthal, Renate
  Becoming Visible, 185
Brissot, Jacques-Pierre, 92
British Critic, 99

British Historical Association, 157
Brittain, Vera, 160
Brown, Rita Mae, 210, 211
Brunehaut, 90
Bruni, Leonardo
  History of the People of Florence, 19
  on women's education, 65
Buckstaff, Florence Griswold, 137
Buer, Mabel, 162
Buffalo Oral History Project, 224–5
Bulwer-Lytton, Edward
Burke, Edmund
  Reflections on the Revolution in France, 54, 82, 89
Burke, Peter, 18–19
Burstein, Miriam Elizabeth, 7, 122
butch/femme, 207–8, 213, 221–5
Butler, Eleanor, 214
Butler, Josephine, 138
Byron, Lord George Gordon, 53, 104

Cabelisin, Apollonia, 69
Cam, Helen Maud, 162
Canadian Historical Association, 182
Carby, Hazel V., 229, 238
Caritat, Marie-Jean, Marquis de Condorcet, 48
Carlyle, Thomas
  The French Revolution, 56
  representation of women, 56
Carr, E. H., 15
Carroll, Berenice A., 180
Carpenter, Edward, 221
Carpenter, Mary, 128
Cartismandua, 37
Carus-Wilson, Eleanora, 162
Caspar, Scott F., 127
catalogs
  misogynistic, 25
  representation of women, 23–5, 38–9
  satirical, 25
Catherine of Aragon, 42
Cavendish, Margaret
  biographer, 6
  Life of William Cavendish, 71
  A True Relation of My Birth Breeding and Life, 77

Chao, Pan, 241n
Charlotte Augusta
  opinion of Hannah More, 115
  opinion of Jane Austen, 115
Child, Lydia Maria
  abolitionist, 133
  History of the Condition of Women, 105, 133
  influence of Germaine de Staël, 105
chronology, 46, 137
Churchill, Sarah, 75
Cicero, 32
civil rights movement, 173–4, 232, 234, 235
Clark, Alice
  suffrage, 140
  Working life of women in the seventeenth century, 140–1, 166
class and class consciousness, 11, 177, 178, 191, 193, 198, 199–203, 223, 229, 236–7, 240
classical
  education, 15–19, 34, 36, 64
  history and historians, 9, 17–33, 52–9
  inheritance, 9–33
  languages, 17–18
  literature, 15
  understandings of gender, 9, 15–16, 20–33, 34, 53
Classics
  women's experience of, 153, 156
  preferred career path for men, 156–7
Cleopatra, 90
Clifford, Anne, Duchess of Dorset and Pembroke, 78, 137
Coignet, Matthieu, 19
Collier, Frances, 140–1
colonisation, 176, 235, 238–40
Common Cause, 137
confessional history, 70
consciousness raising (CR), 174–5, 182, 194–5, 200, 223, 235
constitutional history, 148, 165
contraception, 222, 231
convents
  as archives, 67
  histories of, 68–9
  as sites of female literacy, 68

Conway, Jill Kerr, 182
Cook, Blanche Wiesen, 198, 206
Corbin, Hannah Lee, 125
Cordeilla, 37
Cornazzano, Antonio, 39
Cott, Nancy F., 198
Coulton, G. G., 157
counterculture (female), 205
Creighton, Louise, 156
Creighton, Mandell, 156
cult of true womanhood, 110, 113, 118, 198
cultural history, 179
Cumming, Jane, 216

Dall, Caroline, 146
Daly, Mary, 212
Darwin, Charles, 126
Daughters of Bilitis, 210
Davies, Emily
  champion of women's higher education, 156
  Girton College, 156
Davies, Stevie, 72
Davis, Angela B., 235
Davis, Madelaine D., 224–5
Davis, Natalie Zemon
  on Charlotte Arbaleste, 70
  on gender, 4
  women's history in Canada, 182
  women worthies, 6
defences of women
  political subtexts, 41–2
  representation of women, 38–42
Dentière, Marie
  La guerrre et deslivrance de la ville Genesve, 69
  Très Utile, 68
Derrida, Jacques, 4
Descartes, René, 45
Dickenson, Emily, 215
Dido, 24
difference
  feminist theory, 11, 228, 229, 31
  women's history, 11, 229–40
Dionysius, 19, 20
Dognon, Susan, 164

domestic fiction, 111, 118, 119
domestic heroines/heroism, 72, 107, 112–15, 116, 125, 128
domestic ideology, 133, 165, 167, 232
domestic industry/labour, 146, 166–7, 179
domestic seclusion, 22–3, 26, 29, 35, 55–7, 65, 79, 114, 195
domestic sphere
  as ahistorical, 23, 24–5, 30–1, 55, 58–9, 110, 190, 195
  historicisation of, 76, 101, 107, 109–12, 195–8, 200
  as site of women's oppression, 195–6, 200
domestic womanhood, 110–11, 113–15, 116–17, 118–19, 127
Donoghue, Emma
  Passions between women, 226
Dowriche, Anne
  The French History, 69
DuBois, Carol Ellen
  on first-wave feminism, 142, 223
  critique of Smith-Rosenberg, 200–3, 206

Eastman, Crystal, 221–2
Eckstein, Arthur, 31
economic history, 143, 148–9, 150, 165–6
Economic History Society, 162–3
Edgeworth, Maria, 101, 125
Edinburgh Review, 104
education
  arguments against the education of women, 20–1, 40, 53, 158–9
  arguments in favour of the education of women, 38, 40, 49, 51, 65, 66
  domesticity, 53, 83, 85, 127, 151, 153, 158
  higher education of men, 57–8
  struggle for women's higher education, 130, 133, 140–1, 142, 144, 150–71, 172–88
  women's, 20–1, 38, 64–5, 80, 83–5, 88, 114–15, 116, 118, 123, 168, 175, 196
Eliot, T. S. 17

Ellet, Elizabeth Fries Lummis
  complicit in patriarchal discourses around women, 127
  Daughters of the American Revolution, 127
Ellis, Havelock, 220–1
Elyot, Thomas
  Defence of Good Women, 42
Emerson, Ralph Waldo, 104
Emerton, Ephraim, 152
empiricism, 6, 45–6, 188
Engels, Fredrich, 174
Enlightenment
  modernity, 51–2
  philosophical history (or conjectural), 46–50
  rationality, 48–52
essentialism/essentialist notions, 191, 204–6, 227, 229–31
ethnology, 47
Eusebius
  Ecclesiastical History, 27, 43
Eve, 27
Everest (Levi), Kate, 152
Everett, Edward, 104

Fabian Society, 145, 148
Faderman, Lillian
  influence of Smith-Rosenberg, 216
  Scotch Verdict, 216–17
  Surpassing the love of men, 215–16
  sexology, 216–17, 220–1
family history
  as extension of domestic duties, 70–3
  as political history, 72
  as women's history, 9, 63, 67, 68–73, 74, 77–9, 94, 103, 178–9
Fanshawe, Ann, Lady
  Memoir, 71–2
Fawcett, Millicent Garrett, 138
Febvre, Lucien, 164
female sovereignty, 36, 40–6, 52, 90–1, 114
femmes fatales, 18, 42, 43
femmes forte, 35, 38, 42, 90, 91–2
femininity
  antithetical to history, 24, 111
  bourgeois notions of, 107, 111, 112
  classical notions of 9, 20, 34
  definitions, 23–4
  evangelical notions of, 107, 112
  Protestant notions of, 30–1, 68, 72, 80, 112
  Romantic notions of, 86
feminism
  Enlightenment, 80, 94, 110, 128, 134
  cultural, 203–8, 211–13, 216, 221, 229
  difference, 230–40
  domestic, 113–15, 133, 151
  first-wave, 128, 130, 136–42, 144, 145, 146, 153, 169, 199, 202, 206–8, 221–2
  inter-war, 142, 166–7, 207, 222
  lesbian, 205, 209–12, 223–4
  Liberal, 171, 173–4, 210
  Marxist, 175–6, 201
  'pro-sex', 207–8, 221–3
  radical, 131, 174, 189–92, 195–6, 201, 203–8, 229, 234
  revolutionary, 89–101, 112, 113, 115
  romantic, 101–8, 112
  second-wave, 142, 169, 206–8, 221–2
  socialist, 175–6, 201
  Victorian, 110–12, 128, 134, 135–6
  women's history and, 8–11, 63, 124–9, 130–49, 150–71, 172–88, 189–208, 209–28, 229–40
Feminist Studies, 200
'feminocentric', 216
fiction
  effect on female morality, 119, 123
  as women's history, 74, 102
Firestone, Shulamith, 191, 204
Fitzpatrick, Kathleen, 163
Flexner, Eleanor
  Century of Struggle, 170
Fossé, Augustin du, 93, 95
Foucault, Michel, 218–19, 221
Foxe, John
  Acts and Monuments, 43–4
  representation of women, 43–4
Franklin, Benjamin, 82
Fraser's Magazine, 109
Frédégonde, 90
Freedman, Estelle, 198, 206

Freeman, Edward Augustus, 121
Freeman, Jo, 197
French Revolution
　feminisation of culture, 89, 93–5, 103
　historical representations of women during, 86, 89, 92
　romantic reaction, 51,
　treatment of women during, 54–5, 86, 89, 99
　women's history, 9–10, 86–108, 109–10
Friedan, Betty
　Feminine Mystique, 167, 170–1, 173, 179, 186, 195, 231–3
　homophobia, 210
　influence of Eleanor Flexner, 170, 280n
　National Organisation of Women (NOW) 171, 173
Freud, Sigmund, 214, 218
Fry, Elizabeth, 128
Fuller, Margaret
　clubs, 132
　feminism, 132
　history of Italian Revolution, 107
　influence of Germaine de Staël, 105, 107
　journalism, 107
　role in Risorgimento, 107
　subject of feminist biographies, 128, 138
　Woman in the Nineteenth Century, 107, 132
　'Yankee Corinne', 107

Gage, Matilda Joselyn, 135
Garrett, Margery Lois, 157
gay history, 216, 218–20
gay liberation, 204, 210–11, 219–20, 224
George, M. Dorothy
　Girton graduate, 156
　theories about the impact of industrialisation upon women, 148, 167
Gentleman's Magazine, 82, 96
Giddings, Paula, 232–3
Gierke, Otto von, 159–60
Gilbert, Sue, 215
Godwin, William
　on history and romance writing, 100
　Memoir of Mary Wollstonecraft, 83, 100, 110
　'new philosophy', 101
Goff, Jacques le, 182
Goldman, Emma, 221–2
Goldstein, Vida, 140
Gomme, A. W., 56
Gordon, Dame Helen Cumming, 217
Gordon, Linda
　on women's history, 4, 223
Gramsci, Antoni, 177
Greer, Germaine, 204
Grimke, Angelina and Sarah, 128, 133, 138
Grundy, Isobel, 68
Guevara, Che, 173
Guizot, Franois, 89
Gutwirth, Madelyn, 102
gynaecracie, 42

hagiography, 18, 27, 68, 124
Hale, Sarah Josepha, 127
Hall, Catherine, 183
Hall, Radclyffe, 221
Hamilton, Elizabeth
　comparison between history and romance, 123
　Memoir of Modern Philosophers, 116
　Memoirs of Agrippina, 116
Hammond, Barbara, and Hammond, J. L., 147
Harley, Brilliana, 125
Hays, Mary
　Appeal to the Men of Great Britain, 115
　Emma Courtney, 116
　Female Biography, 115–16, 118
　feminism, 115
　hostile reviews, 116
　Letters and Essays, 115
　modernisation of biography, 118
　relationship with Wollstonecraft and Godwin, 115, 116
　relationship with William Frend, 116
　transitional figure, 115
Henry, Alice, 140
Herder, Johann Gottfried, 52, 104

Herodotus
  Histories, 32
  influence on modern historiography, 32–3
  representation of women, 1, 32–3
Herwegh, Emma, 105, 266n
Herwegh, Georg, 105
Hesiod, 23
Hesse, Carla, 91
Hesseltine, William, 150
Hewitt, Nancy, 202
Heywood, Eliza, 75
Heywood, Thomas, 6, 42
Hill, Bridget, 82, 99
Hill, Georgiana, 147
Hine, Darlene Clark, 238
Hintze, Hedwig, 163–4
historicity
  women and, 1–2, 6, 76, 191
history
  as an academic discipline, 57–9, 150ff.
  democratisation of, 172, 176–9
  as an easy study, 156
  'from below' 177, 192
  as literature, 34, 44, 46
  professionalisation, 57–9, 120, 150–5
  as a science, 34, 44–6, 47, 58, 121, 151, 155, 159
History Workshop
  movement, 177–8, 183
  support of women's history, 183
Hobbes, Thomas, 18
Hogsett, Charlotte, 103
Hollibaugh, Amber, 223
Homer, 23, 30
homosexuality, 212–14, 216, 218–20
hooks, bell, 235
Hotman, Franois, 69
Howard, George E., 157
Howard, Henry Lord
  A Dutiful Defence of the lawfull regiment of woman, 42
Hull House, 149
humanism
  gender blindness, 16
  and history, 16, 21
  Studia humanitas, 16

Hume, David, 48, 80, 116
Hutchins, Barbara Leigh, 147
Hutchinson, Lucy
  Life of Colonel Hutchinson, 72–3
  Victorian images of, 72, 125
hypersexuality, 238

imperial history, 176, 239
industrialisation
  brutalising effect of, 145, 147
  history of, 146ff.
  women's role in, 147–8, 165
Isbell, John, 103

Jackson, Margaret, 223
Jameson, Anna, 124
Jeffreys, Sheila
  defining lesbianism, 226
  first-wave feminism, 223
  sexology, 220–1
Joan of Arc, 105
Johnston, Jill, 211
Jordan, Constance, 39
Joshel, Sandra R, 29
Juvenal, 25

Kames, Lord (Henry Homes), 48, 49
Kaplan, Louis, 150
Kaplan, Temma, 200
Keeble, N. H., 71–2
Kelley, Donald R., 19
Kelly-Gadol, Joan
  'Did Women have a Renaissance?' 64
  on gender, 4
  on the *Querelle des Femmes*, 66
Kemble, J. M., 109
Kemp-Welch, Alice, 66
Kennedy, Elizabeth Lapovsky, 224–5
Kéralio, Louise de (Roberts)
  Collection des meilleurs ouvrages français, 90
  Les Crimes des reines de la France, 90
  Histoire d'Elisabeth, 90
  as *historienne*, 89, 261n
  hostile reactions to journalism, 92
  journalism, 91–2
Kerber, Linda, 181, 182

Kirkham, Margaret, 94
Knowles, Lillian
  Girton graduate, 156
  theories regarding the impact of industrialisation on women, 148, 156, 167
Knox, John
  The First Blast of the Trumpet against the Monstrous Regiment of Women, 42
  representation of women, 37, 42,
Koedt, Anne, 204
Koonz, Claudia
  Becoming Visible, 185
Kraditor, Aileen
  Up from the Pedestal, 195
Kucich, Greg, 8

labour history, 177, 178–9, 192, 193, 202
Ladurie, Emmanuel Le Roy, 182
Langlois, C. V., 157
'Lavender Menace', 209–10
Lawrence, Hannah, 124
Leibniz, Gottfried Wilhelm, 52
Leopardi, Giacomo, 104
Lerner, Gerda
  women's history, 8, 185, 192, 196, 200
'lesbian chauvinism', 211
lesbian continuum, 212–13, 215, 216, 225
lesbian history
  agency, 213, 222–3, 224
  archives, 225
  bar culture, 224
  definitional uncertainty, 217, 225–8
  development, 11, 209–28
  feminist consciousness, 223
  herstory, 225
  identity, 209–28
  impact of queer, 227–8
  literary studies, 226
  resistance, 213, 224
  sexuality, 222, 226
Lessing, Gotthold Ephraim, 52
lettres de cachet, 262n.
Lézardière, Marie-Charlotte-Pauline de, 88–9
l'Hoir, Francesca Santoro, 29,

Lister, Anne
  diaries, 225–6
  'marriage' to Anne Walker, 226
Livy
  History of Rome, 19
  influence on modern historiography, 19, 25–7, 45, 54
  rape, 26
  representation of women, 25–7, 37, 39
Loades, David, 44
local history
  as women's history, 77–80
London School of Economics (LSE)
  scholarships for women, 140, 157
  supportive environment for female scholars, 148, 157, 162–3
Looser, Devoney, 94
Lussan, Marguerite de
Luther, Martin, 37, 40

Macaulay, Catherine Sawbridge
  adoption of feminism, 82–3
  on ancient rights, 136
  History in Letters, 94
  History of England, 80, 82
  hostile reviews, 82, 94
  Letters on Education, 83
  marriage to William Graham, 83
  political historian, 2, 6, 80, 259n.
  role model, 84
  support of American Revolution, 80, 82
  support of Republicanism in France, 82
  treatment in the anti-Jacobin press, 83
  on women's education, 82, 83
Macintosh, Sir James, 104
Maenads, 56
Maitland, Frederick, 157
Maitzen, Rohan A., 7
Manley, Delarivier
  The New Atlantis, 75–6
Marie Antoinette, 53, 54, 90–1
marital law reform, 134, 135–6, 142
Marmontel, Jean Francois, 82,
marriage, 29–30, 32, 33, 168–9, 195, 214
Marshall, Dorothy, 162
Martineau, Harriet, 107

Index

martyrs
  female, 27–8, 43–4
  male, 43–4
  martyrology, 43–4
Marxist history, 2, 177, 192–3
masculinist history
  classical origins, 15–33
  critiques of, 8, 122, 124, 132–3, 137, 184–8, 189–209
  deconstruction of, 4–5, 189–209
  emphasis on public sphere, 186, 188, 195
  as general history, 4–5, 15, 57, 74, 111, 184, 187–8, 230
  historical specificity of men, 4, 188
  new social history as, 176–9, 194
  as pedagogy, 19–23, 28–33, 57–9, 111
  phallocentrism, 187–8, 189
  professionalisation, 57–9
  representation of women, 9–33, 34–59, 91
  use of evidence, 186, 188
masculinist politics, 172–4
Matheson, Erica, 27
matriarchal theory, 126
Mavor, Elizabeth
  Ladies of Llangollen, 214
  'romantic friendships' 214–15
Maza, Sara, 91
McLeod, Glenda, 66
Medici, Catherine de', 36, 40, 90
Meiners, Christoph, 50
Mellor, Anne K., 95
Melman, Billie 7, 110
memoir
  as women's history, 74–5, 76, 77, 79, 111
Messalina
  archetype of female evil, 25, 53, 91
Meun, Jean de
  Romance of the Rose, 66
Michelet, Jules
  friendship with Marie d'Agoult, 105
  support of women's education, 158
  Women of the Revolution, 56
Mickiewicz, Adam, 105
Mignet, F. A., 105
Mikalachki, Jodi, 37

Miles, Rosalind
  Women's History of the World, 183
Millar, John, 48
Millet, Kate, 175, 204
misogyny, 9, 18, 20, 25, 28, 33, 36, 38, 66, 83, 96, 99, 111, 220
Mitchell, Juliet, 175
Mitchell, Rosemary, 7
Montagu, Lady Mary Wortley
  'Account of the Court of King George I', 75–6, 258n.
Moore, Lisa
  Dangerous Intimacies, 226
Moraga, Cherríe, 223
More, Hannah
  Coelebs in Search of a Wife, 113, 116
  complicit in patriarchal discourses around women, 126–7
  Essays designed for Young Ladies, 114
  on female inferiority, 113–14
  Hints towards forming the character of a young princess, 114–15
  opinion of history, 114
  Strictures on Education, 114
Morgan, Lady Sydney Owenson
  Patriotic Sketches, 125
  romantic feminism, 101
Morgan, Robyn, 191
Mott, Lucretia, 128

National Association for the Promotion of Social Science, 144
National Federation of Settlements, 145
National Organisation of Women (NOW), 171, 173, 209–10, 231, 235
national tales
  as women's history, 125
National Union of Women's Suffrage Societies (NUWSS), 141
National Union of Women Teachers, 142
Neilson, Nellie, 154
Nestle, Joan, 209
Newton, Isaac Sir, 46
New York Tribune, 107
Niebuhr, B. G., 52
Nightingale, Florence, 128
Norton, Caroline, 135–6

nuns
  historical writing, 67–9
  'Sister books', 67

objectivity, 6, 47, 58, 139, 188, 192
Ong, Walter J., 16
oral history, 224–5
Orléans, Anne-Marie Louise-Henriette d', 74, 258n
Orléans-Longueville, Marie d', 74
Ormsby, Margaret, 163
Ortner, Sherry, 197
Otis, James, 80
Ozouf, Mona, 182

Pamphilia, 20
Pankhurst, Christabel
  role in militant campaigns, 137
  treatment by male historians, 274n.
Pankhurst, E. Sylvia
  role in militant campaigns, 137
  The Suffragette, 137
Pankhurst, Emmeline
  role in militant campaigns, 137
  treatment by male historians, 274n.
Pantel, Pauline Schmitt, 182
patriarchy
  authority, 40, 78,
  critiques of, 89
  gender relations, 23, 27, 31, 37, 40–4, 45–6, 49, 55, 72–3, 80, 112, 119–20, 122, 184, 191–2
  sexual relations, 204, 206–8, 211
patriotism
  gendering of, 113, 117, 125–6, 270n.
Patzelt, Erna, 164
Paulson, Fredrich, 159
Pericles
  funeral oration, 22, 114
periodisation, 137, 186
Perrot, Michelle
  on gender, 4
  women's history in France, 182, 200
philology, 17,
Pinchbeck, Ivy
  Girton graduate, 156
  study at LSE, 162
  theories about the impact of industrialisation upon women, 148, 167
  Working Women and the Industrial Revolution, 167
Pirie, Jane, 216–17
Pisan, Christine de
  Book of the Body Politic, 65
  Cité des dames, 65–7
  feminine virtue, 65, 118
  first feminist, 66
  influence on modern historiography, 66
  women worthies, 66
Plutarch
  domestic seclusion of women, 23
  opinion of Thucydides, 22–3
  Virtues of Women, 22
  women worthies, 6, 23
political economy, 143, 148
political history
  elitist, 148
  as women's history, 80, 87–8, 165
Polybius
  history as masculine pedagogy, 21
  pragmatic history, 21
  representation of women, 31–2, 54
Ponsonby, Sarah, 214
pornography, 207–8, 221–2
Porter, Jane, 101
postcolonial history, 177, 238–40
poststructuralism, 239–40
Potter, David, 186
Power, Beryl, 140
Power, Eileen
  on Cambridge men, 157
  Girton graduate, 156
  on suffrage, 140
  on women's culture, 196
prostitution, 222
Pushkin, Alexander, 104
Putnam, Bertha, 154

queer history, 227–9
queer politics, 227–9

Index

Querelle des Femmes, 40, 66
Quinet, Edgar, 105
Quintillian, 32

race, 11, 177, 191, 202, 203, 229ff.
radical history, 176–9, 180
'radicalesbian' manifesto, 210
Rang, Brita, 39
Ranke, Leopold von
  exclusion of women, 58–9, 159–60
  historical practice, 58–9
  historicism, 58–9, 104
  seminar teaching, 58
rape
  historical device, 26, 27
  'rape valid', 26
Reformation
  gendering of history, 35–7
  idea of history, 35–6
  impact of sectarianism on historical writing, 35–6
  theology of gender, 37–44
  treatment of women, 36–44
religion
  influence on women's historical writing, 67–77, 195
religious history
  as women's history, 68
Renaissance
  gendering of history, 9, 15–33
  historiography, 17–19
  idea of history, 17–19
  scholarship, 9, 15–19
  treatment of women, 15, 21
Rendall, Jane
  on Elizabeth Hamilton, 117
  Enlightenment, 8
  History Workshop, 183
  on women's history, 8
republican motherhood, 53, 55, 81, 116
Rich, Adrienne, 212, 215
Richardson, Samuel
  Pamela, 118–19
Riley, Denise, 145
Robertson, William, 48
Rogers, Thorold, 156

Roland, Marie-Jeanne Madame, 84
romance writing
  opposed to history, 51, 74–5
  as women's history, 74–5, 76
romantic friendships, 212–17, 220–1, 223, 225
Romanticism
  impact on historical writing, 8, 10, 86, 100, 103
  nationalism, 52–3
Roper, Lyndal, 37
Rosaldo, Michelle Zimbalist, 197
Rose, Willie Lee, 181
Rose Report, 181
Rousseau, Jean-Jacques, 53, 88
Ruehl, Sonja, 221
Russell, John Sir, 123

sadomasochism, 207
Sahli, Nancy, 198
Salmon, Lucy Maynard
  on the professionalisation of history, 154
  on women's culture, 196
  women's higher education, 140
  women's suffrage, 140
salons
  as 'centres of Enlightenment', 88
  intellectual culture of, 87–8, 105
  political importance of, 87–8, 105
  women's role in, 87
Samuel, Raphael, 177
Sandford, Mrs John
  Lives of English Female Worthies, 120
Sanger, Margaret, 221–2
Sappho, 90
Schmidt, Erich, 159
Schreiner, Olive, 141
Sclafert, Thérèse, 164
Scott, Joan Wallach
  'Gender: A Useful Category of Historical Analysis', 3
  gender, 3–5
  on women's history, 3
  textuality, 4

Scudéry, Madeleine de
   Artamenes, 75, 76
   influence of, 106
   Les Femmes illustres, 90
secret history
   as women's history, 76, 102
Sedgwick, Eve Kosofsky, 226
Seneca Falls Convention, 132, 134, 135
sensibility, 49, 52
separate spheres, 15, 23, 31, 32, 35, 50, 111, 128, 133, 144, 146, 167, 195, 201, 202, 206, 223, 239
Settlement Houses, 144
sex radicalism, 221–31, 229, 290n
sex wars, 207–8, 209–12, 221, 224
sexology
   defining homosexuality, 219–20
   defining lesbian 215–21, 225
sexual preference
   as desire, 205
   'compulsory heterosexuality' 212, 216
   discrimination, 209–10, 224, 229
   as political choice, 205, 211–12
sexual revolution, 203–4, 207–8, 223
Shepherd, Amanda, 41
Skelton, Isabel, 140
Sklar, Kathryn Kish, 79, 198
slavery, 132, 133, 134, 176, 194, 201, 235, 238, 239
Smiles, Samuel, 111
Smith, Bonnie G.
   'Contribution of Women to Modern Historiography', 6
   on history of women, 6–8, 275n
   on Mercy Otis Warren, 82
   on Ranke, 58–9, 159
   on women polymaths, 88
Smith, Lucy Toulmin, 146
Smith-Rosenberg, Carroll
   female networks and feminism, 198, 201–3, 220
   female sexuality, 198, 213–14, 216, 218, 227
   'Female World of Love and Ritual', 197–8, 199, 200, 206, 212–13
   romantic friendships, 197, 206, 212–16

social history, 143, 148–9, 150, 165–6, 178–9, 180, 192
social motherhood, 144
social policy, 143
social purity, 130, 133, 142, 222
social sciences
   and first-wave feminism, 142–6
social surveys, 143
sociology, 48, 143, 148, 182, 197, 206
St Augustine
   City of God, 66
St Jerome, 38
St Paul
   on female silence, 39, 68
Staël, Germaine de
   Considérations de la Révolution, 103
   as Corinne, 102, 139
   Corinne, 101, 103, 104, 105, 107, 125
   Corinne as allegory of revolution, 102–3
   Corinne as role model, 102
   De l'Allemagne, 103
   Delphine, 102, 104, 125
   enemy of Napoleon, 101, 103, 104
   erotic life, 103, 265n.
   on feminine genius, 101–2, 104, 106
   influence upon American historical writing, 104
   influence upon feminism, 102
   influence on modern historiography, 104
   influence upon Romanticism, 87, 103
   influence upon women's writing, 102, 106, 125, 139
   masculine understanding, 104
   opinion of England, 107
   originator of nationalism, 103, 104
   relationship with father (Jacques Necker), 101, 103
   role in French Revolution, 86, 101, 103
   salon, 101,
   use of fictional narrative as history, 77, 101–2
Stanley, Liz, 221
Stanton, Elizabeth Cady
   History of Woman Suffrage, 135
   influence of Margaret Fuller, 132

Index

Seneca Falls Declaration, 135
subject of feminist biography, 138, 141
stasis (civil strife), 30–2
Steedman, Carolyn, 183
Steinman, Paula, 130
Stenton, Doris Mary
  English Woman in History, 137
Stodart, M. A., 121
Stone, Lucy, 141
Stopes, Charlotte Carmichael
  British Freewomen, 136
Strachey, Lytton, 118, 269n
Strachey, Ray
  The Cause, 138, 141
  militant hostility towards, 141
Strickland, Agnes, 119, 123
Strickland, Elizabeth, 123
Stuart, Lady Louisa, 76
Stuart, Mary, Queen of Scots, 40, 91, 105
Stubbs, William, 121, 156
subaltern history, 177
suffrage
  ancient rights of women, 136–7, 146
  art, 139
  autobiography, 138–9
  campaigns, 133, 134, 144
  constitutionalist campaigns, 136–7, 141
  constitutionalist histories of, 137, 141
  histories of, 134–5, 136, 139, 141–2, 145
  journals, 136
  memorialising the campaigns, 138
  militant campaigns, 137–9, 141
  militant histories of, 137–9, 141
  preservation, 142
Suffrage Annuals and Women's Who's Who, 138
The Suffragette, 136
Suffragette Fellowship, 138

Tacitus
  Agricola, 28–9
  Annals, 28–30
  differences between German and Roman women, 28–30
  Germania, 28–9
  Histories, 28–30
  influence on modern historiography, 18, 27–30, 45, 50, 52, 90
  representation of women, 25–30, 36–7, 53, 54, 55, 57
Taylor, Barbara, 183
Thierry, Augustin, 105
Thirsk, Joan, 7
Thomas, Antoine-Léonard, 50
Thomas, M. Carey, 153
Thompson, E. P.
  The Making of the English Working Class, 178, 193
  working-class culture as political culture, 178, 193–4, 198, 199
Thrupp, Sylvia, 163
Thucydides
  elision/seclusion of women, 18, 20, 21–2, 114, 195
  history as masculine pedagogy, 21
  influence on modern historiography, 18, 30–2, 45
  Peloponnesian War, 18–19, 21, 30–1
  representation of women, 30, 33, 57
Ticknor, George, 104
Tiger, Lionel
  Men in Groups, 285n.
Tocqueville, Alex de, 105
Tomaselli, Sylvana, 48
Toynbee Hall, 144, 147
Trieschke, Heinrich von, 160
Trumbach, Randolph, 219
Tudor, Elizabeth, 42, 90, 114
Tudor, Mary, 36, 42, 73
Turgot, Anne-Robert-Jacques, 48, 82
Turner, Frederick Jackson
  'Frontier thesis', 186
  women historians critique, 186
Tyron, Rolla Milton, 147

Ulrichs, Karl, 219
The Una, 146
University of Chicago
  supportive of women social scientists, 149

Valla, Lorenzo, 22
Valois, Marguerite de
  Memoirs, 73–4
Varga, Lucie, 164–5
Vassar, Matthew, 151–2
Vicinus, Martha
  on female biography, 120
  on lesbian history, 225, 227
Vico, Giambattista
  The New Science, 47, 107
  influence on Romanticism, 52
Victoria, Queen, 123, 124
Virgil
  Aeneid, 24
  femininity as ahistorical, 24
  representation of gender, 24–5
Vitae Sanctorum, 38
Voltaire (François Marie Arouet), 48

Walkowitz, Judith, 223
Walpole, Horace, 80,
Warner, Marina, 27
Warren, Mercy Otis
  History of the American Revolution, 81–2
  influence of Catherine Sawbridge Macaulay, 84
  letters, 83
  'maternal' history, 81
  political historian, 6, 80,
  role in American revolution, 81–2, 125
Washington, Martha and George, 80
Webb, Jessie, 163
Weeks, Jeffrey, 219
Welter, Barbara, 195
Wiedemann, Thomas E. J., 30,
Wilamowitz-Moellendorff, Ulrich von, 159, 245n.
Williams, Helen Maria
  attack on Burke, 95
  feminism, 95
  ideas about sexual passion, 96
  influence on Romanticism, 87
  James Boswell's comments, 263n.
  Letters from France, 93–4, 98, 99
  Narrative of Events which have taken place in France, 96

  opinion of French Revolution, 93, 95, 103
  opinion of women's participation in the French Revolution, 95
  relationship with John Hurford Stone, 96
  salon, 93, 95–6
  treatment in anti-Jacobin press, 93, 96
  use of epistolary form, 94
  use of fictional narrative as history, 77, 94–5
Wokler, Robert, 49
Wolley, Mary, 153
Wollstonecraft, Mary
  birth of Fanny Imlay, 84
  birth of Mary Godwin, 100
  critique of history, 85, 135
  death in childbirth, 100
  feminism, 84–5
  genderless voice in HMV, 99
  Historical and Moral View of the Origin and Progress of the French Revolution (HMV), 97–9
  HMV as philosophical history, 98
  ideas about sexual passion, 97
  influence on Romanticism, 87
  marriage to William Godwin, 100
  pregnancy/maternity, 97
  opinion of the French Revolution, 84, 86, 93, 97–8, 103
  opinion of women's role in the French Revolution, 98–9
  opinion on women's education, 84
  relationship with Catherine Sawbridge Macaulay, 83–4
  relationship with Gilbert Imlay, 97, 100
  relationship with Helen Maria Williams, 93, 99
  relationship with Henry Fuseli, 97
  response to Edmund Burke, 84, 93, 99
  subject of feminist biographies, 128, 138
  suicide attempt, 84, 100
  Vindication of the Rights of Man, 84
  Vindication of the Rights of Woman, 84, 85, 98
  treatment in anti-Jacobin press, 83–4, 93, 99–101, 113

Index

woman
  as historical category, 4, 11, 48–51
woman question, 130–49
women
  absence from history, 1–2, 15–23, 76, 77, 133, 142, 180, 185, 237
  acting 'above their sex', 35, 63, 85, 89, 118
  collecting, 78–9
  of colour, 173, 229–40
  declining civil status, 130, 134–7
  economic dependence on men, 145–6
  as fragmented subject, 239–40
  historical subjectivity, 9, 23, 34, 37, 39, 67, 70, 71, 100, 103, 111, 217–18
  historical voice, 20, 26, 69, 71, 73, 74–5, 90, 256n.
  as indicators of civilisation, 33, 48–51, 98
  as markers of social upheaval, 25–32, 36–7, 42, 54–6, 73, 91–2
  moral influence, 112–15, 122, 124, 125, 133
  outside history, 1, 4–5, 24, 34–5, 37, 53–6, 58–9, 195
  philanthropy, 143
  public, 67, 100
  scholars as 'third sex', 64
  separatism, 195–8, 203–8, 210–17, 229
  as sex class, 174
  as 'the Sex', 34, 50–1
  as 'unhistoried minority', 230
  white, 170, 171, 173, 229–40
women historians
  discrimination, 180–1
  employment, 152, 156–71, 180ff.
  Ph.D.s, 150, 152, 154, 161
women's colleges
  American, 150–5, 161
  British, 156–8, 162
Women's Freedom League (WFL), 141, 142
Women's Social and Political Union (WSPU), 141
women's history
  in the academy, 10, 150ff.
  'add women and stir' approach, 2, 186
  agency, 111, 133, 184, 194, 213, 222–3, 224, 229, 236
  as amateur history, 120–1, 156
  as feminine/feminist pedagogy, 63–4, 65, 122, 150–71
  and feminism, 131, 132–3, 189–208
  contribution, 196
  feminisation, 111, 126–8, 183
  feminist consciousness, 63, 66, 131, 134, 138, 194, 197–8, 199–203, 205–6, 223, 231
  as 'herstory' 172, 185, 229, 237
  homogenising effect, 230–6
  and lesbian history, 209, 215–28
  male support of, 157
  men's antagonism towards, 109, 120
  networks, 150, 155, 158, 161, 182, 194, 196–8, 199, 200
  new versus old, 169
  oppression, 131, 134–7, 142, 190–2, 197, 204
  outside the academy, 183
  particular history, 4–5, 66, 74–5, 111, 188
  resistance, 194, 201, 202, 213, 224, 229, 236
  sexuality, 222
  'womanist' accounts of the past, 126
  and women's culture, 194–208
women's liberation
  bra burning, 175
  coming of, 171, 172
  heterosexism/homophobia, 210
  history of, 231ff.
  influence on women's history, 2, 10, 172, 179–88
  politics of 172–6
  racism, 229–30, 233–5
women worthies, 6–7, 66, 110
Wood, G. A., 160
Wood, Marianne, 216–17
Woodbury, Helen Laura (Sumner)
  Equal Suffrage, 139–40,
  on women's work, 147
Woolf, Daniel R., 8

Woolf, Virginia
   Parody of Pericles' funeral oration, 22
   A Room of One's Own, 86, 124
work
   conditions of women's, 142–5, 232–3
   history of women's, 145ff., 166ff.
   impact of war on women's, 165
   men's, 178
   sexual division of labour, 145, 178–9
   worker's education, 148, 177

Yeo, Eileen, 144

Zeitlin, Froma I., 27